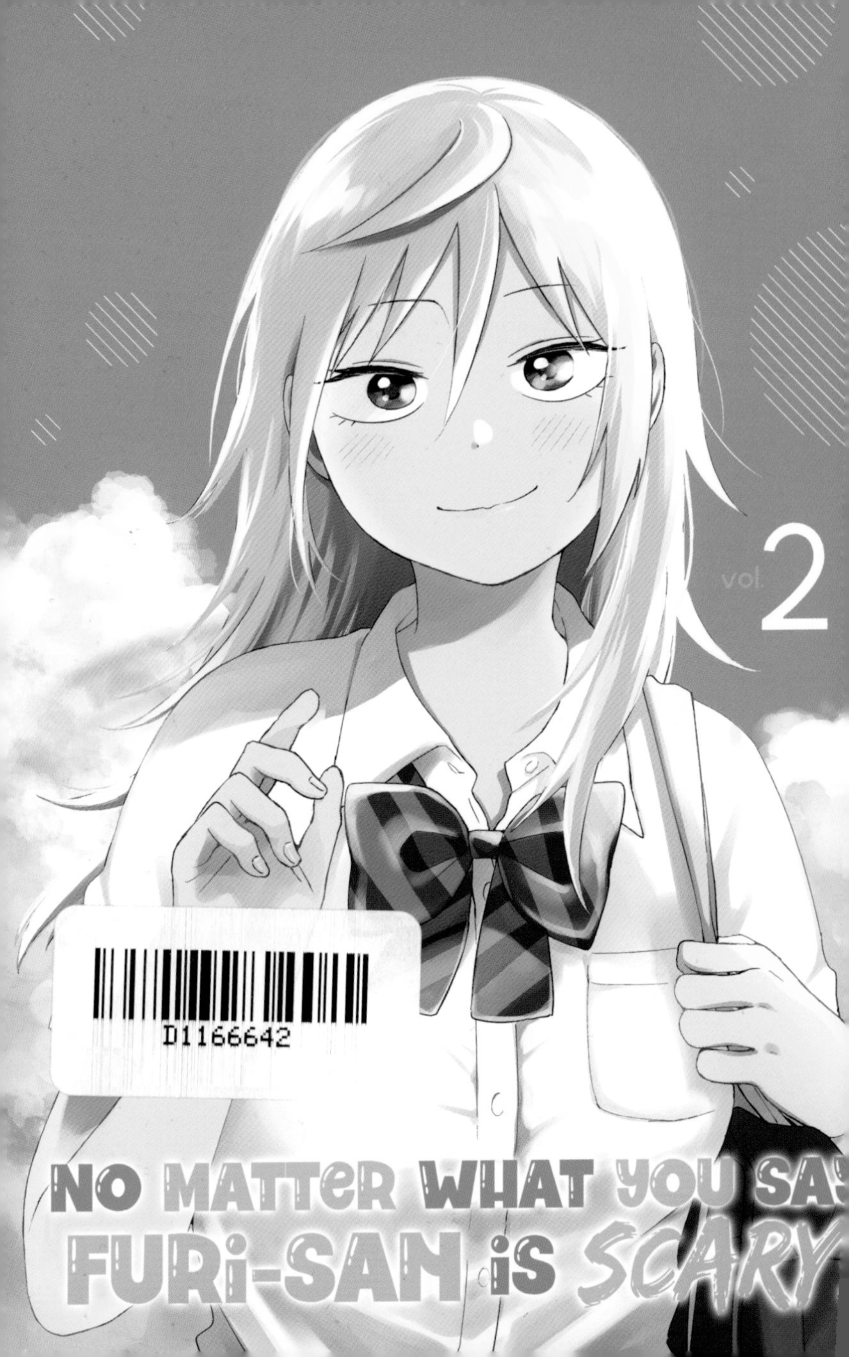
vol. 2
NO MATTER WHAT YOU SA
FURi-SAN iS SCARY

Contents

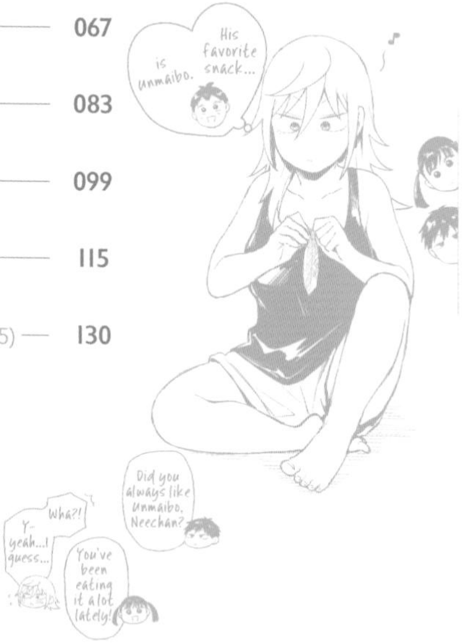

His favorite snack... is unmaibo.
Did you always like unmaibo, Neechan?
You've been eating it a lot lately!
Wha?!
Y-yeah...I guess...

Chapter 9

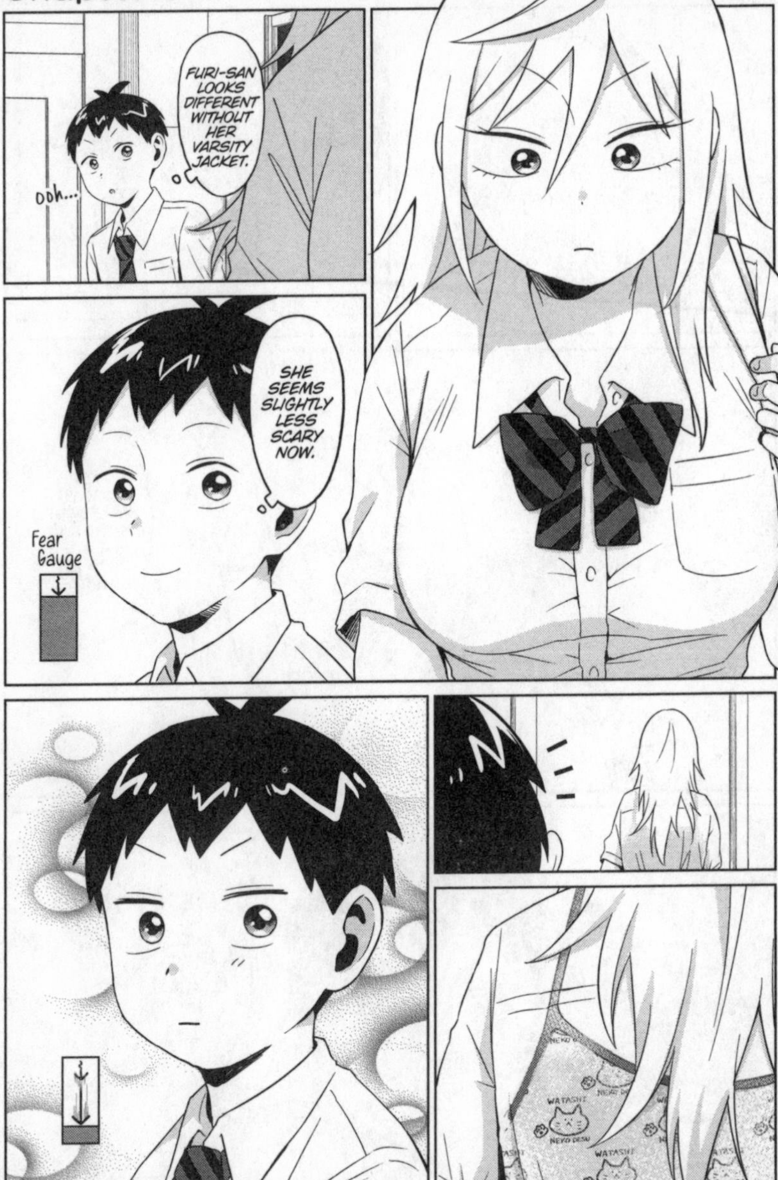
FURI-SAN LOOKS DIFFERENT WITHOUT HER VARSITY JACKET.
ooh...
SHE SEEMS SLIGHTLY LESS SCARY NOW.
Fear Gauge
WATASHI NEKO DESU

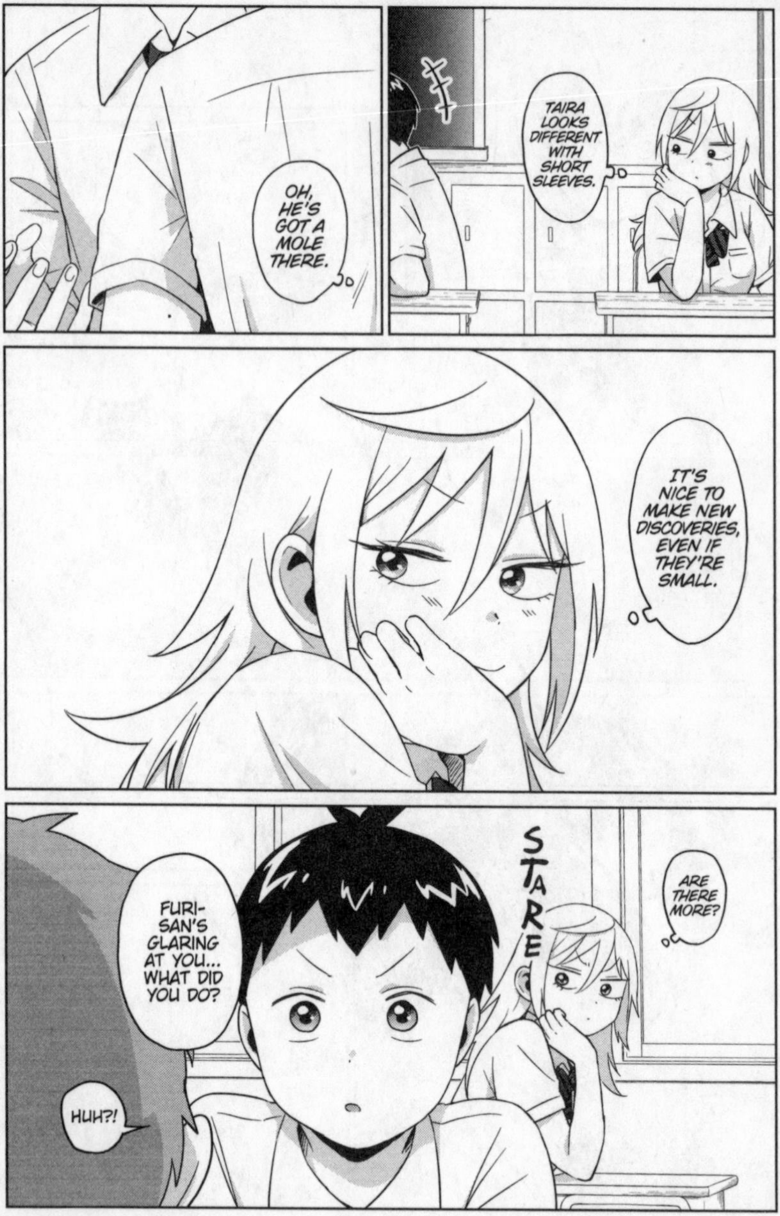
TAIRA LOOKS DIFFERENT WITH SHORT SLEEVES.
OH, HE'S GOT A MOLE THERE.
IT'S NICE TO MAKE NEW DISCOVERIES, EVEN IF THEY'RE SMALL.
ARE THERE MORE?
STARE
FURI-SAN'S GLARING AT YOU... WHAT DID YOU DO?
HUH?!

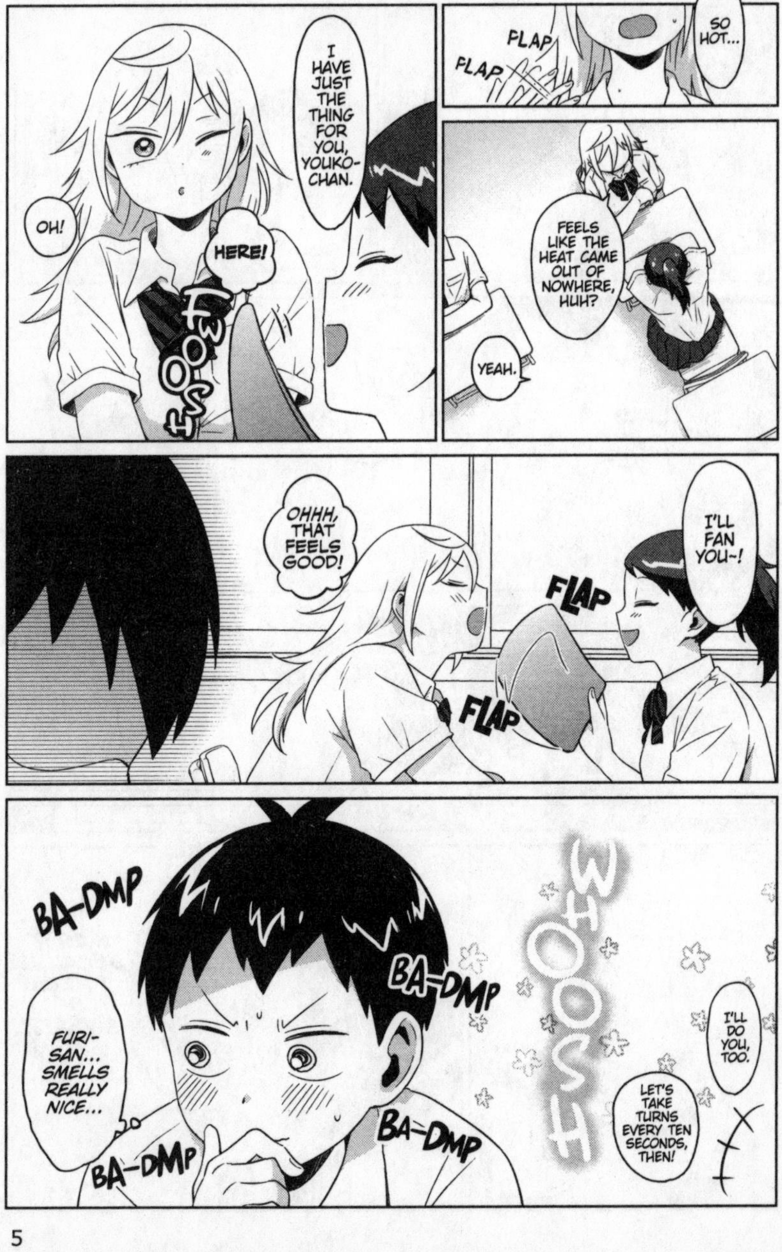
SO HOT...
FLAP
FLAP
FEELS LIKE THE HEAT CAME OUT OF NOWHERE, HUH?
YEAH.
I HAVE JUST THE THING FOR YOU, YOUKO-CHAN.
OH!
HERE!
FWOOSH
I'LL FAN YOU~!
FLAP
OHHH, THAT FEELS GOOD!
FLAP
I'LL DO YOU, TOO.
LET'S TAKE TURNS EVERY TEN SECONDS, THEN!
WHOOSH
BA-DMP
BA-DMP
BA-DMP
FURI-SAN... SMELLS REALLY NICE...
BA-DMP

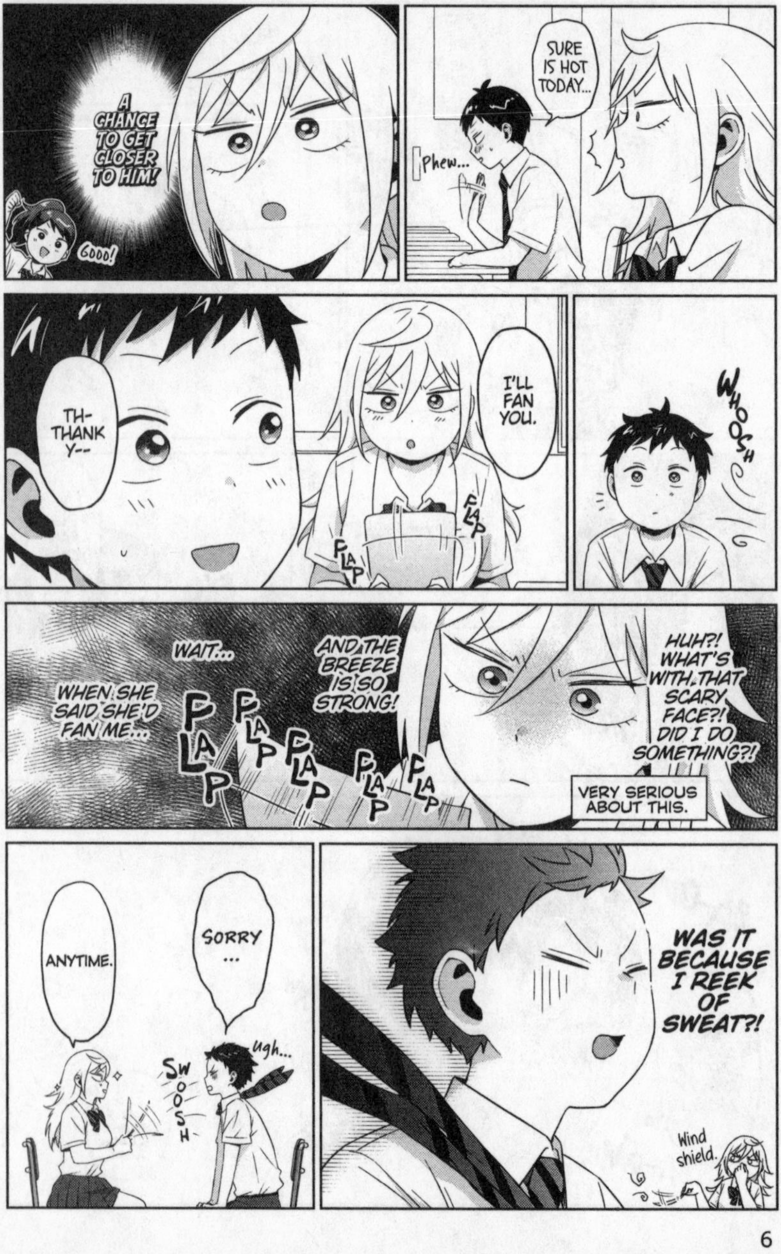

SURE IS HOT TODAY...
Phew...
A CHANCE TO GET CLOSER TO HIM!
GOOD!
WHOOSH
I'LL FAN YOU.
FLAP
FLAP
TH- THANK Y--
HUH?! WHAT'S WITH THAT SCARY FACE?! DID I DO SOMETHING?!
VERY SERIOUS ABOUT THIS.
AND THE BREEZE IS SO STRONG!
FLAP
FLAP
FLAP
FLAP
FLAP
WAIT...
WHEN SHE SAID SHE'D FAN ME...
WAS IT BECAUSE I REEK OF SWEAT?!
Wind shield.
SORRY ...
ugh...
ANYTIME.
SWOOSH

Chapter 10

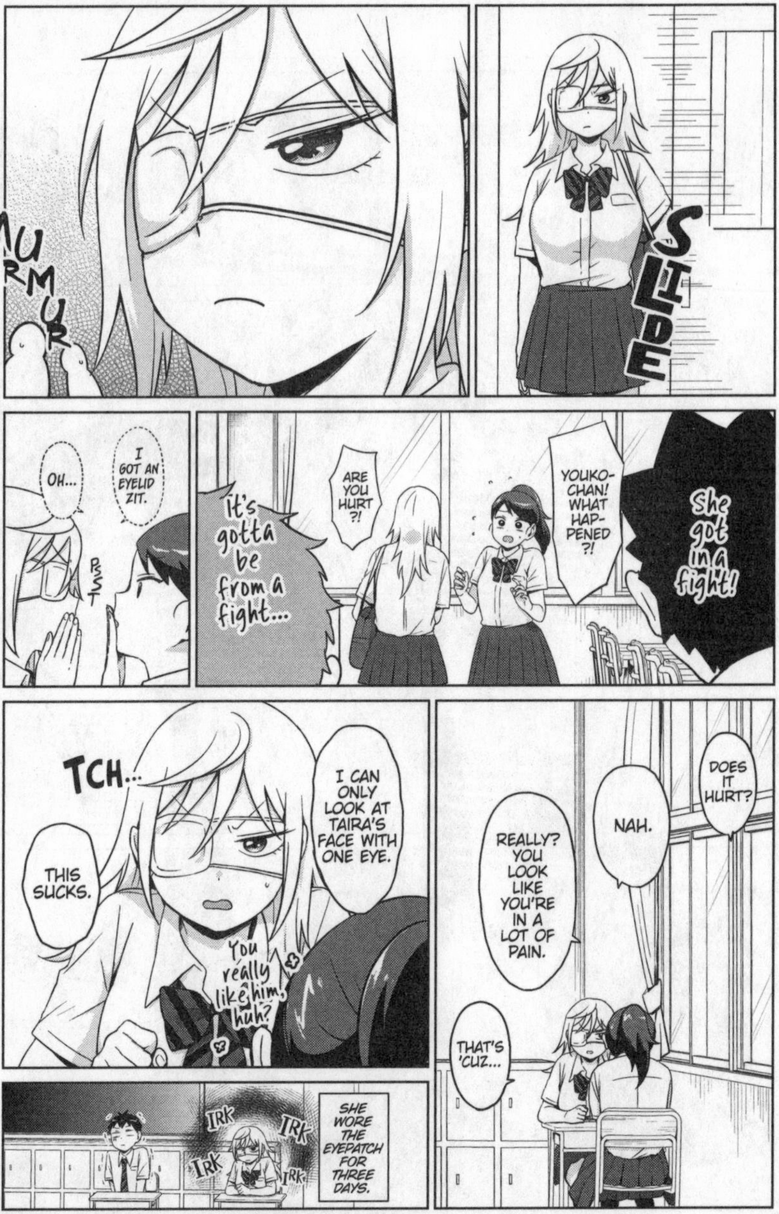
SLIDE
MURMUR MURMUR
She got in a fight!
YOUKO-CHAN! WHAT HAPPENED?!
ARE YOU HURT?!
It's gotta be from a fight...
I GOT AN EYELID ZIT.
OH...
PSST
DOES IT HURT?
NAH.
REALLY? YOU LOOK LIKE YOU'RE IN A LOT OF PAIN.
THAT'S 'CUZ...
I CAN ONLY LOOK AT TAIRA'S FACE WITH ONE EYE.
TCH...
THIS SUCKS.
You really like him, huh?
SHE WORE THE EYEPATCH FOR THREE DAYS.
IRK
IRK
IRK
IRK

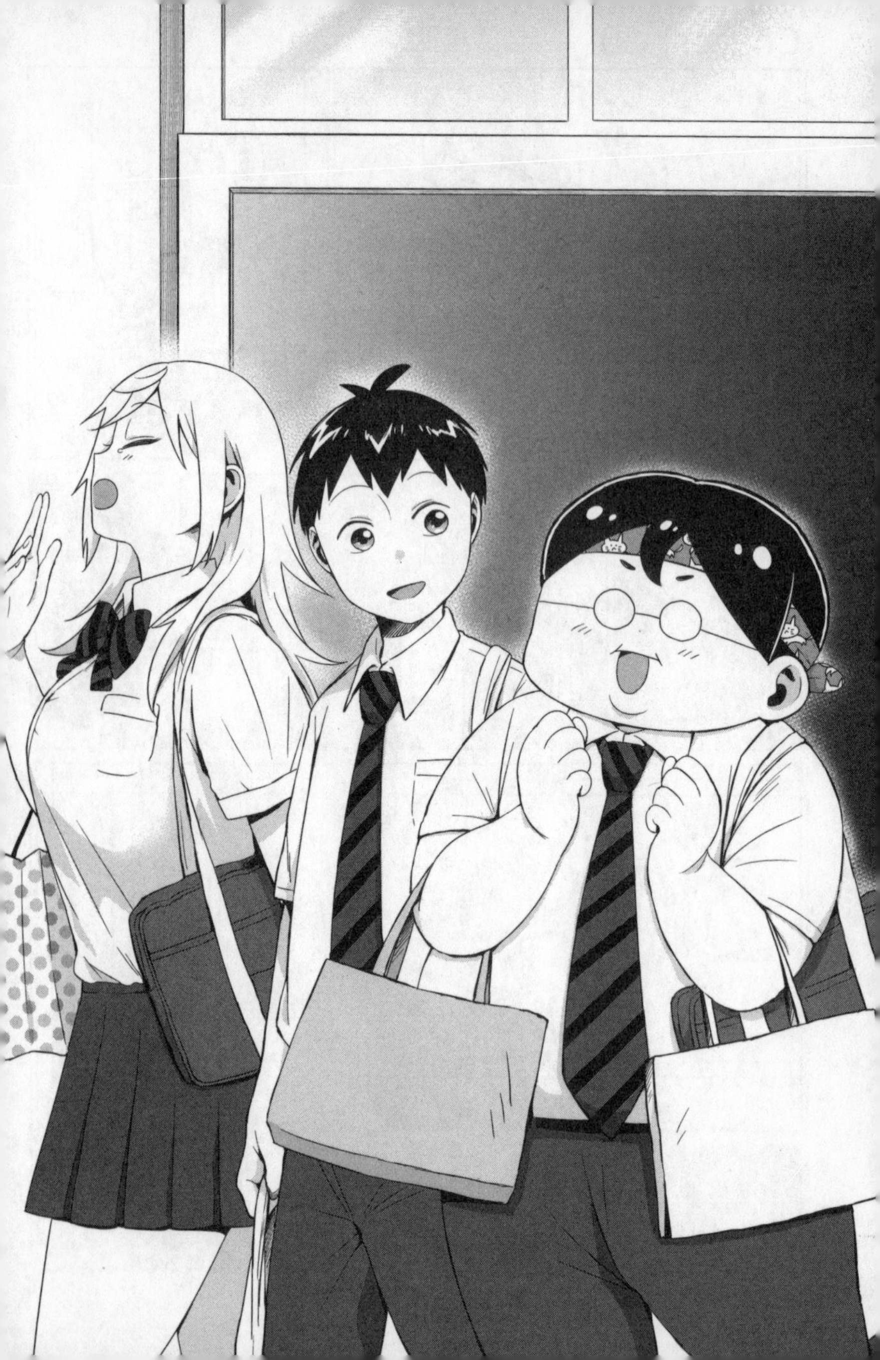

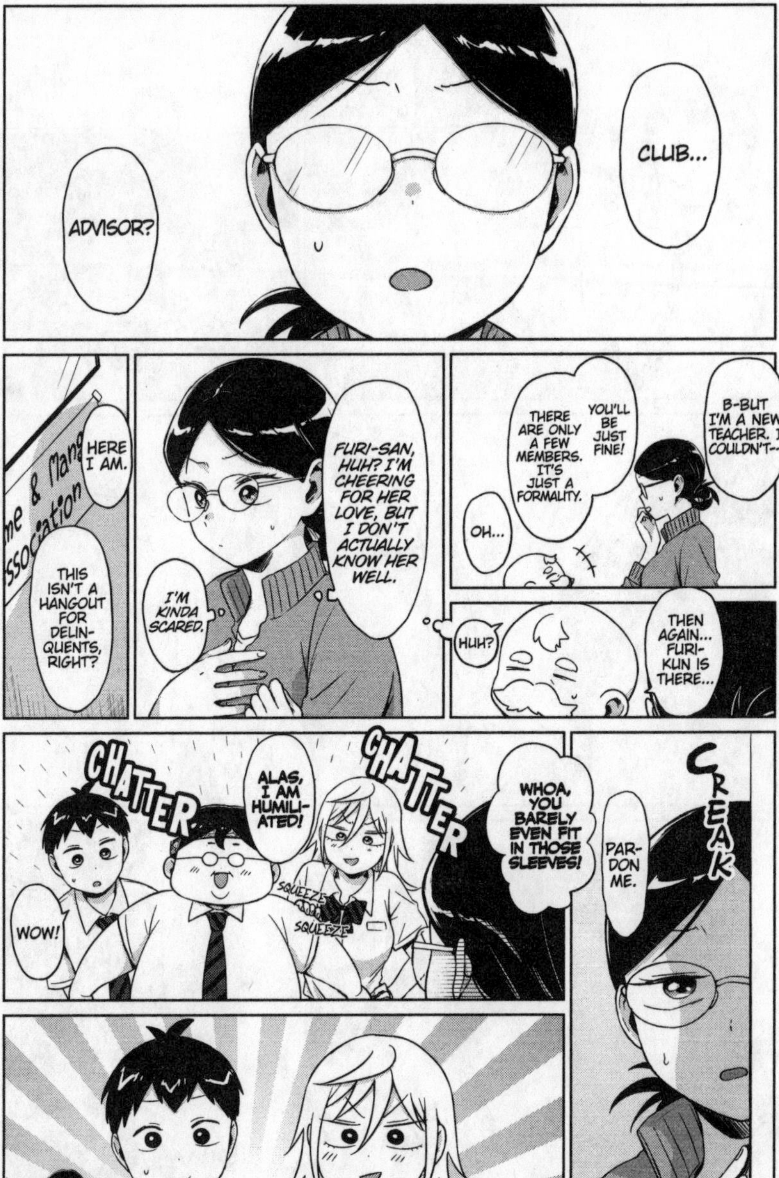
CLUB...
ADVISOR?
B-BUT I'M A NEW TEACHER. I COULDN'T--
YOU'LL BE JUST FINE!
THERE ARE ONLY A FEW MEMBERS. IT'S JUST A FORMALITY.
OH...
THEN AGAIN... FURI-KUN IS THERE...
HUH?
FURI-SAN, HUH? I'M CHEERING FOR HER LOVE, BUT I DON'T ACTUALLY KNOW HER WELL.
I'M KINDA SCARED.
HERE I AM.
THIS ISN'T A HANGOUT FOR DELIN-QUENTS, RIGHT?
CREAK
PARDON ME.
WHOA, YOU BARELY EVEN FIT IN THOSE SLEEVES!
CHATTER
ALAS, I AM HUMILIATED!
CHATTER
SQUEEZE
SQUEEZE
WOW!

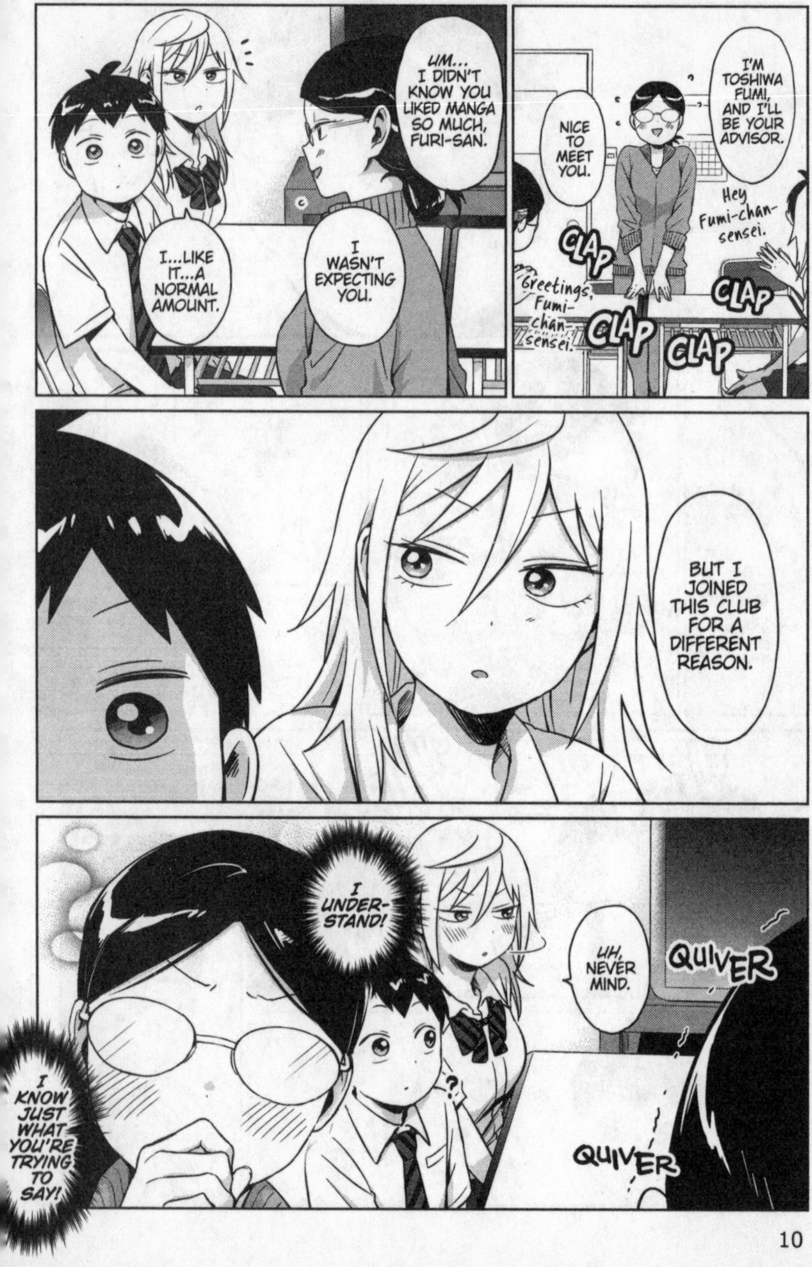
I'M TOSHIWA FUMI, AND I'LL BE YOUR ADVISOR.
NICE TO MEET YOU.
Hey Fumi-chan-sensei.
CLAP
CLAP
Greetings, Fumi-chan-sensei.
CLAP
CLAP
UM... I DIDN'T KNOW YOU LIKED MANGA SO MUCH, FURI-SAN.
I WASN'T EXPECTING YOU.
I...LIKE IT...A NORMAL AMOUNT.
BUT I JOINED THIS CLUB FOR A DIFFERENT REASON.
QUIVER
UH, NEVER MIND.
I UNDER-STAND!
QUIVER
I KNOW JUST WHAT YOU'RE TRYING TO SAY!

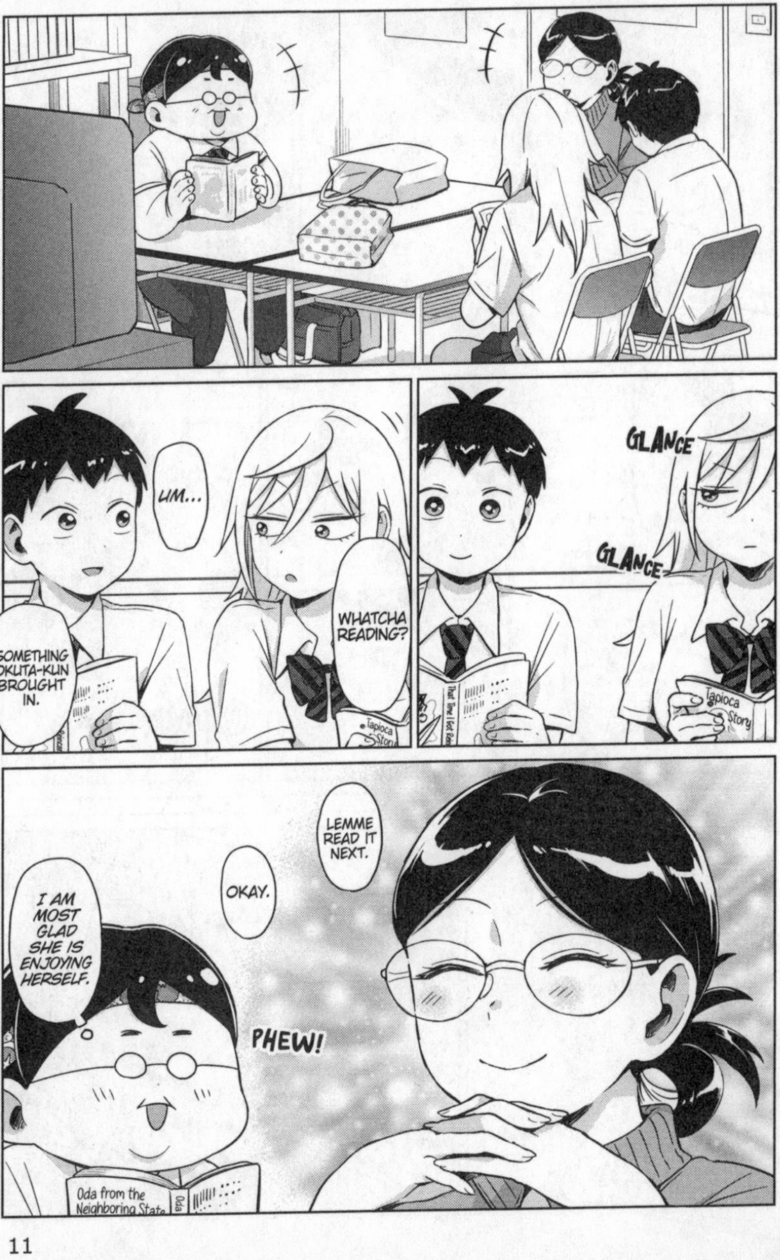
GLANCE
GLANCE
Tapioca Story
UM...
WHATCHA READING?
SOMETHING OKUTA-KUN BROUGHT IN.
Tapioca Story
LEMME READ IT NEXT.
OKAY.
I AM MOST GLAD SHE IS ENJOYING HERSELF.
PHEW!
Oda from the Neighboring State
Oda

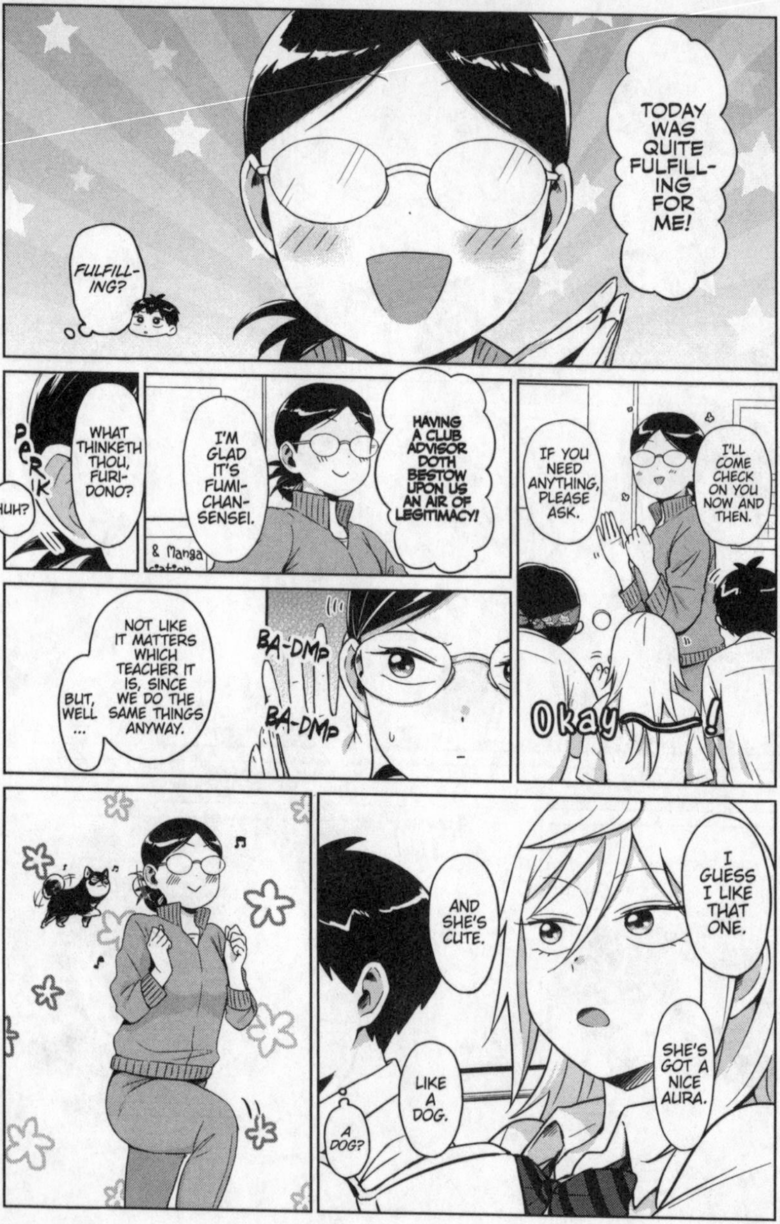
TODAY WAS QUITE FULFILL-ING FOR ME!
FULFILL-ING?
I'LL COME CHECK ON YOU NOW AND THEN.
IF YOU NEED ANYTHING, PLEASE ASK.
Okay—!
HAVING A CLUB ADVISOR DOTH BESTOW UPON US AN AIR OF LEGITIMACY!
I'M GLAD IT'S FUMI-CHAN-SENSEI.
& Manga
WHAT THINKETH THOU, FURI-DONO?
PERIK
HUH?
BA-DMP
BA-DMP
NOT LIKE IT MATTERS WHICH TEACHER IT IS, SINCE WE DO THE SAME THINGS ANYWAY.
BUT, WELL...
I GUESS I LIKE THAT ONE.
AND SHE'S CUTE.
SHE'S GOT A NICE AURA.
LIKE A DOG.
A DOG?

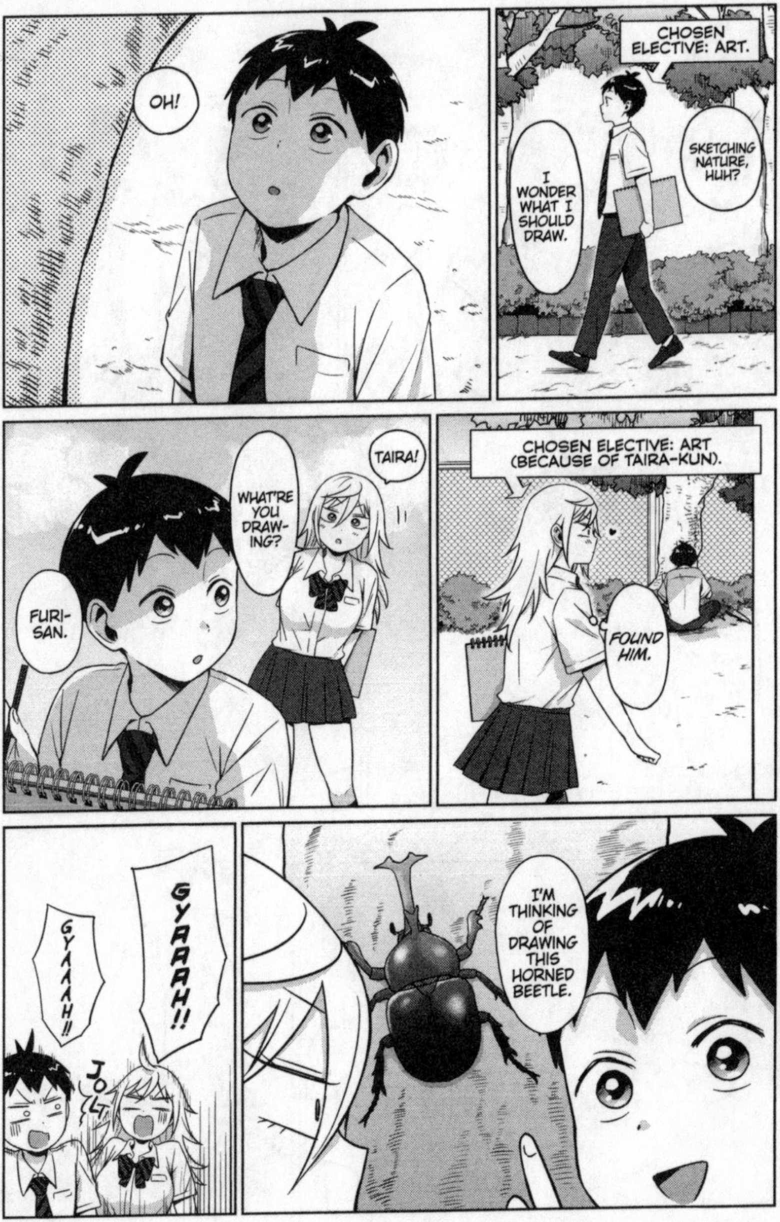

CHOSEN ELECTIVE: ART.
SKETCHING NATURE, HUH?
I WONDER WHAT I SHOULD DRAW.
OH!
CHOSEN ELECTIVE: ART (BECAUSE OF TAIRA-KUN).
FOUND HIM.
TAIRA!
WHAT'RE YOU DRAWING?
FURI-SAN.
I'M THINKING OF DRAWING THIS HORNED BEETLE.
GYAAAAH!!
GYAAAAH!!
JOLT

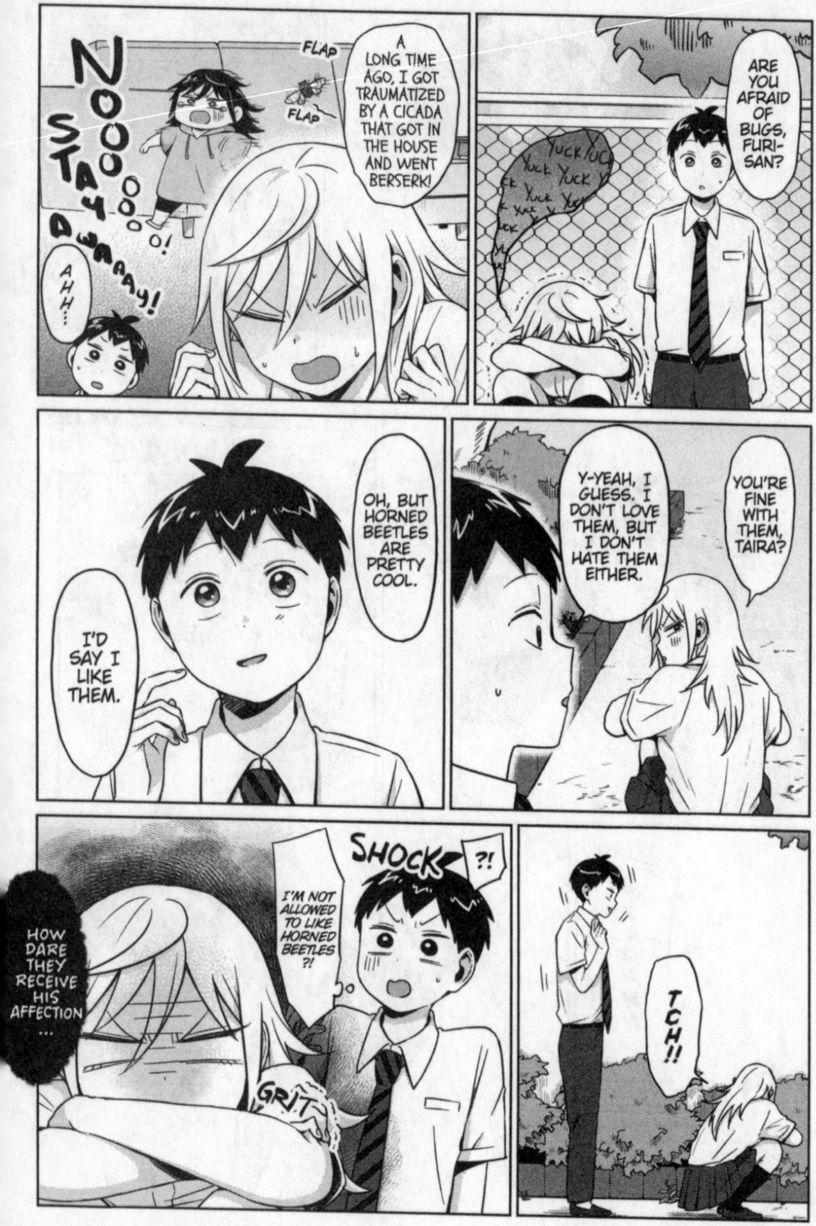

ARE YOU AFRAID OF BUGS, FURI-SAN?
YUCK YUCK YUCK YUCK YUCK YUCK
A LONG TIME AGO, I GOT TRAUMATIZED BY A CICADA THAT GOT IN THE HOUSE AND WENT BERSERK!
FLAP
FLAP
NOOOOOOOO!
STAY AWAAAAY!
AHH...
YOU'RE FINE WITH THEM, TAIRA?
Y-YEAH, I GUESS. I DON'T LOVE THEM, BUT I DON'T HATE THEM EITHER.
OH, BUT HORNED BEETLES ARE PRETTY COOL.
I'D SAY I LIKE THEM.
TCH!!
SHOCK
?!
I'M NOT ALLOWED TO LIKE HORNED BEETLES ?!
HOW DARE THEY RECEIVE HIS AFFECTION ...
GRIT

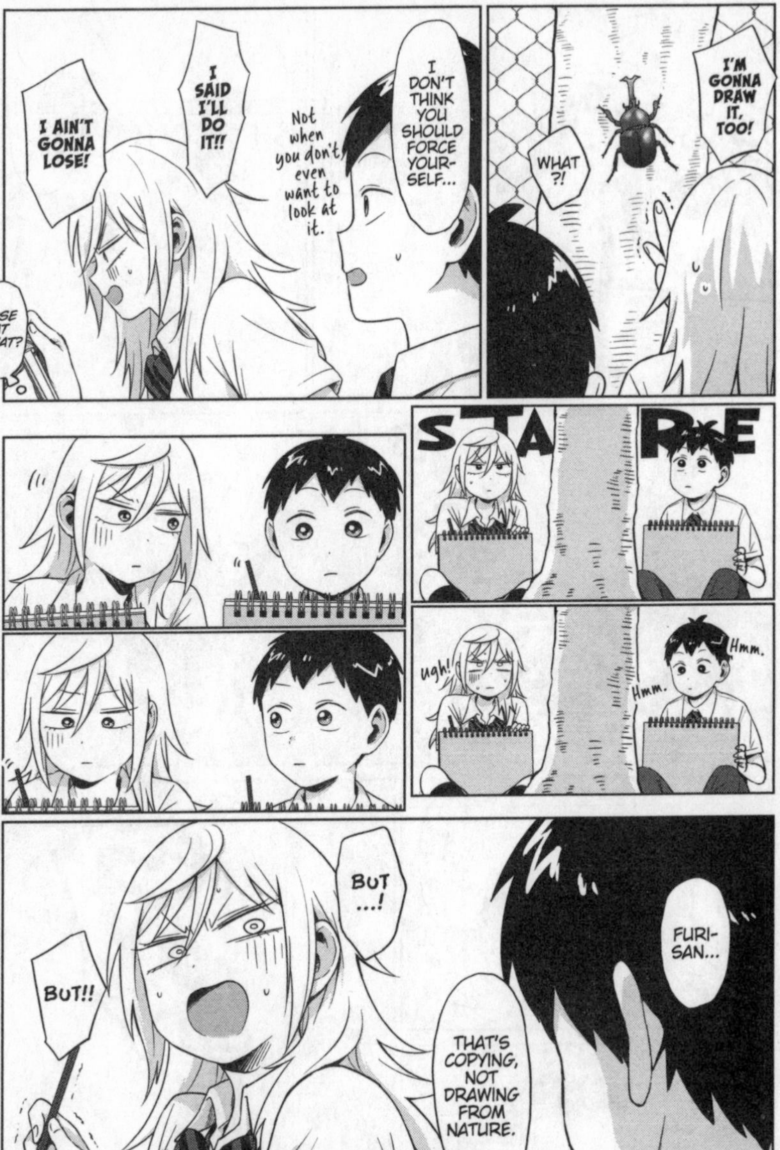
I'M GONNA DRAW IT, TOO!
WHAT ?!
I DON'T THINK YOU SHOULD FORCE YOUR-SELF...
Not when you don't even want to look at it.
I SAID I'LL DO IT!!
I AIN'T GONNA LOSE!
LOSE AT WHAT?
STARE
Hmm.
Hmm.
ugh!
FURI-SAN...
THAT'S COPYING, NOT DRAWING FROM NATURE.
BUT ...!
BUT!!

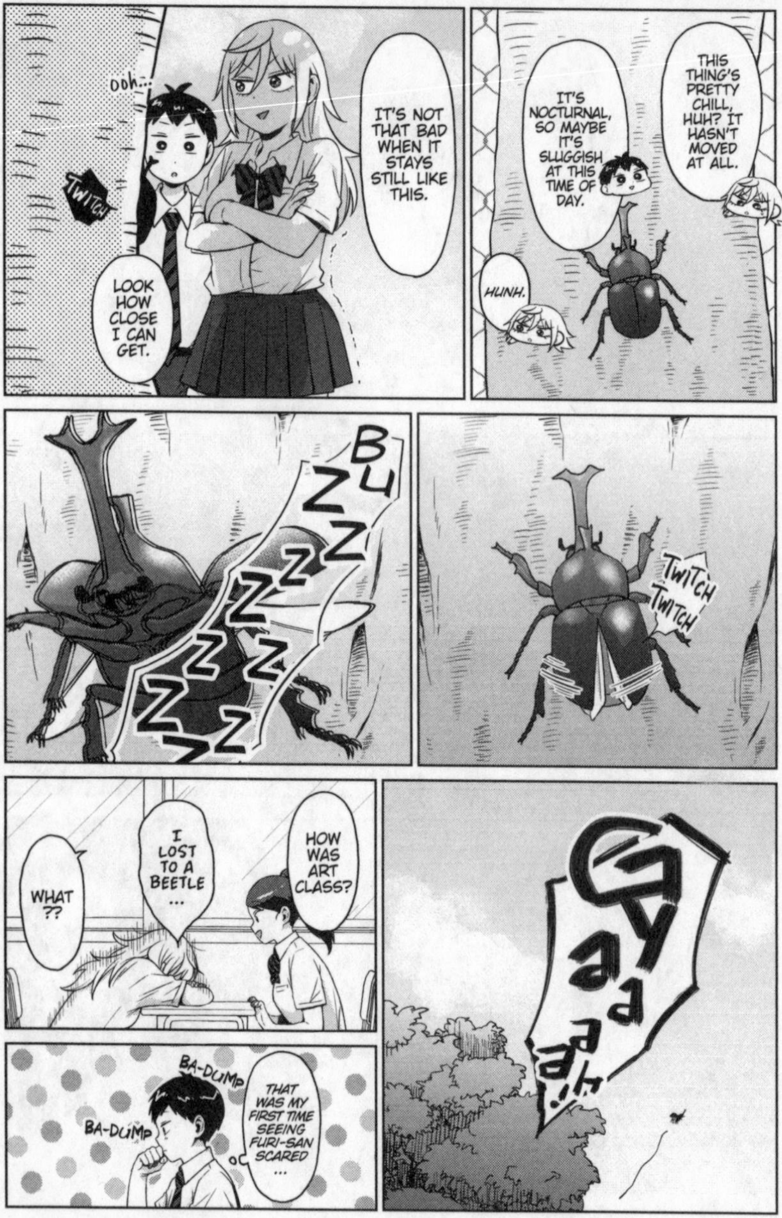
THIS THING'S PRETTY CHILL, HUH? IT HASN'T MOVED AT ALL.
IT'S NOCTURNAL, SO MAYBE IT'S SLUGGISH AT THIS TIME OF DAY.
HUNH.
IT'S NOT THAT BAD WHEN IT STAYS STILL LIKE THIS.
ooh...
TWITCH
LOOK HOW CLOSE I CAN GET.
TWITCH TWITCH
BuZZZZZZZZZ
Gyaaaah!!
HOW WAS ART CLASS?
I LOST TO A BEETLE ...
WHAT ??
BA-DUMP
BA-DUMP
THAT WAS MY FIRST TIME SEEING FURI-SAN SCARED ...

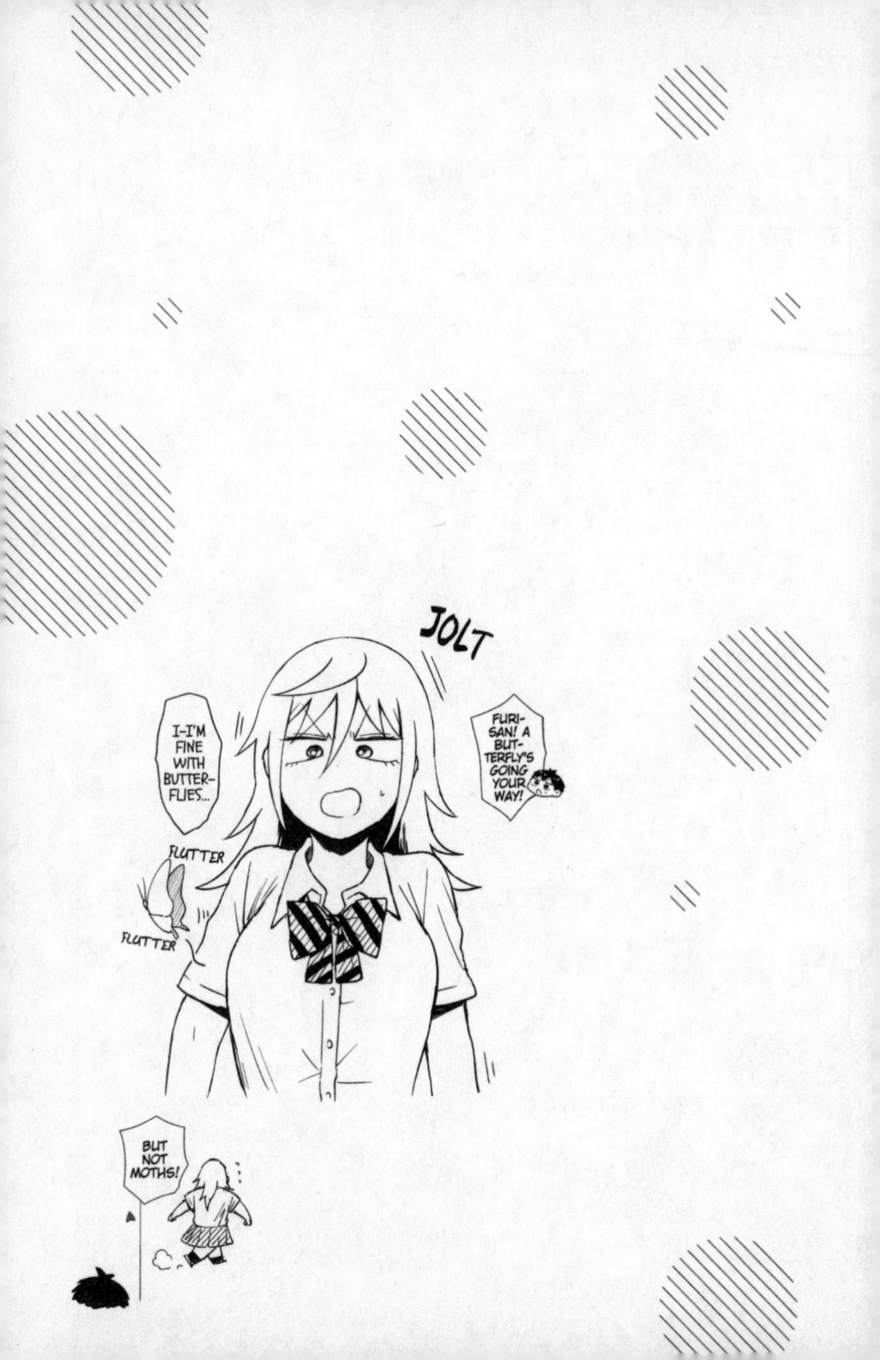
FURI-SAN! A BUTTERFLY'S GOING YOUR WAY!
JOLT
I-I'M FINE WITH BUTTERFLIES...
FLUTTER
FLUTTER
BUT NOT MOTHS!

Chapter 11

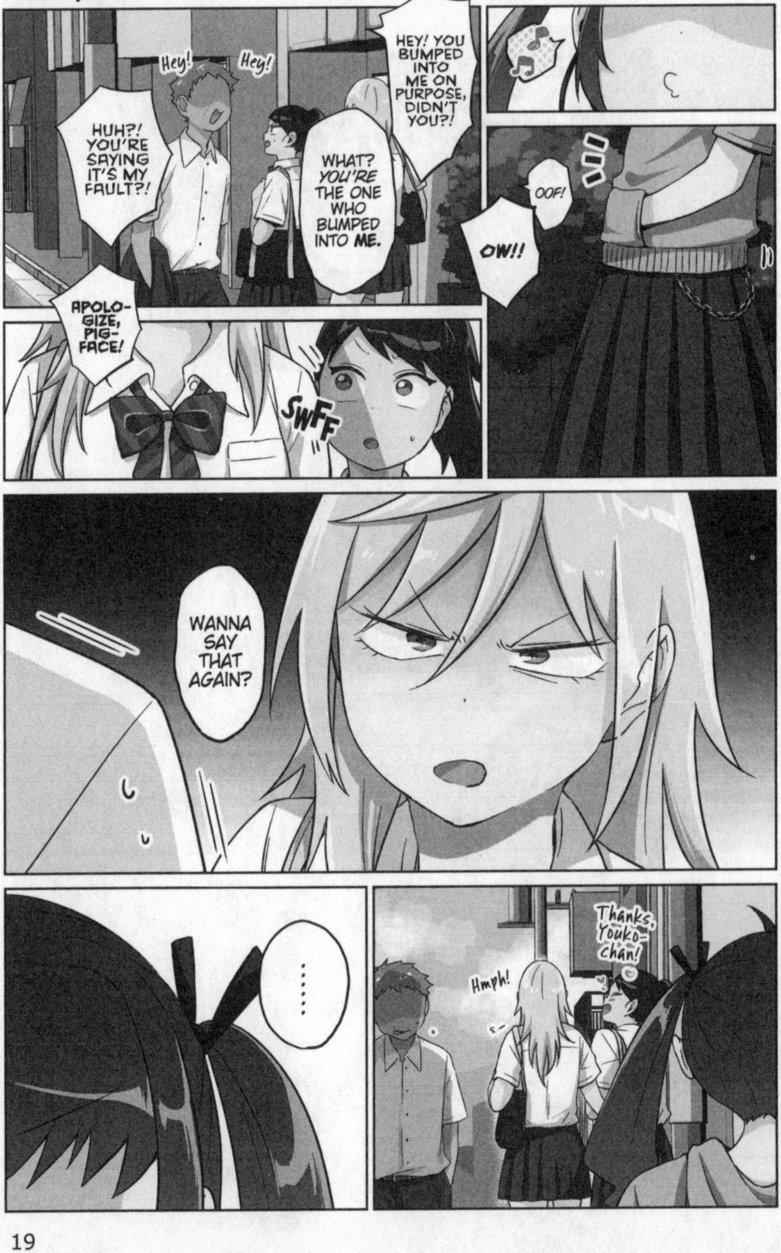
OOF!
OW!!
HEY! YOU BUMPED INTO ME ON PURPOSE, DIDN'T YOU?!
Hey!
Hey!
WHAT? YOU'RE THE ONE WHO BUMPED INTO ME.
HUH?! YOU'RE SAYING IT'S MY FAULT?!
APOLOGIZE, PIG-FACE!
SWFF
WANNA SAY THAT AGAIN?
Thanks, Youko-chan!
Hmph!
……

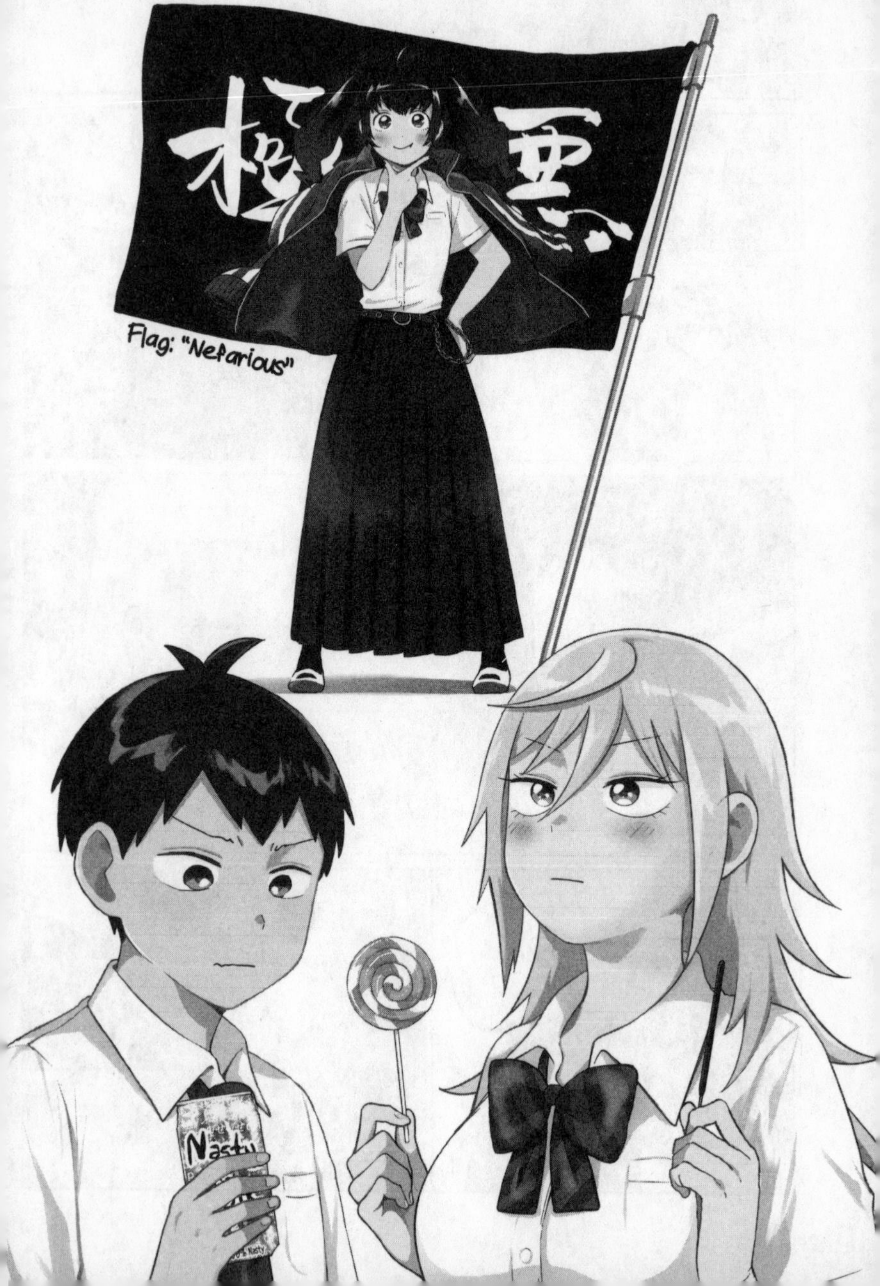
極悪
Flag: "Nefarious"
Nasty

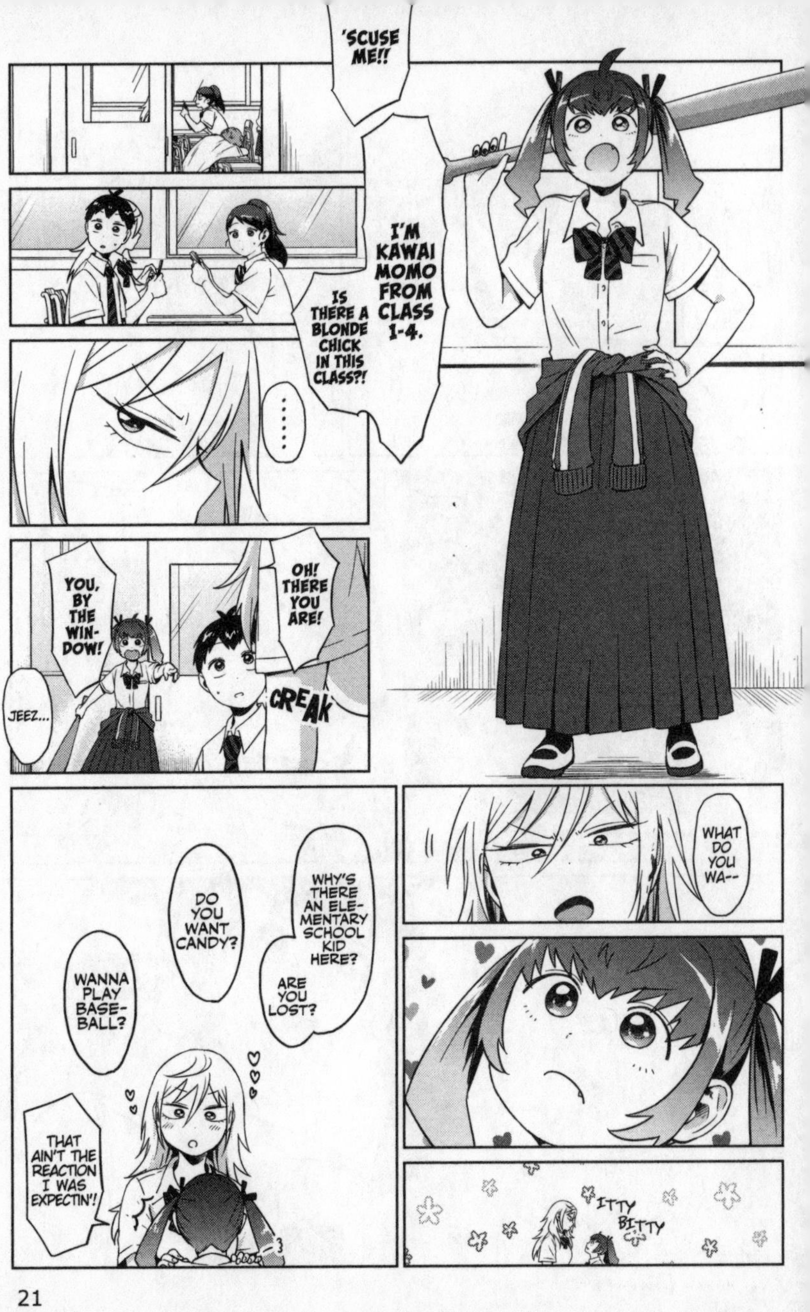
'SCUSE ME!!
I'M KAWAI MOMO FROM CLASS 1-4.
IS THERE A BLONDE CHICK IN THIS CLASS?!
......
OH! THERE YOU ARE!
YOU, BY THE WIN-DOW!
CREAK
JEEZ...
WHAT DO YOU WA--
ITTY BITTY
WHY'S THERE AN ELE-MENTARY SCHOOL KID HERE?
ARE YOU LOST?
DO YOU WANT CANDY?
WANNA PLAY BASE-BALL?
THAT AIN'T THE REACTION I WAS EXPECTIN'!

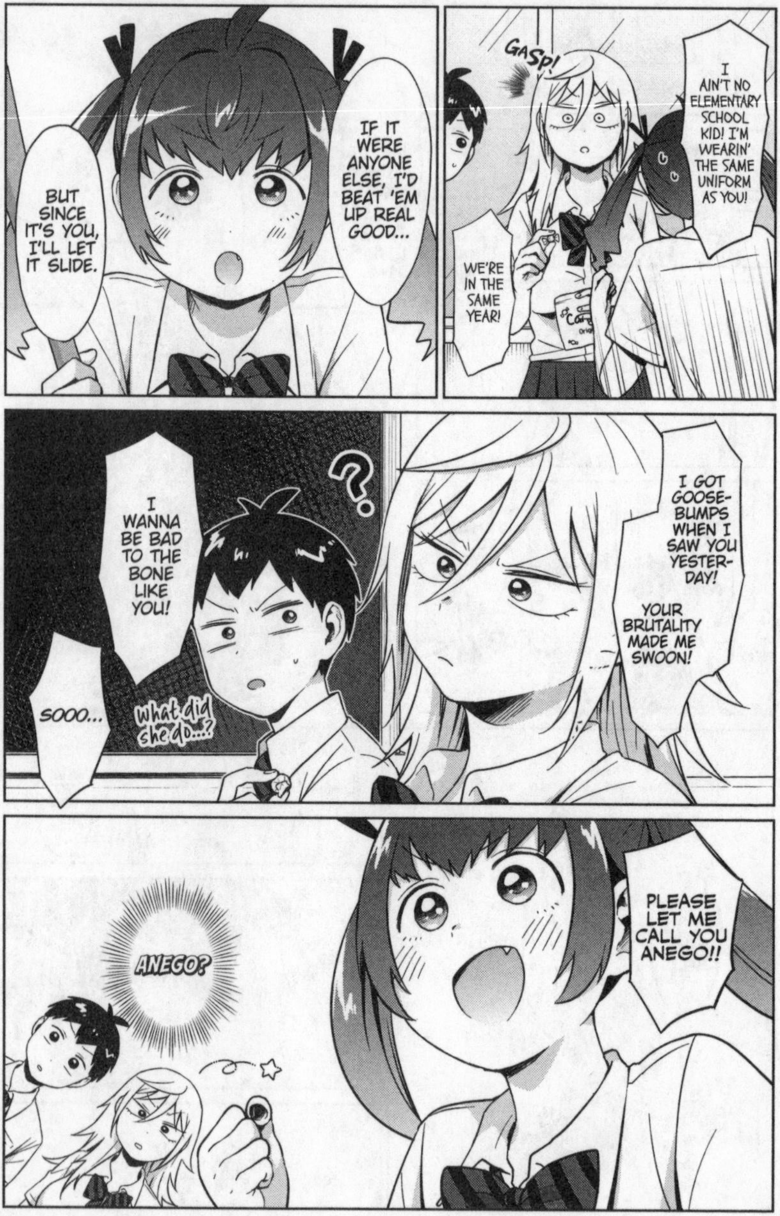
GASP!
I AIN'T NO ELEMENTARY SCHOOL KID! I'M WEARIN' THE SAME UNIFORM AS YOU!
WE'RE IN THE SAME YEAR!
IF IT WERE ANYONE ELSE, I'D BEAT 'EM UP REAL GOOD...
BUT SINCE IT'S YOU, I'LL LET IT SLIDE.
I GOT GOOSE-BUMPS WHEN I SAW YOU YESTER-DAY!
YOUR BRUTALITY MADE ME SWOON!
I WANNA BE BAD TO THE BONE LIKE YOU!
what did she do...?
SOOO...
PLEASE LET ME CALL YOU ANEGO!!
ANEGO?

Anego: An extra-respectful word for "big sister."

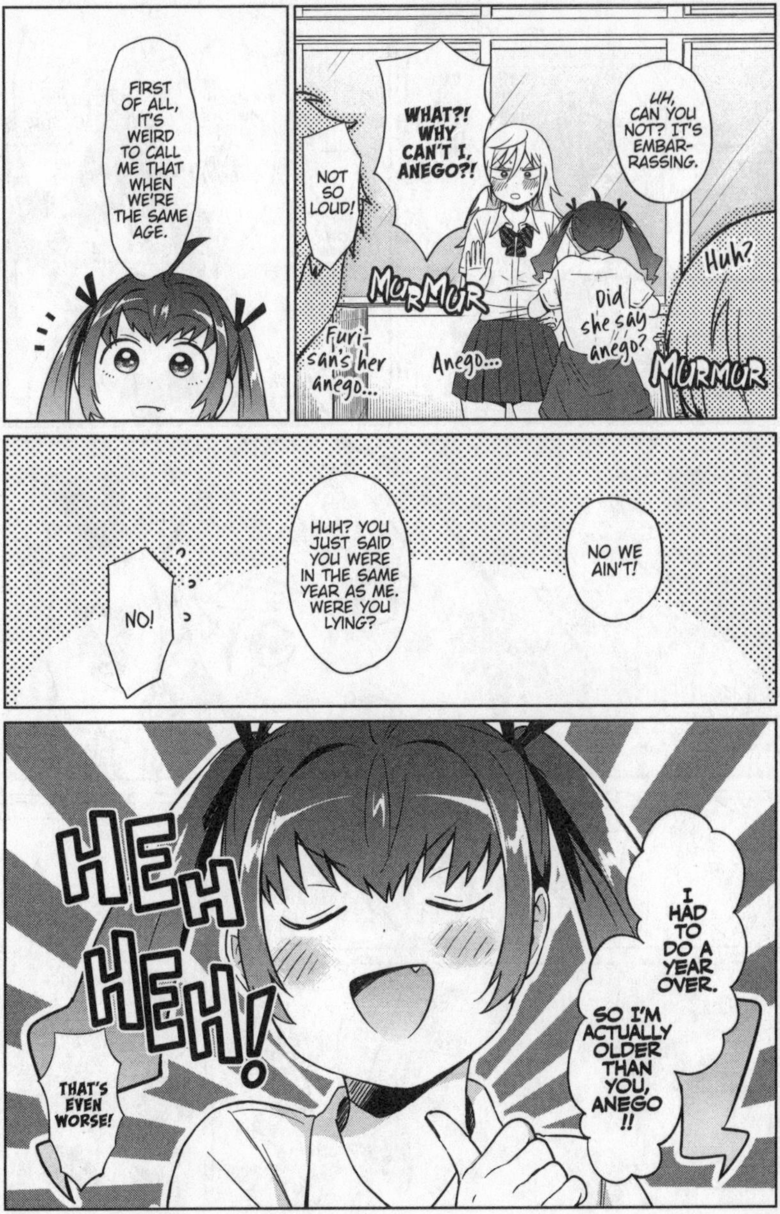
UH, CAN YOU NOT? IT'S EMBARRASSING.
WHAT?! WHY CAN'T I, ANEGO?!
NOT SO LOUD!
Huh?
Did she say anego?
MURMUR
Anego...
MURMUR
Furi-san's her anego...
FIRST OF ALL, IT'S WEIRD TO CALL ME THAT WHEN WE'RE THE SAME AGE.
NO WE AIN'T!
HUH? YOU JUST SAID YOU WERE IN THE SAME YEAR AS ME. WERE YOU LYING?
NO!
I HAD TO DO A YEAR OVER.
SO I'M ACTUALLY OLDER THAN YOU, ANEGO!!
HEH HEH HEH!
THAT'S EVEN WORSE!

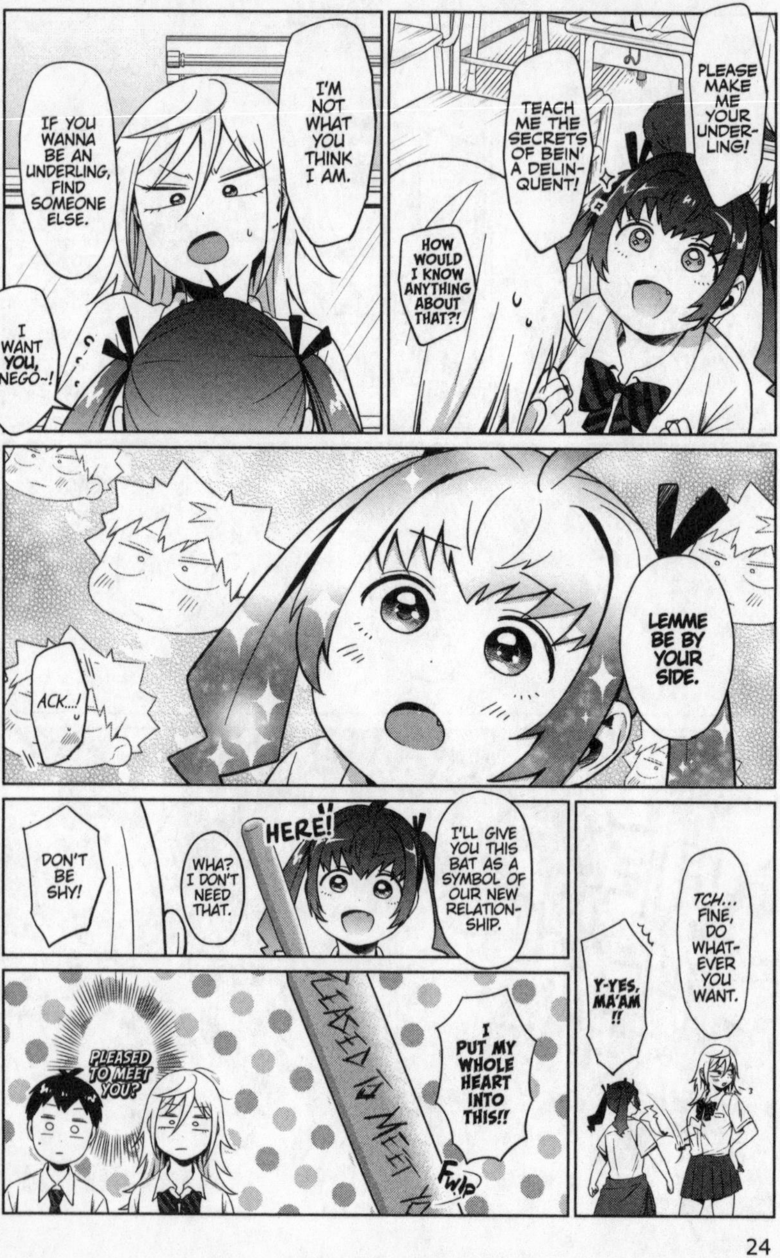
PLEASE MAKE ME YOUR UNDERLING!
TEACH ME THE SECRETS OF BEIN' A DELINQUENT!
HOW WOULD I KNOW ANYTHING ABOUT THAT?!
I'M NOT WHAT YOU THINK I AM.
IF YOU WANNA BE AN UNDERLING, FIND SOMEONE ELSE.
I WANT **YOU**, ANEGO~!
LEMME BE BY YOUR SIDE.
ACK...!
TCH... FINE, DO WHATEVER YOU WANT.
Y-YES, MA'AM!!
I'LL GIVE YOU THIS BAT AS A SYMBOL OF OUR NEW RELATIONSHIP.
HERE!
WHA? I DON'T NEED THAT.
DON'T BE SHY!
I PUT MY WHOLE HEART INTO THIS!!
FWIP
PLEASED TO MEET YOU?

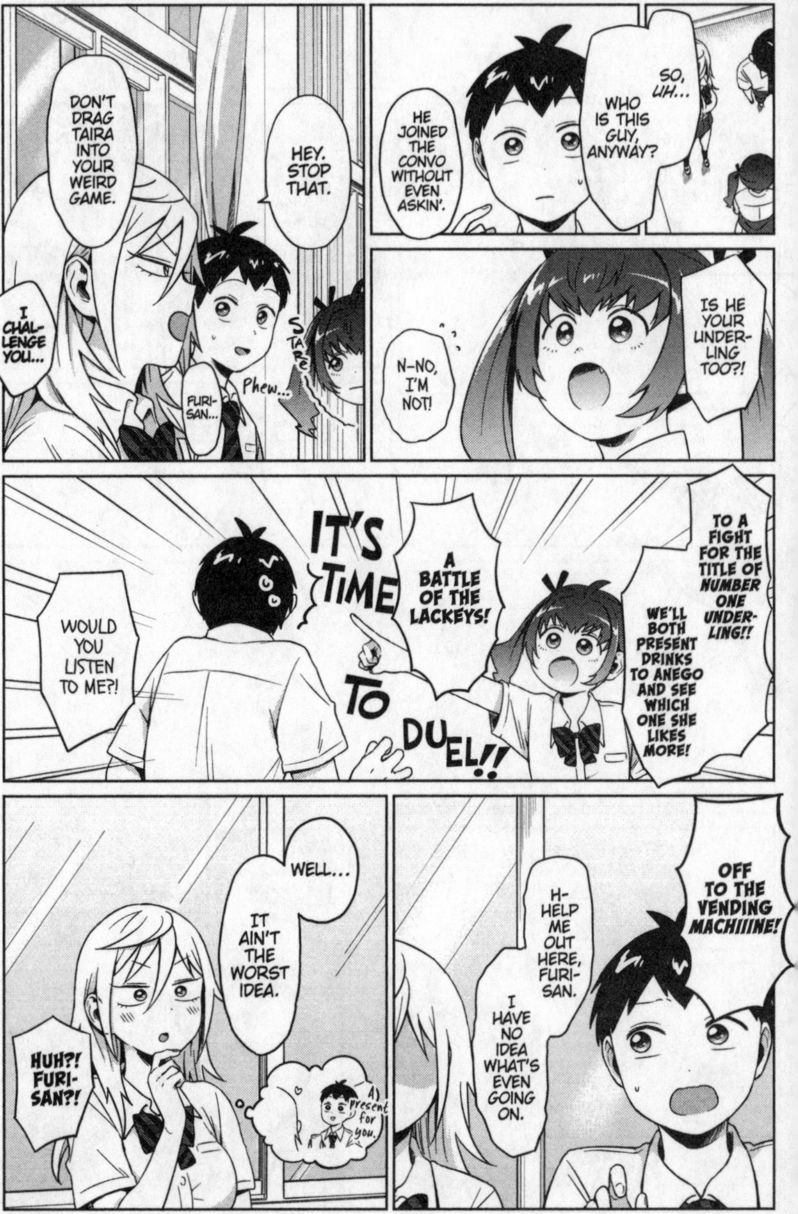
SO, UH... WHO IS THIS GUY, ANYWAY?
HE JOINED THE CONVO WITHOUT EVEN ASKIN'.
IS HE YOUR UNDERLING TOO?!
N-NO, I'M NOT!
HEY. STOP THAT.
DON'T DRAG TAIRA INTO YOUR WEIRD GAME.
STARE
Phew...
FURI-SAN...
I CHALLENGE YOU...
TO A FIGHT FOR THE TITLE OF NUMBER ONE UNDERLING!!
WE'LL BOTH PRESENT DRINKS TO ANEGO AND SEE WHICH ONE SHE LIKES MORE!
A BATTLE OF THE LACKEYS!
IT'S TIME TO DUEL!!
WOULD YOU LISTEN TO ME?!
OFF TO THE VENDING MACHIIINE!
H-HELP ME OUT HERE, FURI-SAN.
I HAVE NO IDEA WHAT'S EVEN GOING ON.
WELL...
IT AIN'T THE WORST IDEA.
A present for you.
HUH?! FURI-SAN?!

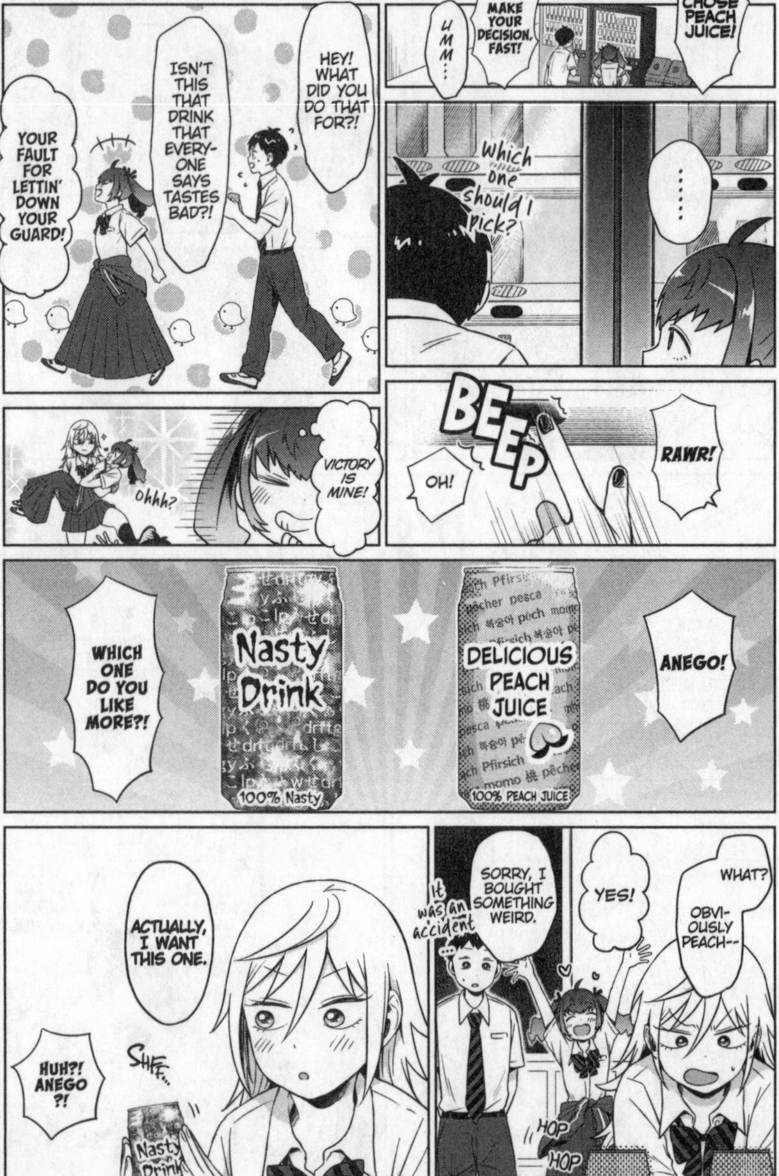
I CHOSE PEACH JUICE!
MAKE YOUR DECISION, FAST!
UMM...
......
Which one should I pick?
RAWR!
BEEP
OH!
VICTORY IS MINE!
Ohhh?
HEY! WHAT DID YOU DO THAT FOR?!
ISN'T THIS THAT DRINK THAT EVERY-ONE SAYS TASTES BAD?!
YOUR FAULT FOR LETTIN' DOWN YOUR GUARD!
ANEGO!
DELICIOUS PEACH JUICE
100% PEACH JUICE
Nasty Drink
100% Nasty
WHICH ONE DO YOU LIKE MORE?!
WHAT?
OBVI-OUSLY PEACH--
YES!
SORRY, I BOUGHT SOMETHING WEIRD.
It was an accident
HOP
HOP
ACTUALLY, I WANT THIS ONE.
SHFF...
Nasty Drink
HUH?! ANEGO ?!

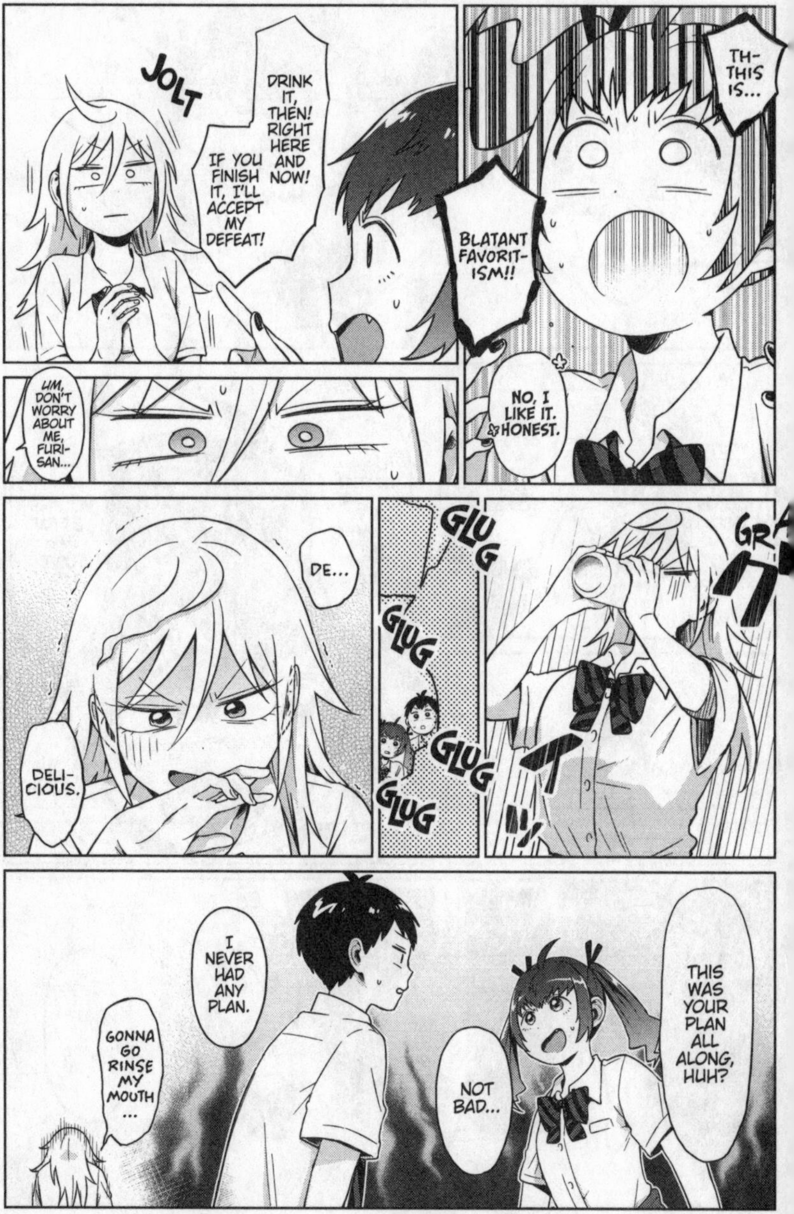
TH-THIS IS...
BLATANT FAVORIT-ISM!!
NO, I LIKE IT. HONEST.
JOLT
DRINK IT, THEN! RIGHT HERE AND NOW!
IF YOU FINISH IT, I'LL ACCEPT MY DEFEAT!
UM, DON'T WORRY ABOUT ME, FURI-SAN...
GRA
GLUG
GLUG
GLUG
GLUG
DE...
DELI-CIOUS.
THIS WAS YOUR PLAN ALL ALONG, HUH?
NOT BAD...
I NEVER HAD ANY PLAN.
GONNA GO RINSE MY MOUTH...

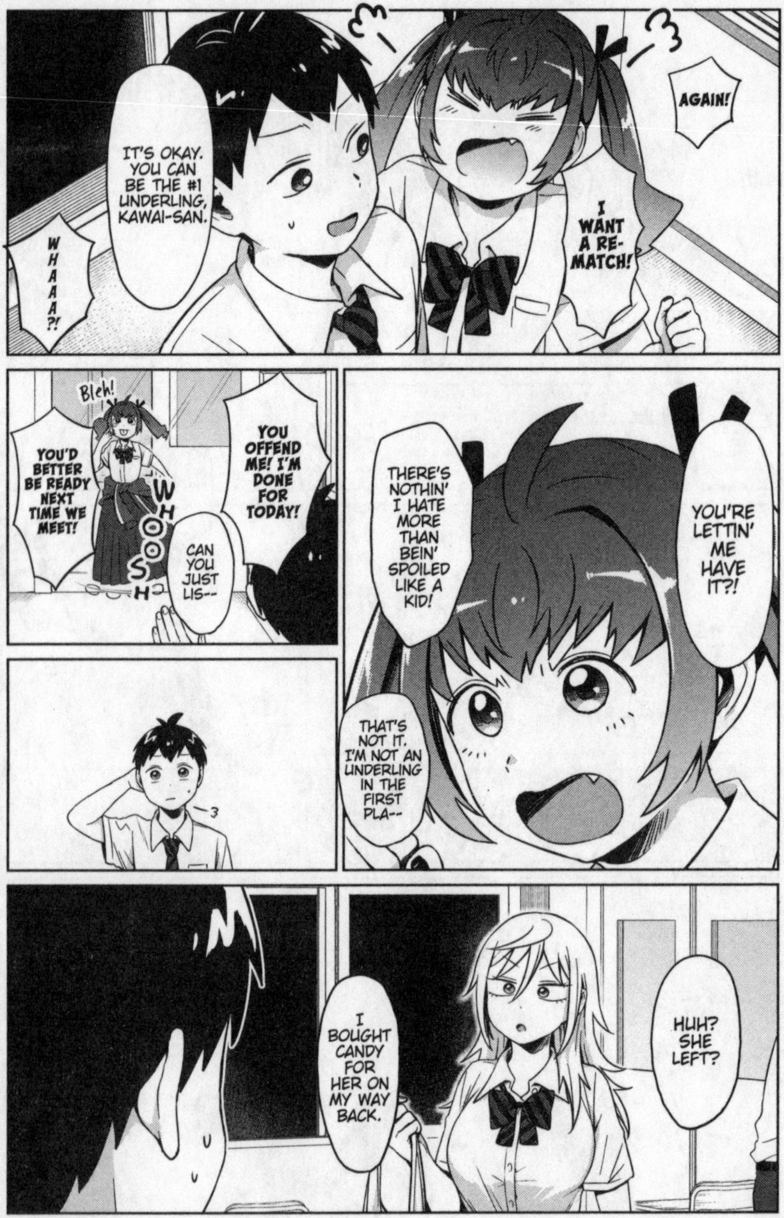
AGAIN!
I WANT A RE-MATCH!
IT'S OKAY. YOU CAN BE THE #1 UNDERLING, KAWAI-SAN.
WHAAAA?!
YOU'RE LETTIN' ME HAVE IT?!
THERE'S NOTHIN' I HATE MORE THAN BEIN' SPOILED LIKE A KID!
THAT'S NOT IT. I'M NOT AN UNDERLING IN THE FIRST PLA--
YOU OFFEND ME! I'M DONE FOR TODAY!
Bleh!
YOU'D BETTER BE READY NEXT TIME WE MEET!
WHOOSH
CAN YOU JUST LIS--
HUH? SHE LEFT?
I BOUGHT CANDY FOR HER ON MY WAY BACK.

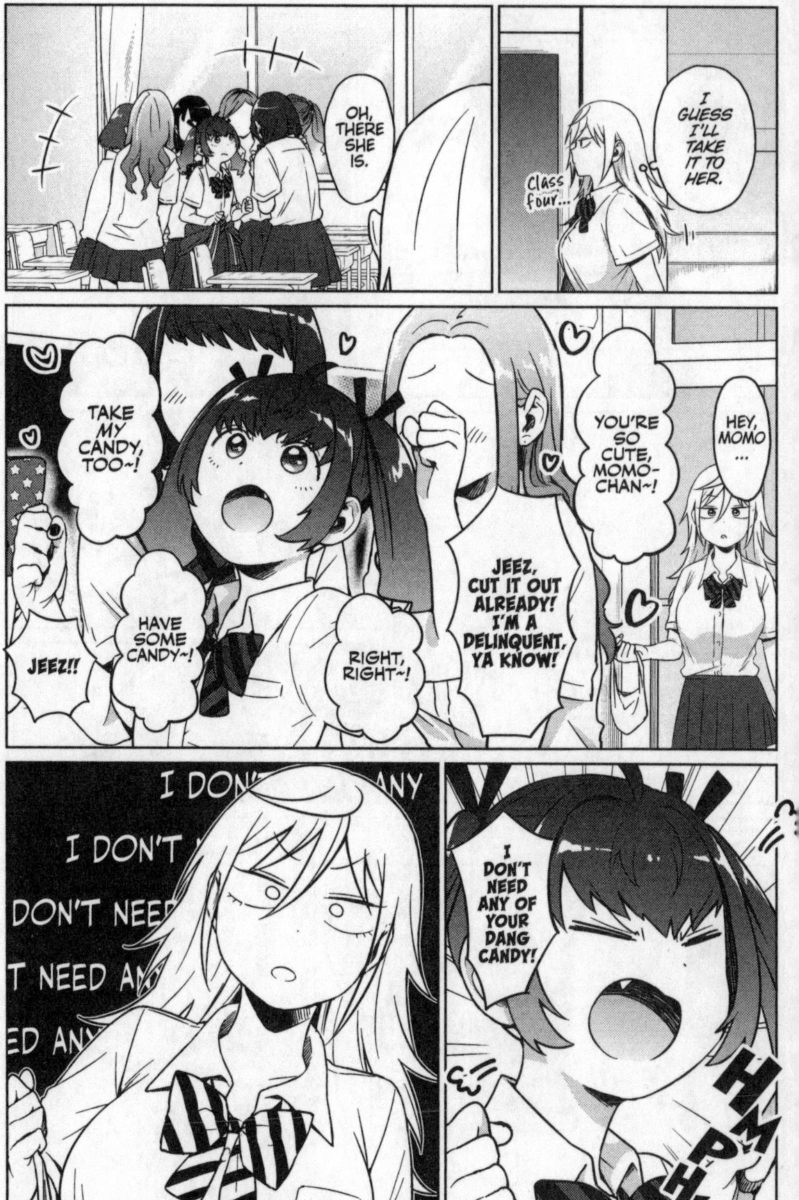
I GUESS I'LL TAKE IT TO HER.
Class four...
OH, THERE SHE IS.
HEY, MOMO...
YOU'RE SO CUTE, MOMO-CHAN~!
JEEZ, CUT IT OUT ALREADY! I'M A DELINQUENT, YA KNOW!
TAKE MY CANDY, TOO~!
RIGHT, RIGHT~!
HAVE SOME CANDY~!
JEEZ!!
I DON'T NEED ANY OF YOUR DANG CANDY!
HMPH!
I DON
ANY
I DON'T
DON'T NEE
T NEED AN
ED ANY

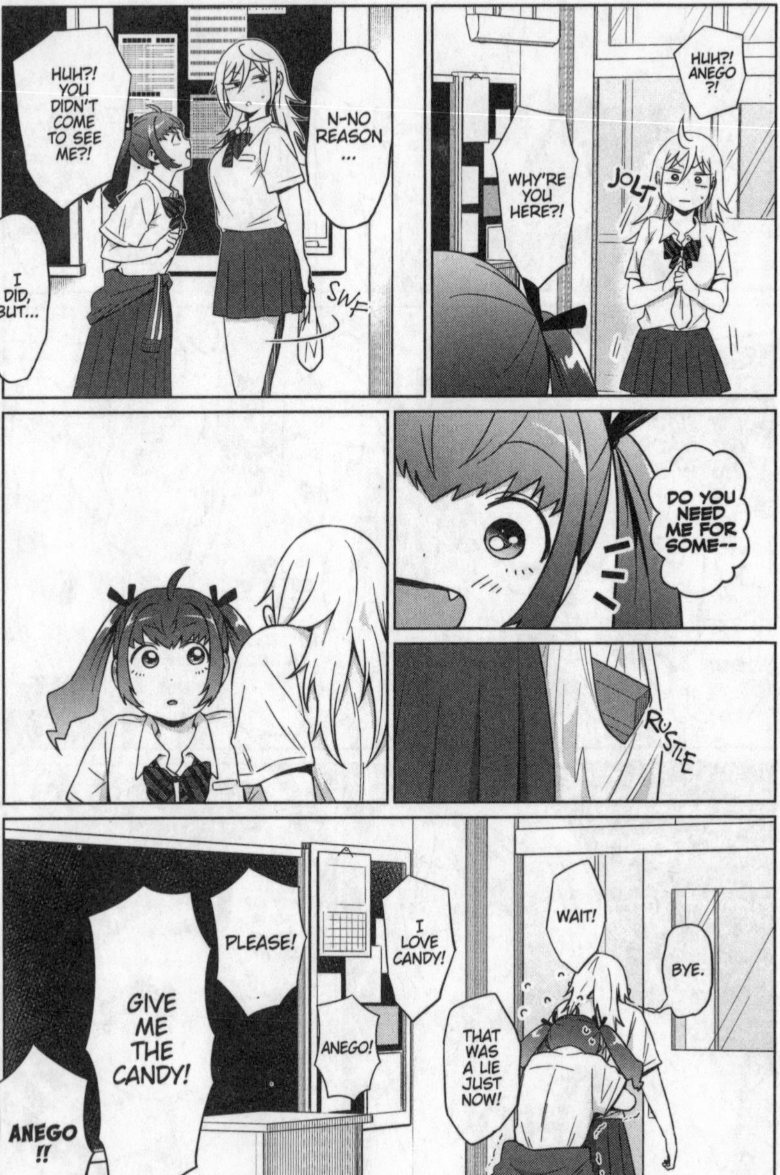
HUH?! ANEGO ?!
WHY'RE YOU HERE?!
JOLT
N-NO REASON ...
HUH?! YOU DIDN'T COME TO SEE ME?!
SWF
I DID, BUT...
DO YOU NEED ME FOR SOME--
RUSTLE
BYE.
WAIT!
THAT WAS A LIE JUST NOW!
I LOVE CANDY!
ANEGO!
PLEASE!
GIVE ME THE CANDY!
ANEGO !!

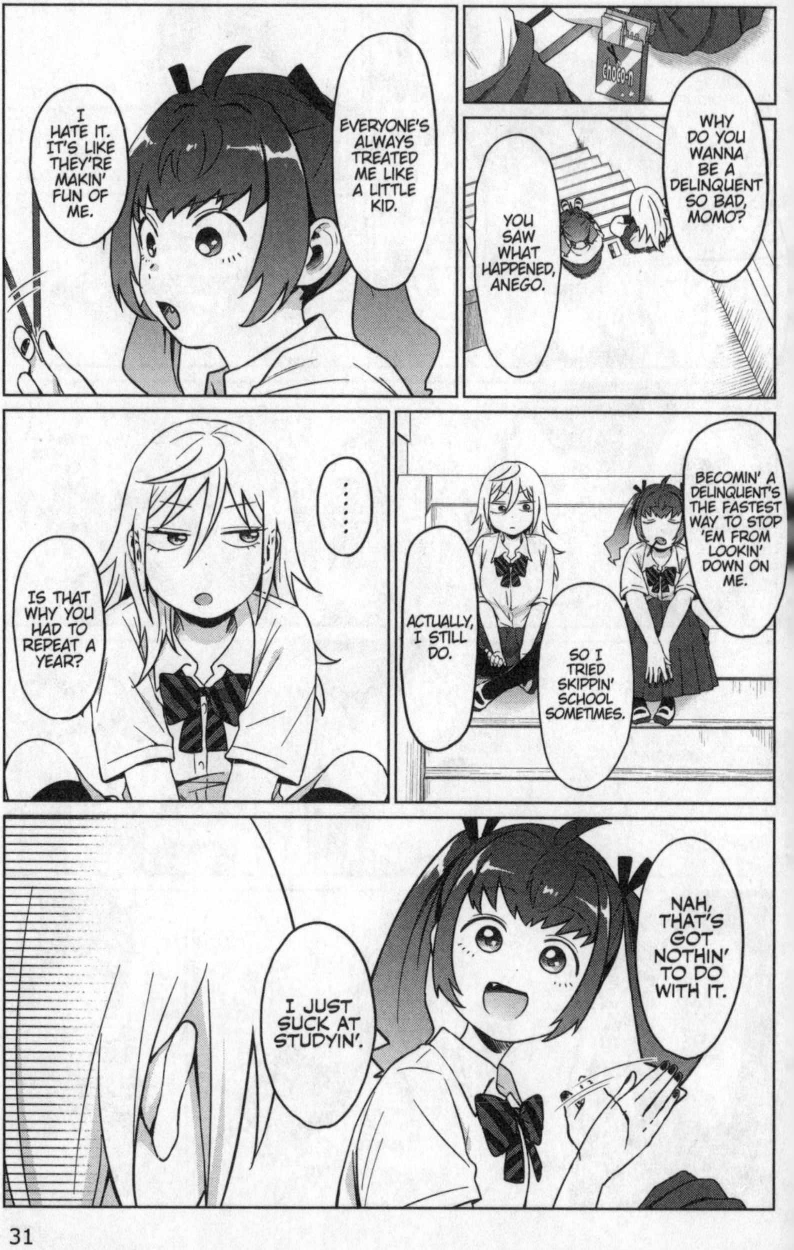
choco-n
WHY DO YOU WANNA BE A DELINQUENT SO BAD, MOMO?
YOU SAW WHAT HAPPENED, ANEGO.
EVERYONE'S ALWAYS TREATED ME LIKE A LITTLE KID.
I HATE IT. IT'S LIKE THEY'RE MAKIN' FUN OF ME.
BECOMIN' A DELINQUENT'S THE FASTEST WAY TO STOP 'EM FROM LOOKIN' DOWN ON ME.
SO I TRIED SKIPPIN' SCHOOL SOMETIMES.
ACTUALLY, I STILL DO.
......
IS THAT WHY YOU HAD TO REPEAT A YEAR?
NAH, THAT'S GOT NOTHIN' TO DO WITH IT.
I JUST SUCK AT STUDYIN'.

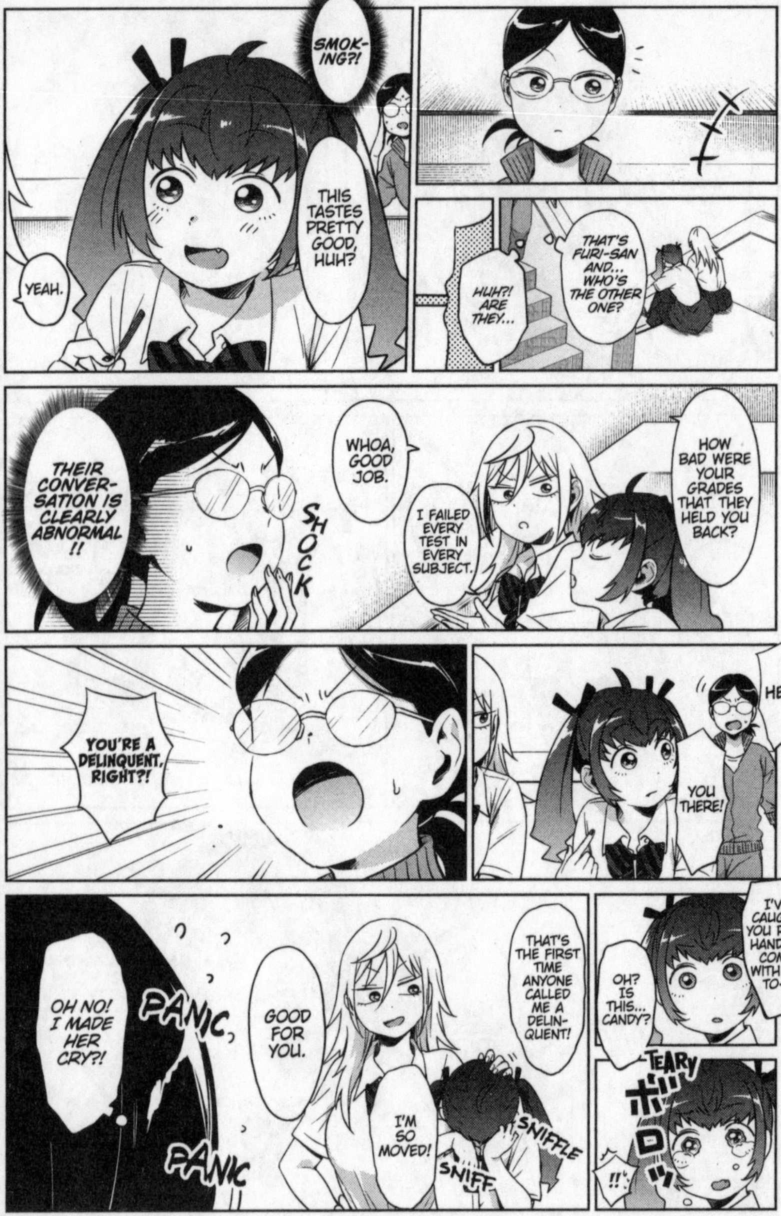
THAT'S FURI-SAN AND... WHO'S THE OTHER ONE?
HUH?! ARE THEY...
SMOK-ING?!
THIS TASTES PRETTY GOOD, HUH?
YEAH.
HOW BAD WERE YOUR GRADES THAT THEY HELD YOU BACK?
I FAILED EVERY TEST IN EVERY SUBJECT.
WHOA, GOOD JOB.
SHOCK
THEIR CONVER-SATION IS CLEARLY ABNORMAL !!
HEY!
YOU THERE!
YOU'RE A DELINQUENT, RIGHT?!
I'VE CAUGHT YOU RED-HANDED! COME WITH ME TO--
OH? IS THIS... CANDY?
TEARY
ボロッ
!!
THAT'S THE FIRST TIME ANYONE CALLED ME A DELIN-QUENT!
I'M SO MOVED!
SNIFFLE
SNIFF
GOOD FOR YOU.
PANIC
OH NO! I MADE HER CRY?!
PANIC

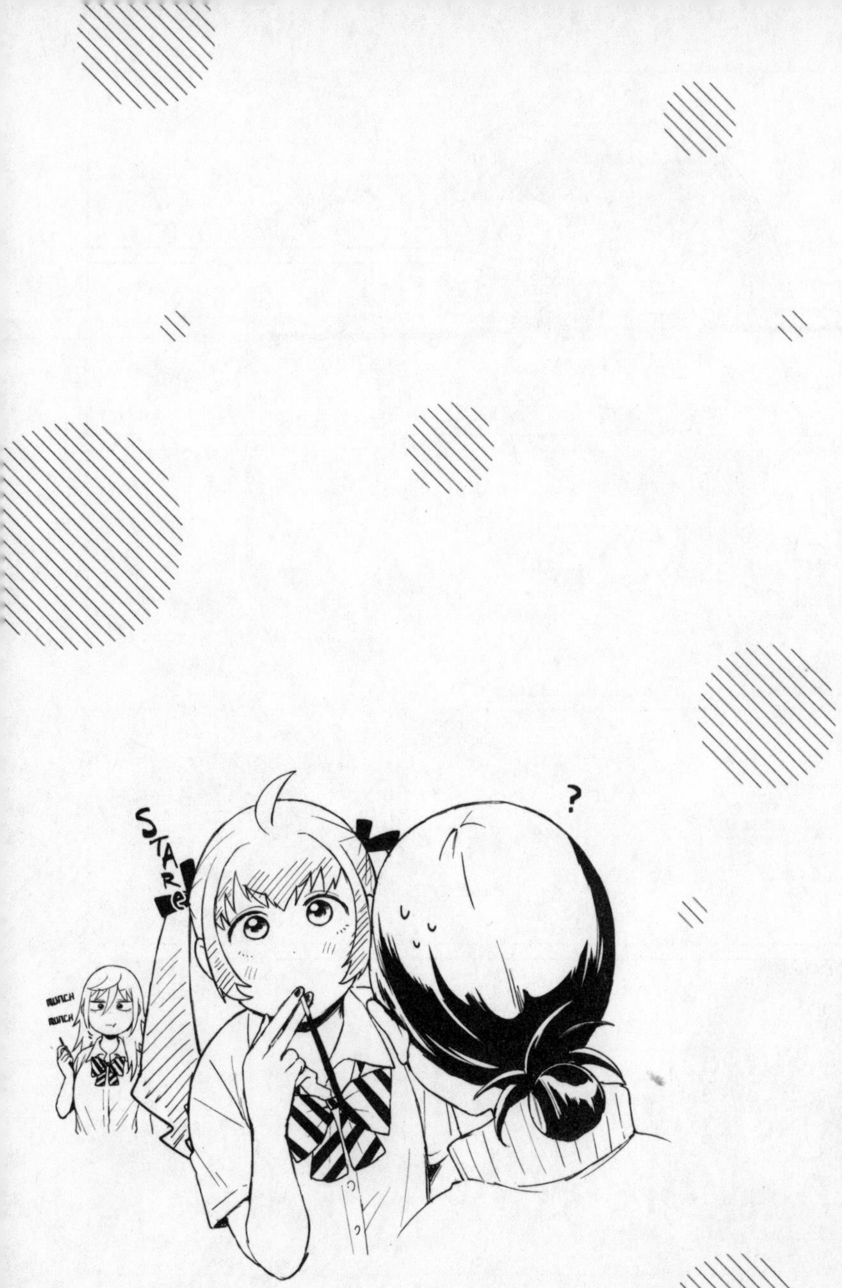
?
STARE
MUNCH
MUNCH

Chapter 12

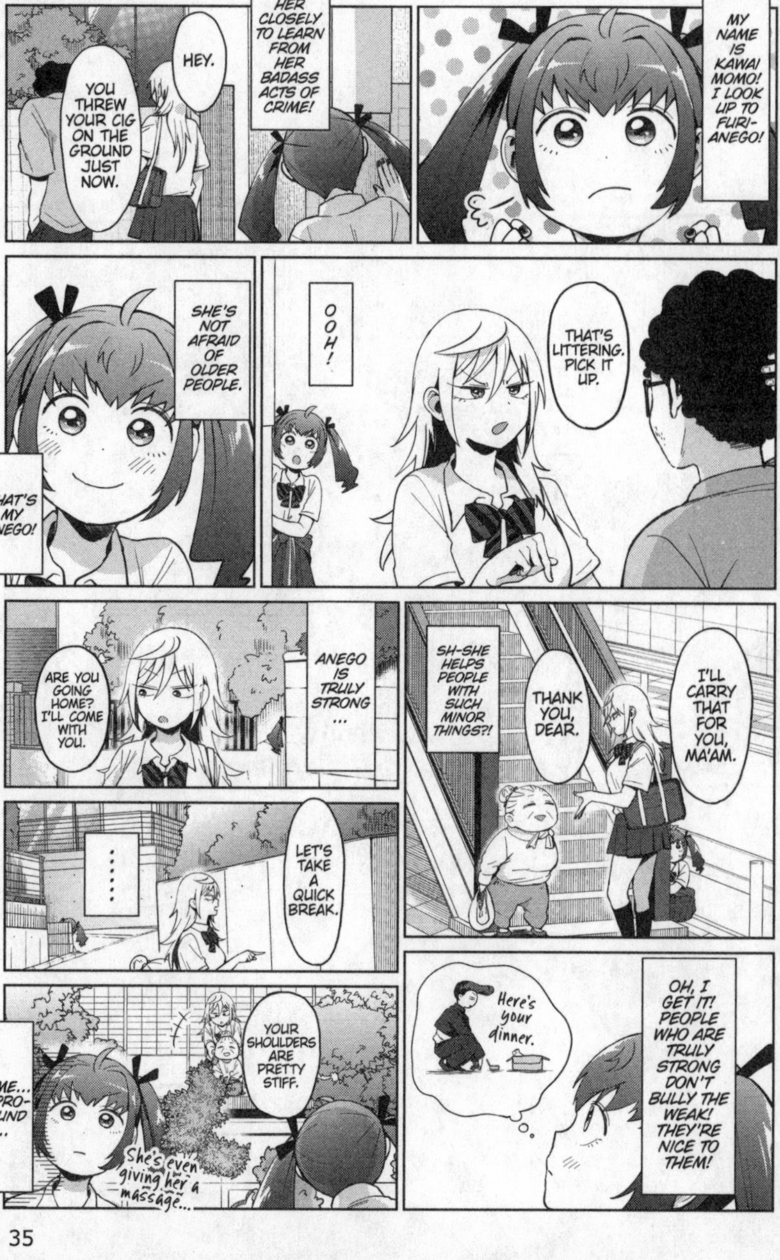

MY NAME IS KAWAI MOMO! I LOOK UP TO FURI-ANEGO!
I WATCH HER CLOSELY TO LEARN FROM HER BADASS ACTS OF CRIME!
HEY.
YOU THREW YOUR CIG ON THE GROUND JUST NOW.
THAT'S LITTERING. PICK IT UP.
OOH!
SHE'S NOT AFRAID OF OLDER PEOPLE.
THAT'S MY ANEGO!
I'LL CARRY THAT FOR YOU, MA'AM.
THANK YOU, DEAR.
SH-SHE HELPS PEOPLE WITH SUCH MINOR THINGS?!
ANEGO IS TRULY STRONG...
ARE YOU GOING HOME? I'LL COME WITH YOU.
LET'S TAKE A QUICK BREAK.
......
OH, I GET IT! PEOPLE WHO ARE TRULY STRONG DON'T BULLY THE WEAK! THEY'RE NICE TO THEM!
Here's your dinner.
YOUR SHOULDERS ARE PRETTY STIFF.
CRIME... IS PRO-FOUND...
She's even giving her a massage...

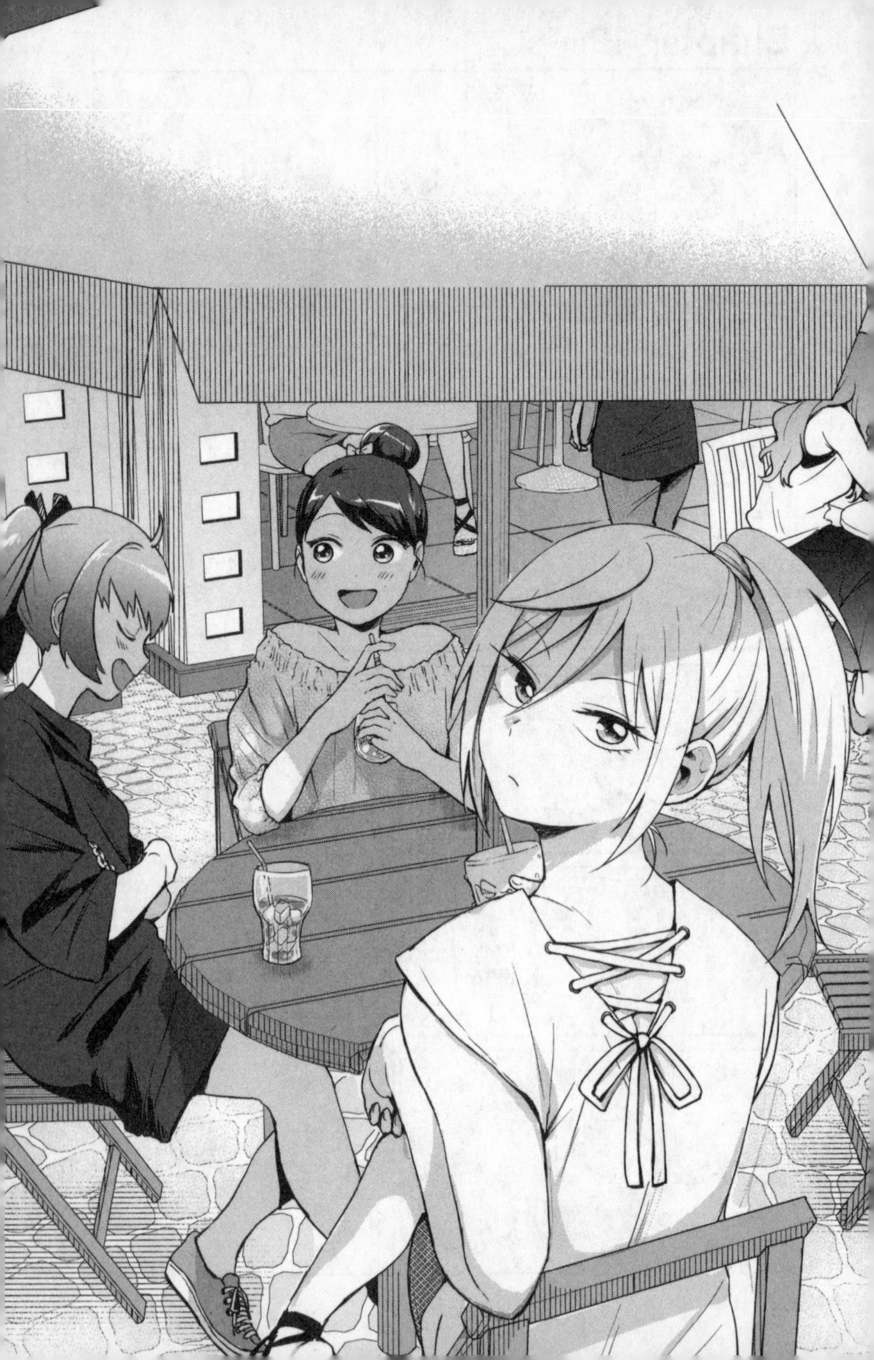

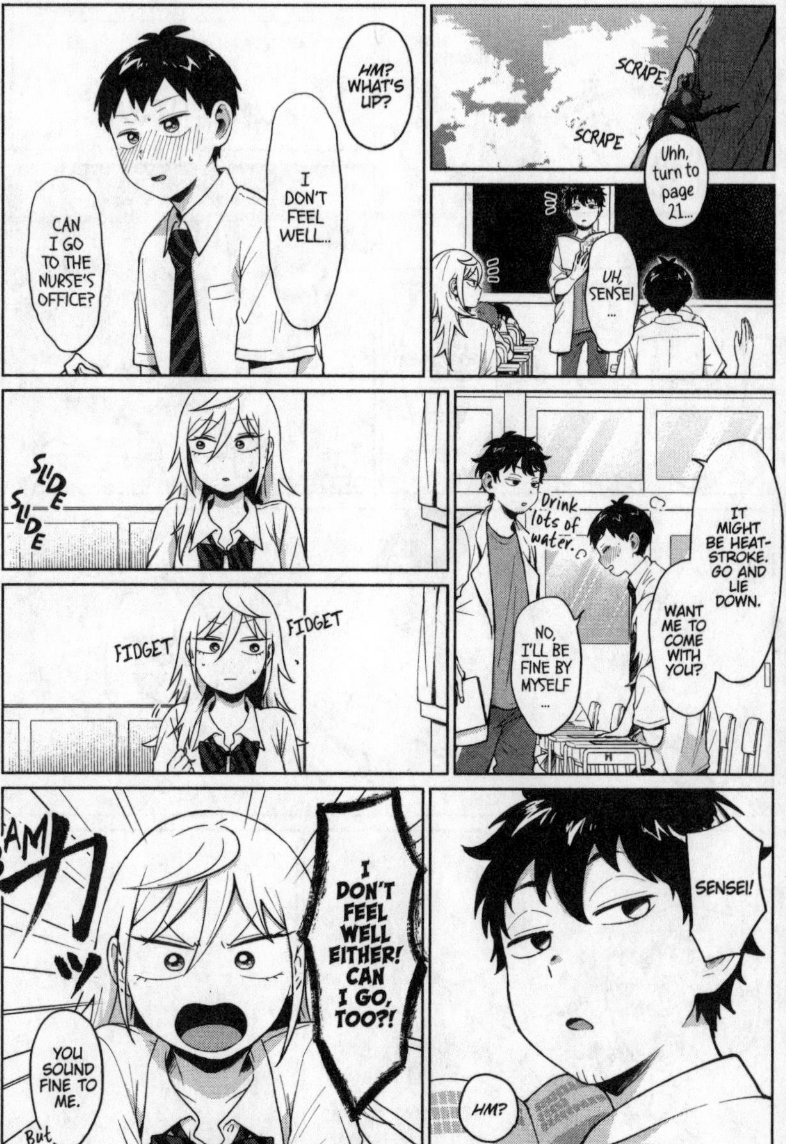
SCRAPE
SCRAPE
Uhh, turn to page 21...
UH, SENSEI ...
HM? WHAT'S UP?
I DON'T FEEL WELL...
CAN I GO TO THE NURSE'S OFFICE?
IT MIGHT BE HEAT-STROKE. GO AND LIE DOWN.
WANT ME TO COME WITH YOU?
NO, I'LL BE FINE BY MYSELF ...
Drink lots of water.
SLIDE
SLIDE
FIDGET
FIDGET
SENSEI!
HM?
BAM
I DON'T FEEL WELL EITHER! CAN I GO, TOO?!
YOU SOUND FINE TO ME.
But sure, whatever.

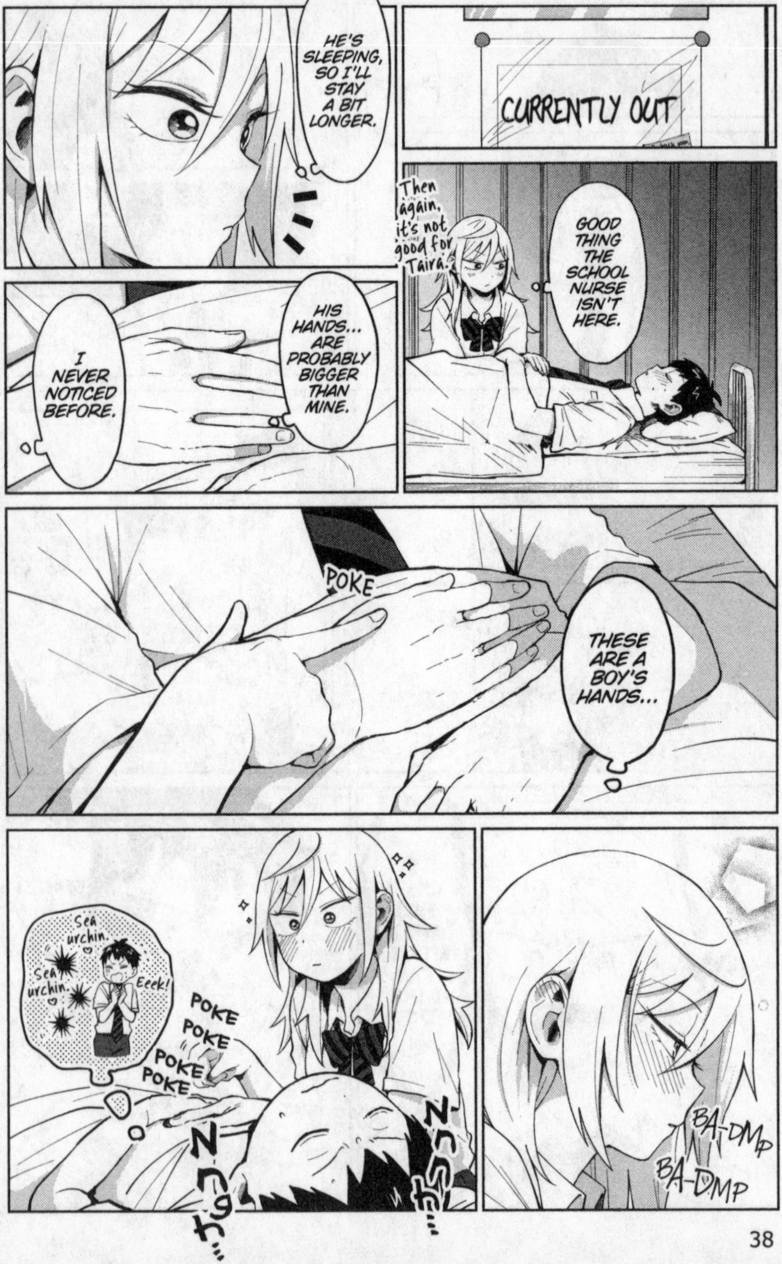
CURRENTLY OUT
GOOD THING THE SCHOOL NURSE ISN'T HERE.
Then again, it's not good for Taira.
HE'S SLEEPING, SO I'LL STAY A BIT LONGER.
HIS HANDS... ARE PROBABLY BIGGER THAN MINE.
I NEVER NOTICED BEFORE.
POKE
THESE ARE A BOY'S HANDS...
BA-DMP
BA-DMP
POKE POKE POKE POKE
Sea urchin.
Sea urchin.
Eeek!
N-nnh...
N-ngh...

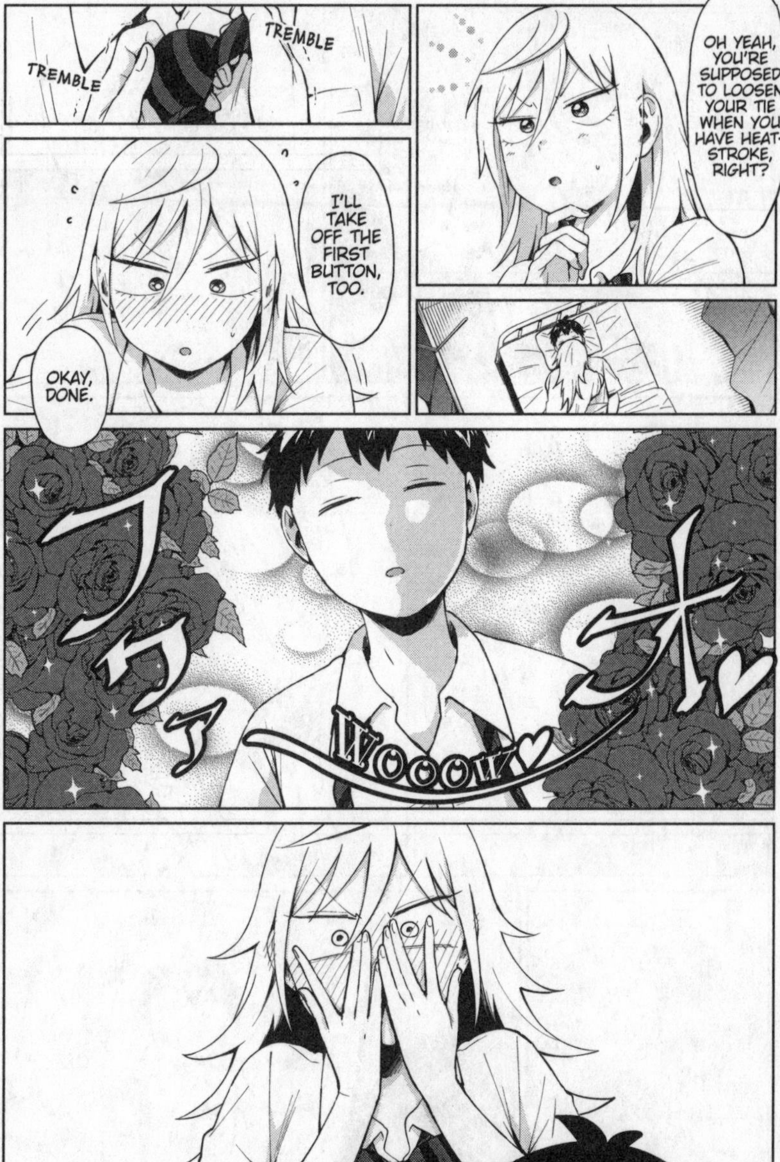
OH YEAH, YOU'RE SUPPOSED TO LOOSEN YOUR TIE WHEN YOU HAVE HEAT-STROKE, RIGHT?
TREMBLE
TREMBLE
I'LL TAKE OFF THE FIRST BUTTON, TOO.
OKAY, DONE.
フワァオ♥
WOOOW♥

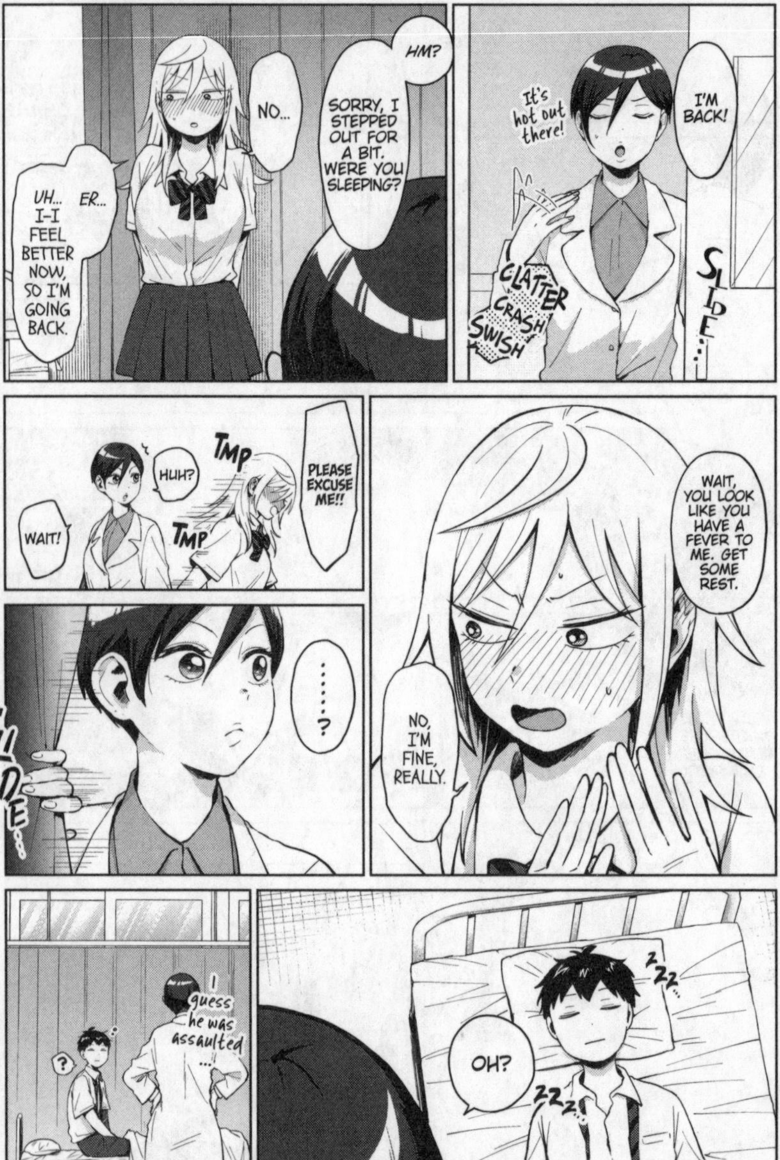
I'M BACK!
It's hot out there!
SLIDE...
CLATTER
CRASH
SWISH
HM?
SORRY, I STEPPED OUT FOR A BIT. WERE YOU SLEEPING?
NO...
UH... ER... I-I FEEL BETTER NOW, SO I'M GOING BACK.
WAIT, YOU LOOK LIKE YOU HAVE A FEVER TO ME. GET SOME REST.
NO, I'M FINE, REALLY.
PLEASE EXCUSE ME!!
TMP
HUH?
TMP
WAIT!
......?
SLIDE...
ZZZ...
OH?
ZZZ...
I guess he was assaulted...!
?

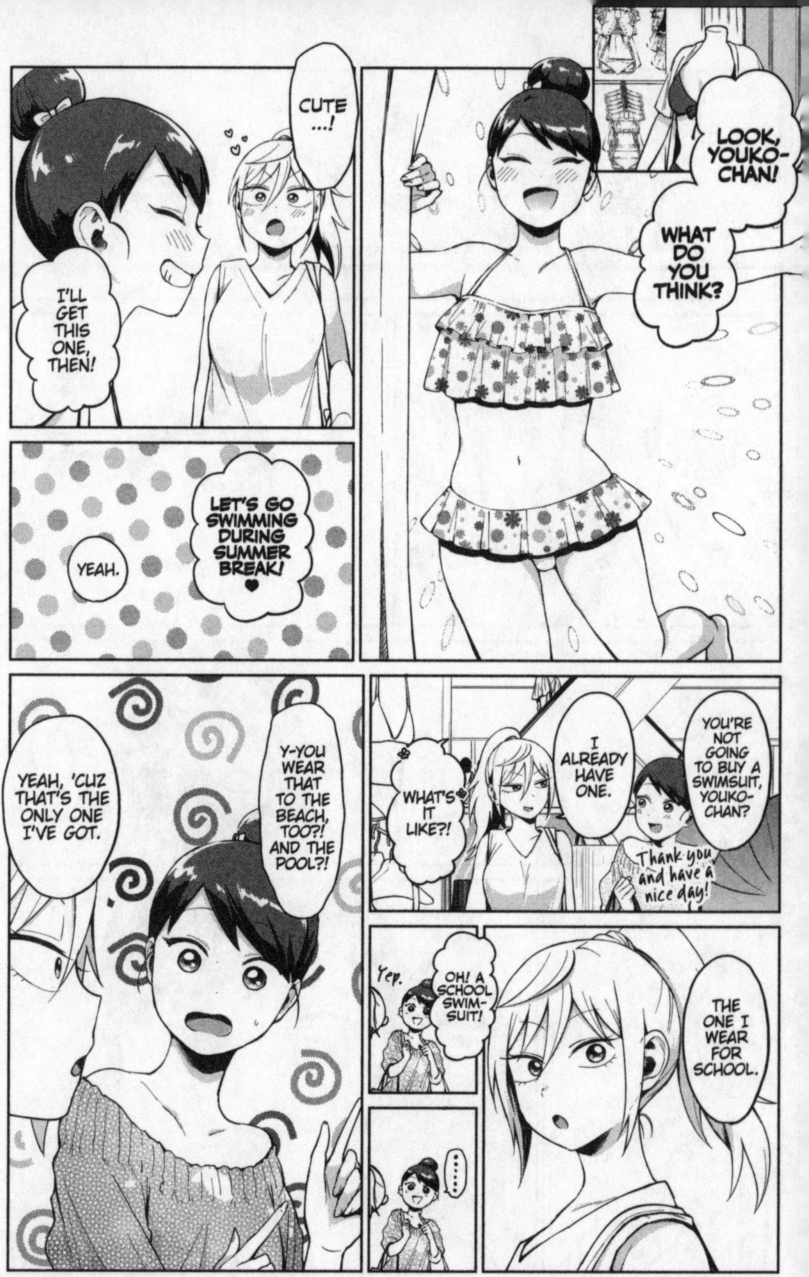
LOOK, YOUKO-CHAN!
WHAT DO YOU THINK?
CUTE ...!
I'LL GET THIS ONE, THEN!
LET'S GO SWIMMING DURING SUMMER BREAK! ❤
YEAH.
YOU'RE NOT GOING TO BUY A SWIMSUIT, YOUKO-CHAN?
Thank you and have a nice day!
I ALREADY HAVE ONE.
WHAT'S IT LIKE?!
THE ONE I WEAR FOR SCHOOL.
OH! A SCHOOL SWIM-SUIT!
Yep.
......
Y-YOU WEAR THAT TO THE BEACH, TOO?! AND THE POOL?!
YEAH, 'CUZ THAT'S THE ONLY ONE I'VE GOT.

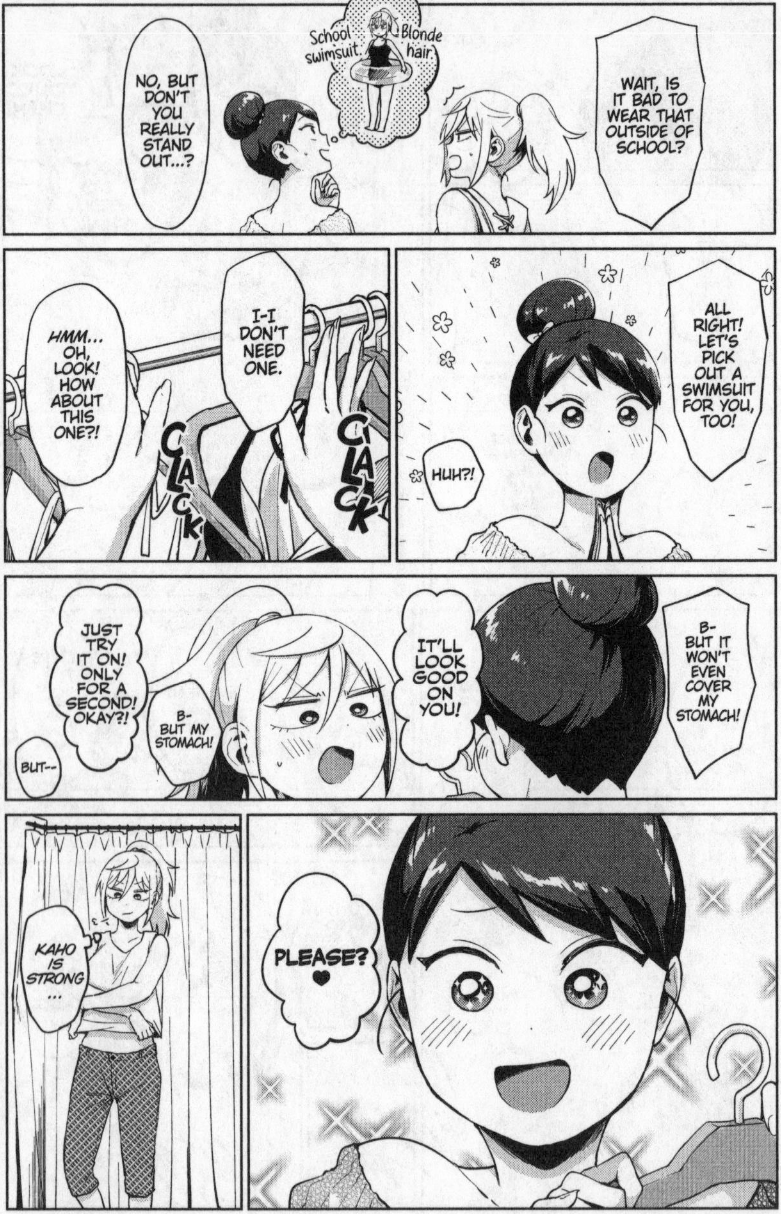
WAIT, IS IT BAD TO WEAR THAT OUTSIDE OF SCHOOL?
Blonde hair.
School swimsuit.
NO, BUT DON'T YOU REALLY STAND OUT...?
ALL RIGHT! LET'S PICK OUT A SWIMSUIT FOR YOU, TOO!
HUH?!
CLACK
I-I DON'T NEED ONE.
CLACK
HMM... OH, LOOK! HOW ABOUT THIS ONE?!
B-BUT IT WON'T EVEN COVER MY STOMACH!
IT'LL LOOK GOOD ON YOU!
B-BUT MY STOMACH!
JUST TRY IT ON! ONLY FOR A SECOND! OKAY?!
BUT--
PLEASE? ♥
KAHO IS STRONG...

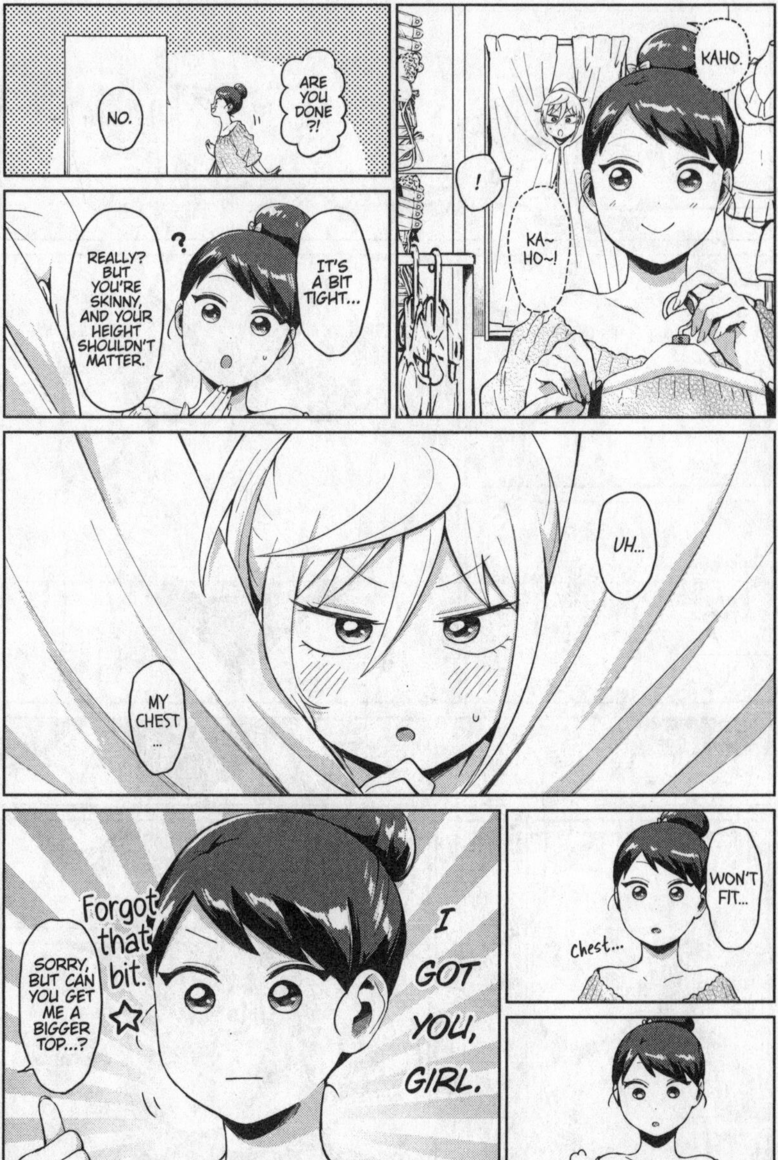
KAHO.
!
KA~ HO~!
ARE YOU DONE ?!
NO.
IT'S A BIT TIGHT...
REALLY? BUT YOU'RE SKINNY, AND YOUR HEIGHT SHOULDN'T MATTER.
UH...
MY CHEST ...
WON'T FIT...
Chest...
I GOT YOU, GIRL.
Forgot that bit.
SORRY, BUT CAN YOU GET ME A BIGGER TOP...?

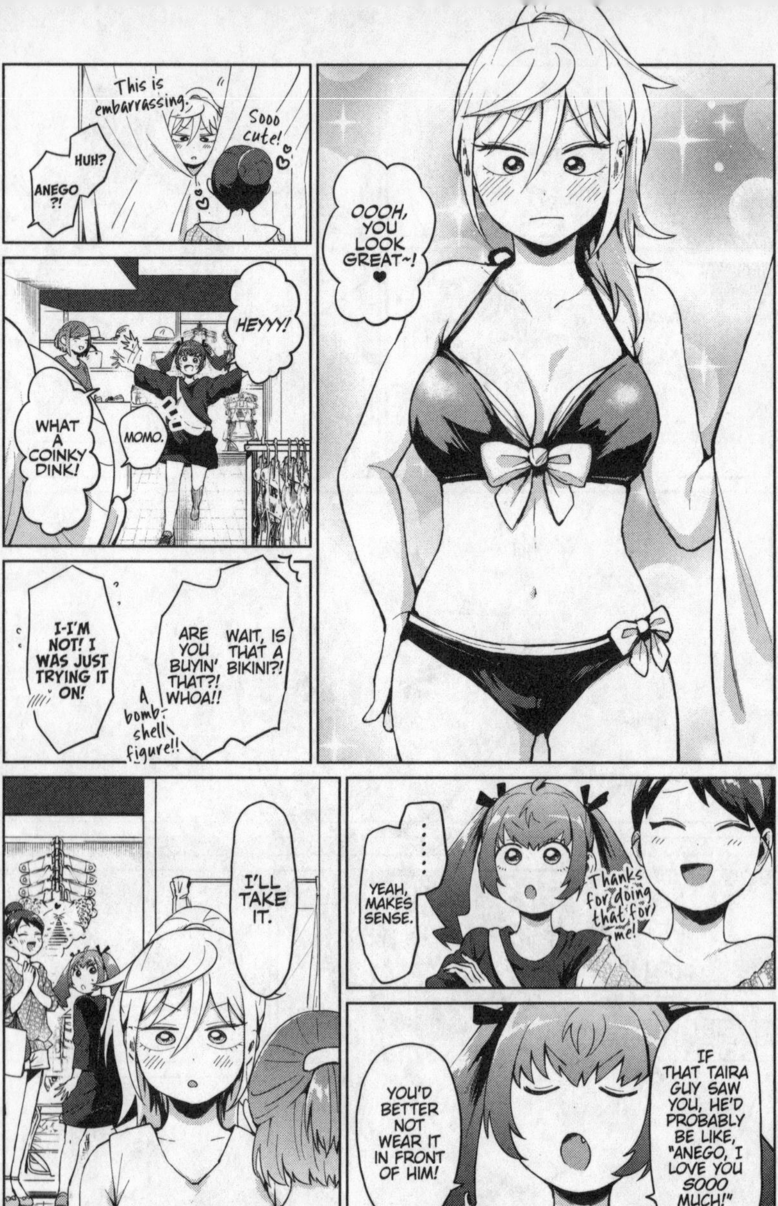
OOOH, YOU LOOK GREAT~! ♥
This is embarrassing.
Sooo cute!
HUH?
ANEGO ?!
HEYYY!
MOMO.
WHAT A COINKY DINK!
WAIT, IS THAT A BIKINI?!
ARE YOU BUYIN' THAT?! WHOA!!
A bombshell figure!!
I-I'M NOT! I WAS JUST TRYING IT ON!
Thanks for doing that for me!
...... YEAH, MAKES SENSE.
IF THAT TAIRA GUY SAW YOU, HE'D PROBABLY BE LIKE, "ANEGO, I LOVE YOU SOOO MUCH!" ♡
YOU'D BETTER NOT WEAR IT IN FRONT OF HIM!
I'LL TAKE IT.

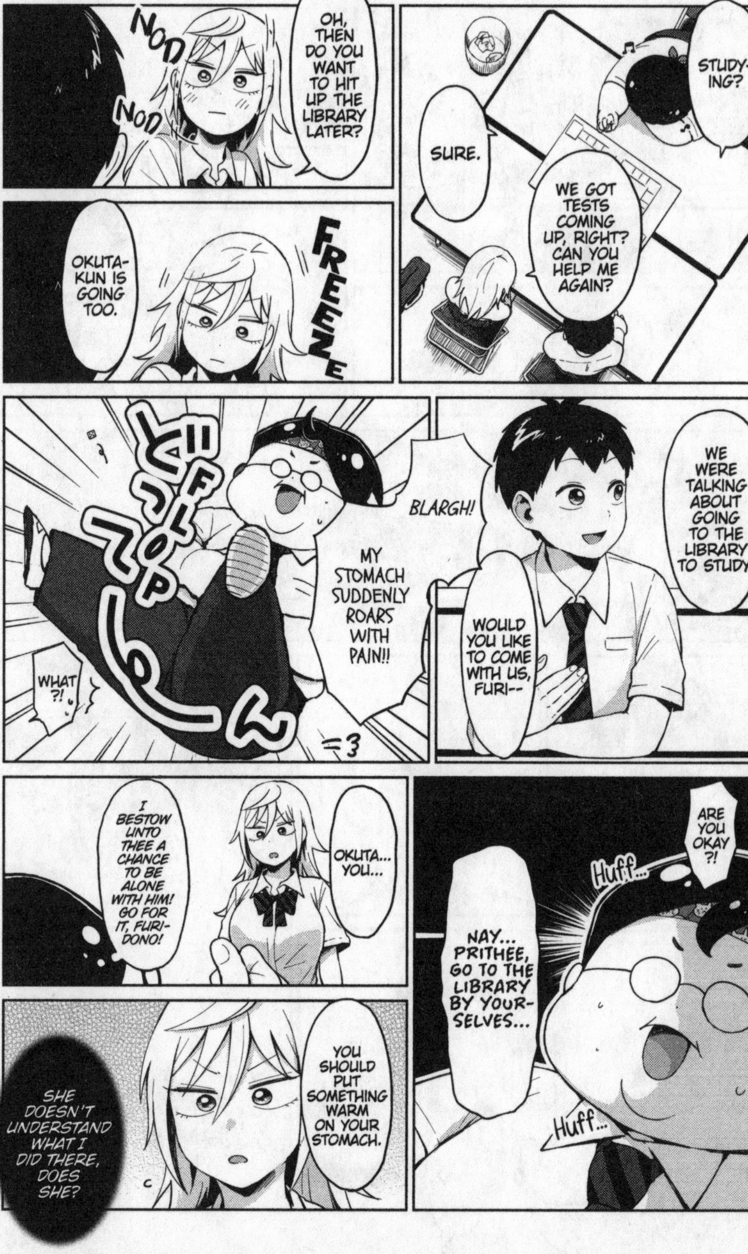
STUDY-ING?
WE GOT TESTS COMING UP, RIGHT? CAN YOU HELP ME AGAIN?
SURE.
OH, THEN DO YOU WANT TO HIT UP THE LIBRARY LATER?
NOD
NOD
FREEZE
OKUTA-KUN IS GOING TOO.
WE WERE TALKING ABOUT GOING TO THE LIBRARY TO STUDY.
WOULD YOU LIKE TO COME WITH US, FURI--
BLARGH!
MY STOMACH SUDDENLY ROARS WITH PAIN!!
FLOP
WHAT ?!
ARE YOU OKAY ?!
Huff...
NAY... PRITHEE, GO TO THE LIBRARY BY YOUR-SELVES...
Huff...
OKUTA... YOU...
I BESTOW UNTO THEE A CHANCE TO BE ALONE WITH HIM! GO FOR IT, FURI-DONO!
YOU SHOULD PUT SOMETHING WARM ON YOUR STOMACH.
SHE DOESN'T UNDERSTAND WHAT I DID THERE, DOES SHE?

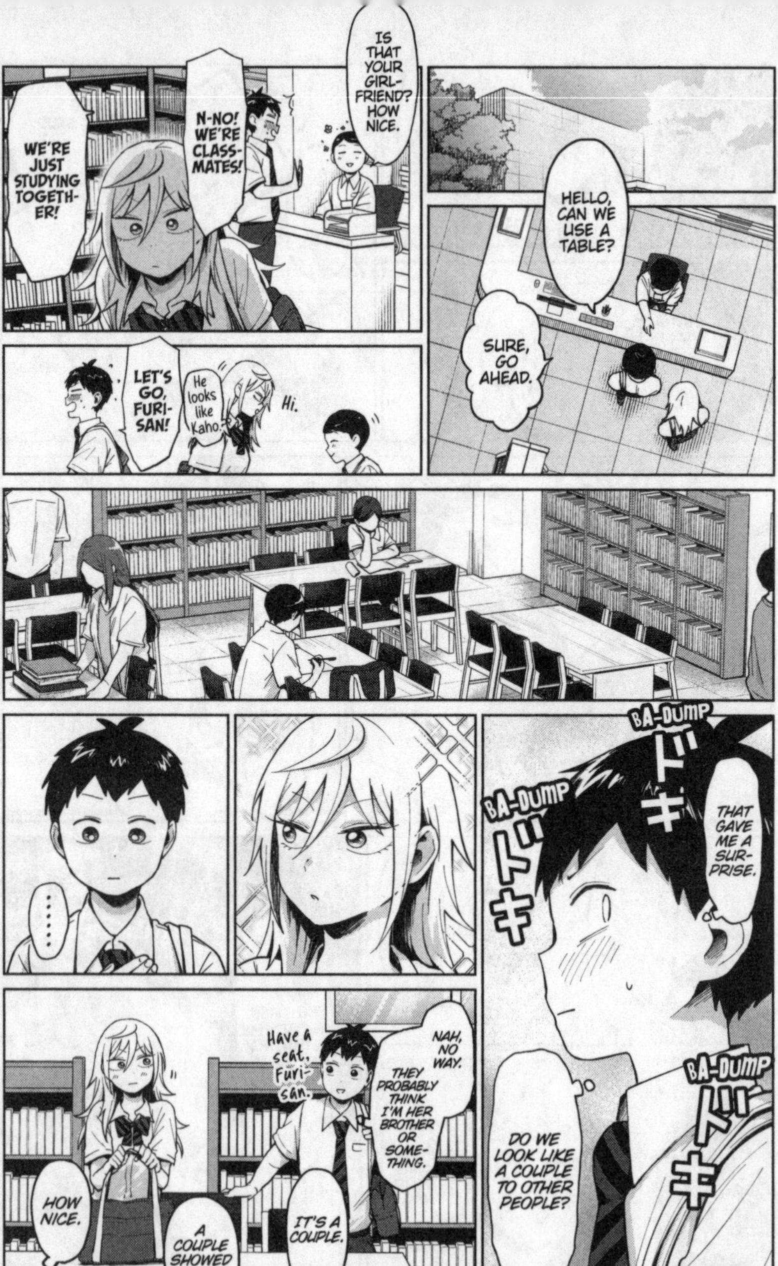
HELLO, CAN WE USE A TABLE?
SURE, GO AHEAD.
IS THAT YOUR GIRL-FRIEND? HOW NICE.
N-NO! WE'RE CLASS-MATES!
WE'RE JUST STUDYING TOGETH-ER!
Hi.
He looks like Kaho.
LET'S GO, FURI-SAN!
BA-DUMP
ドキ
BA-DUMP
ドキ
THAT GAVE ME A SUR-PRISE.
BA-DUMP
ドキ
DO WE LOOK LIKE A COUPLE TO OTHER PEOPLE?
......
NAH, NO WAY.
THEY PROBABLY THINK I'M HER BROTHER OR SOME-THING.
Have a seat, Furi-san.
IT'S A COUPLE.
A COUPLE SHOWED UP.
HOW NICE.

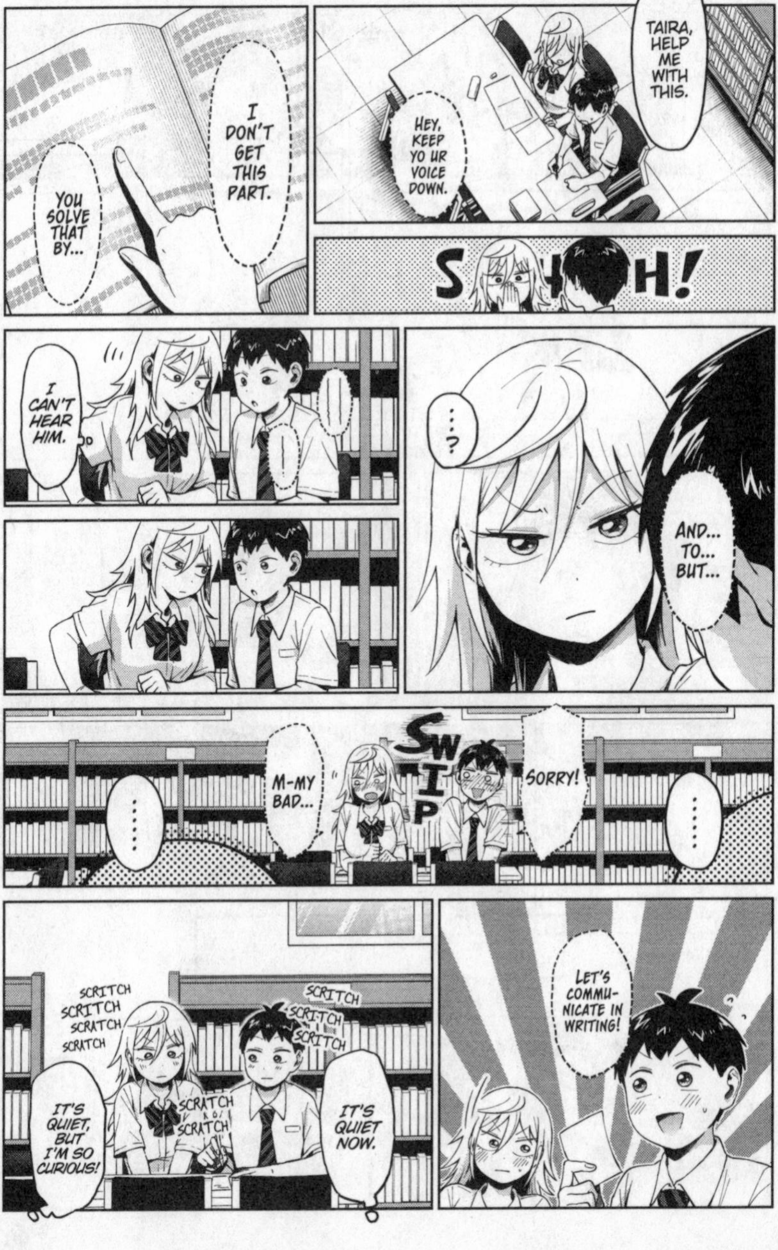
TAIRA, HELP ME WITH THIS.
HEY, KEEP YO UR VOICE DOWN.
S H H!
I DON'T GET THIS PART.
YOU SOLVE THAT BY...
...?
AND... TO... BUT...
I CAN'T HEAR HIM.
......
SORRY!
SWIP
M-MY BAD...
......
LET'S COMMUNICATE IN WRITING!
SCRITCH SCRITCH SCRITCH
IT'S QUIET NOW.
SCRITCH SCRITCH SCRATCH SCRATCH
SCRATCH SCRATCH
IT'S QUIET, BUT I'M SO CURIOUS!

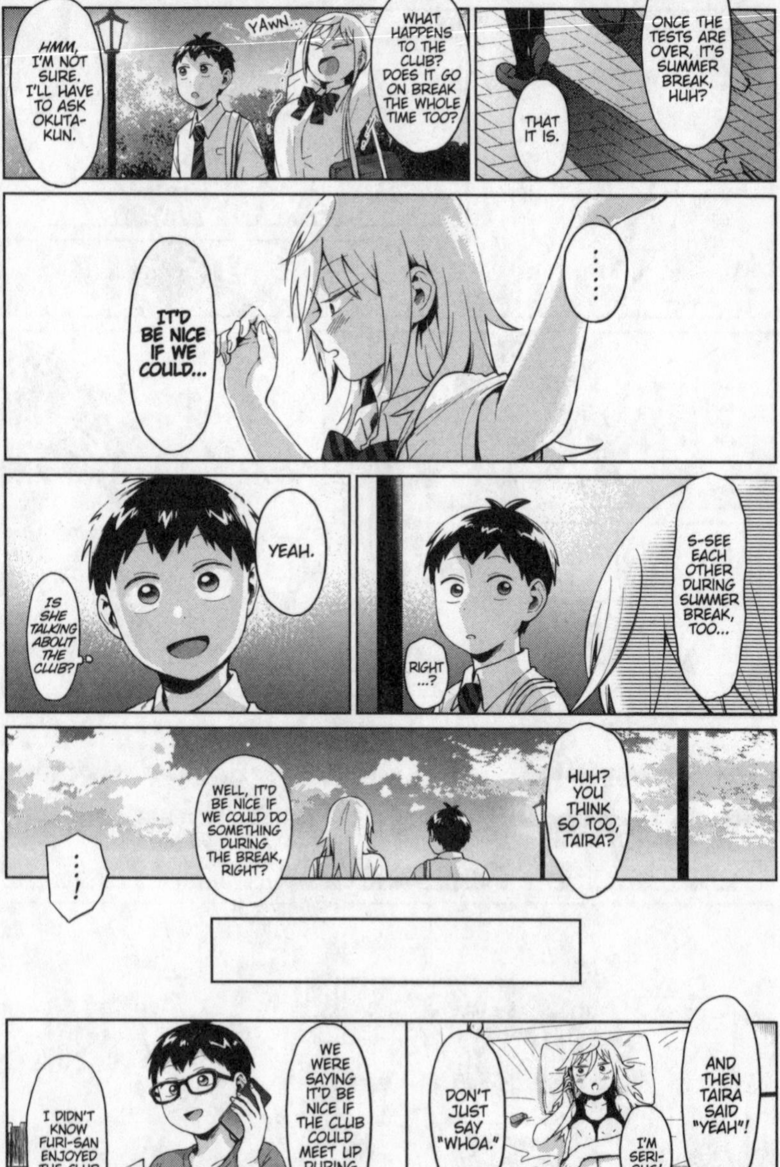
ONCE THE TESTS ARE OVER, IT'S SUMMER BREAK, HUH?
THAT IT IS.
WHAT HAPPENS TO THE CLUB? DOES IT GO ON BREAK THE WHOLE TIME TOO?
YAWN...
HMM, I'M NOT SURE. I'LL HAVE TO ASK OKUTA-KUN.
......
IT'D BE NICE IF WE COULD...
S-SEE EACH OTHER DURING SUMMER BREAK, TOO...
RIGHT ...?
YEAH.
IS SHE TALKING ABOUT THE CLUB?
HUH? YOU THINK SO TOO, TAIRA?
WELL, IT'D BE NICE IF WE COULD DO SOMETHING DURING THE BREAK, RIGHT?
...!
AND THEN TAIRA SAID "YEAH"!
I'M SERI-OUS!
DON'T JUST SAY "WHOA."
WE WERE SAYING IT'D BE NICE IF THE CLUB COULD MEET UP DURING SUMMER BREAK.
I DIDN'T KNOW FURI-SAN ENJOYED THE CLUB SO MUCH.

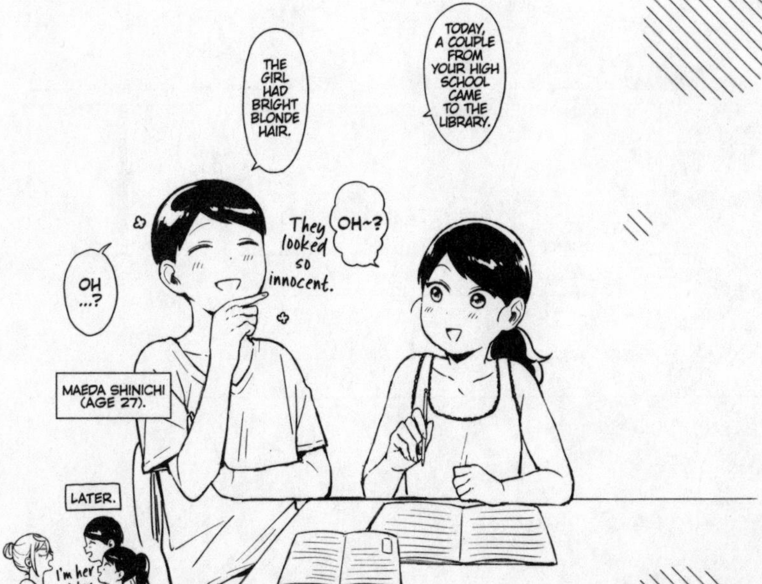
TODAY, A COUPLE FROM YOUR HIGH SCHOOL CAME TO THE LIBRARY.
THE GIRL HAD BRIGHT BLONDE HAIR.
OH~?
They looked so innocent.
OH ...?
MAEDA SHINICHI (AGE 27).
LATER.
I'm her older brother.

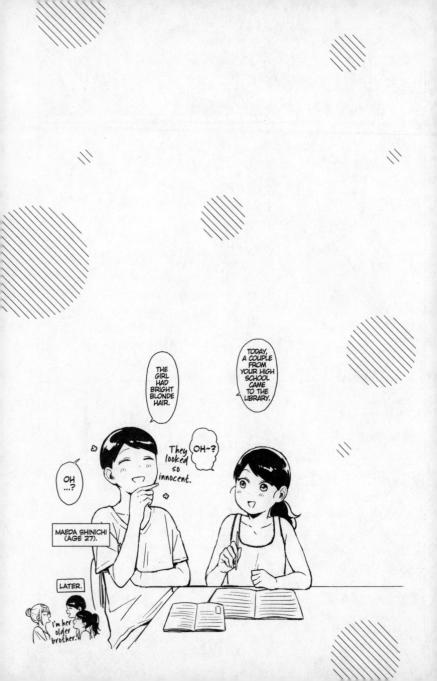

Chapter 13

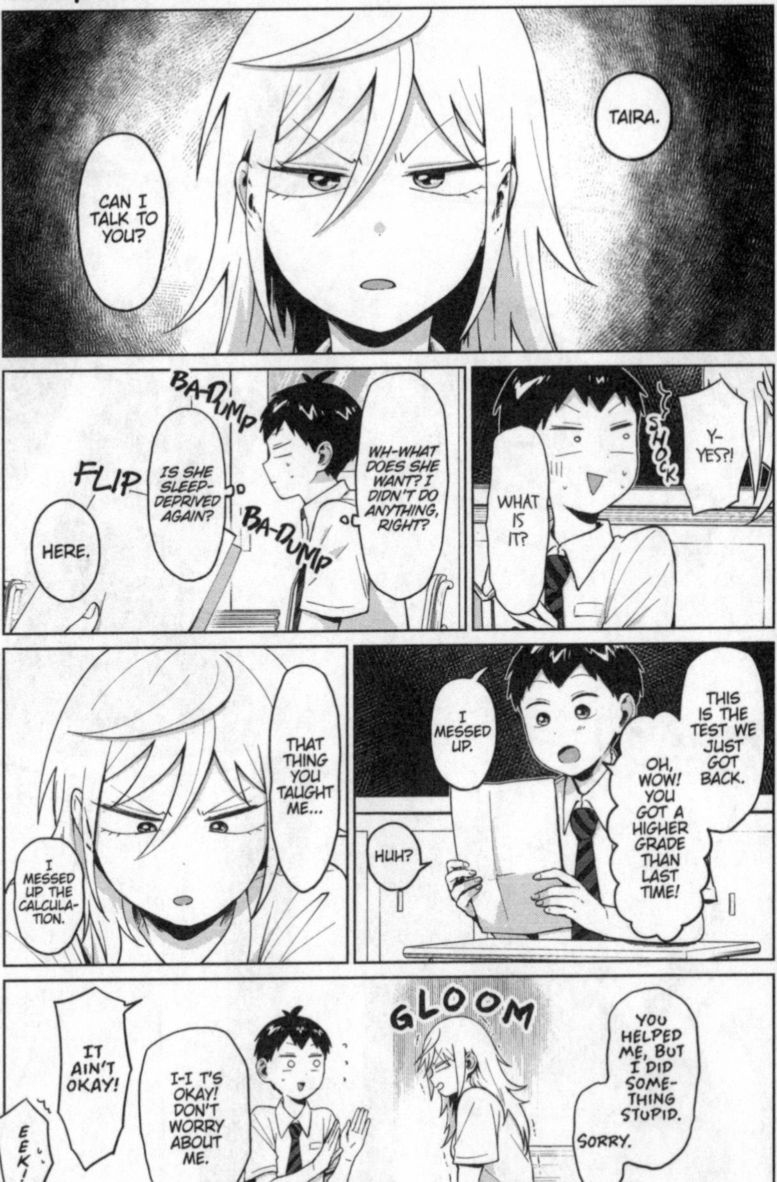

TAIRA.
CAN I TALK TO YOU?
Y- YES?!
SHOCK
WHAT IS IT?
WH-WHAT DOES SHE WANT? I DIDN'T DO ANYTHING, RIGHT?
BA-DUMP
IS SHE SLEEP-DEPRIVED AGAIN?
BA-DUMP
FLIP
HERE.
THIS IS THE TEST WE JUST GOT BACK.
OH, WOW! YOU GOT A HIGHER GRADE THAN LAST TIME!
I MESSED UP.
HUH?
THAT THING YOU TAUGHT ME...
I MESSED UP THE CALCULATION.
YOU HELPED ME, BUT I DID SOMETHING STUPID.
SORRY.
GLOOM
I-I T'S OKAY! DON'T WORRY ABOUT ME.
IT AIN'T OKAY!
EEK!

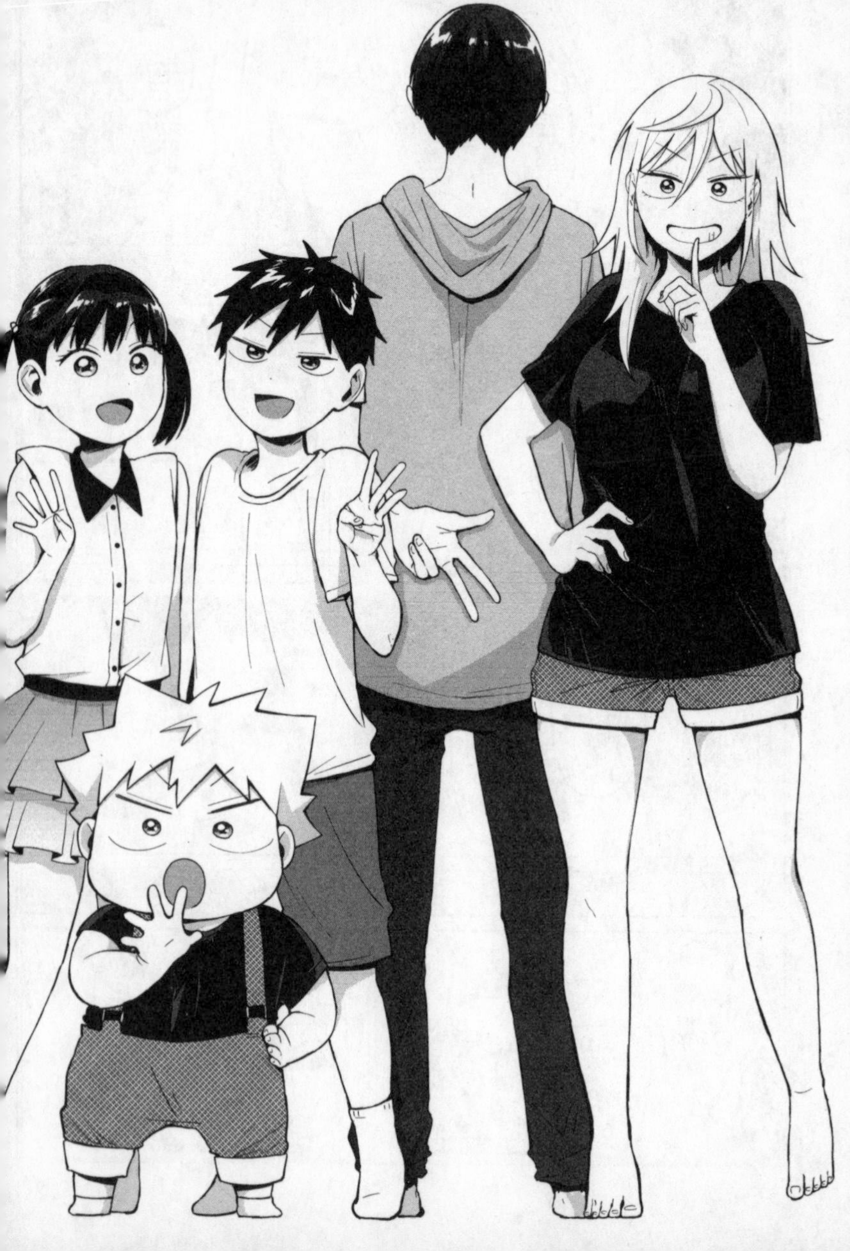

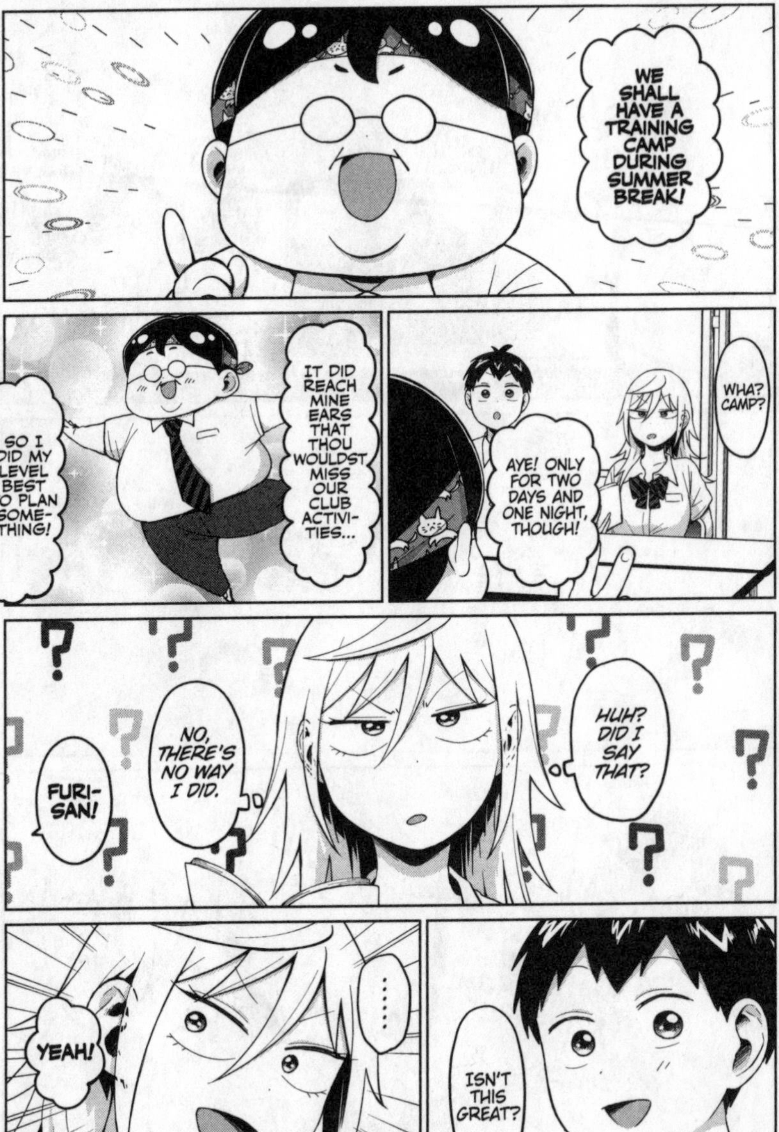
WE SHALL HAVE A TRAINING CAMP DURING SUMMER BREAK!
WHA? CAMP?
AYE! ONLY FOR TWO DAYS AND ONE NIGHT, THOUGH!
IT DID REACH MINE EARS THAT THOU WOULDST MISS OUR CLUB ACTIVITIES...
SO I DID MY LEVEL BEST TO PLAN SOME-THING!
HUH? DID I SAY THAT?
NO, THERE'S NO WAY I DID.
FURI-SAN!
ISN'T THIS GREAT?
......
YEAH!

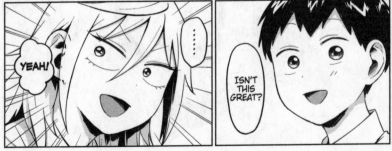

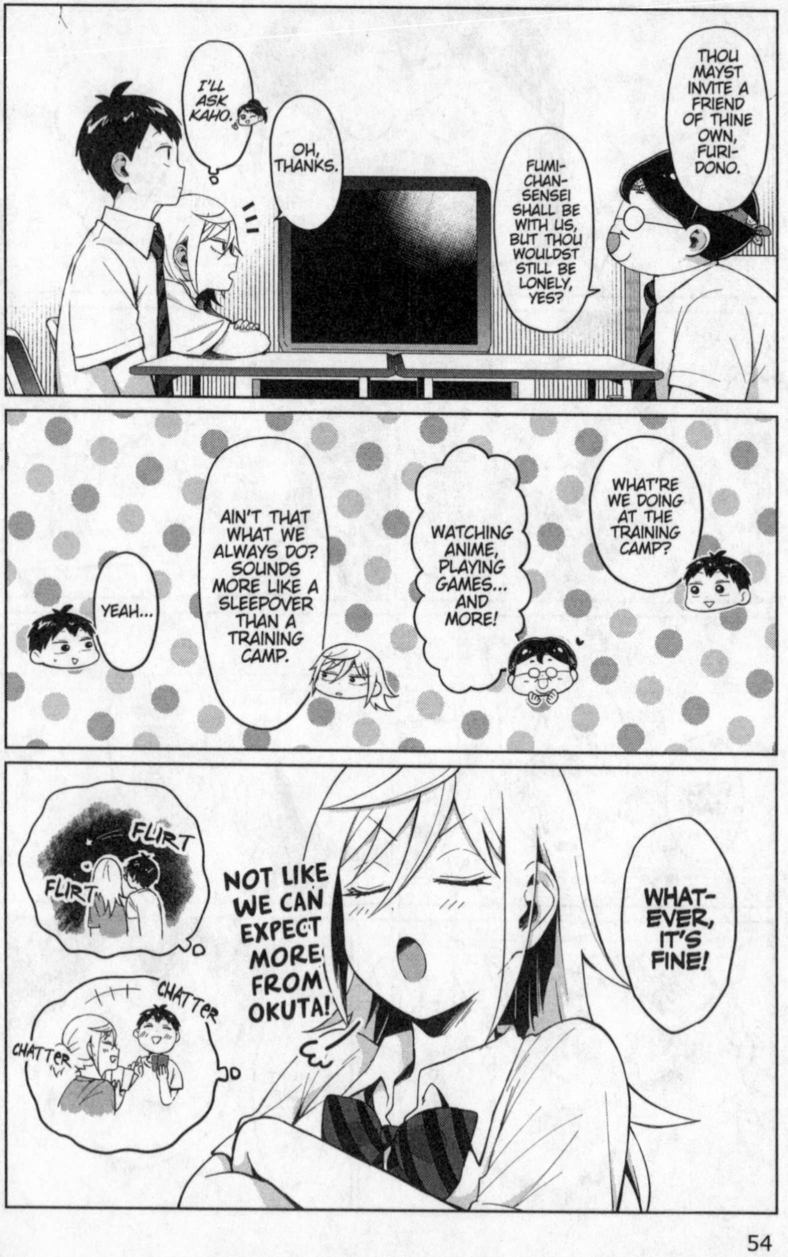
THOU MAYST INVITE A FRIEND OF THINE OWN, FURI-DONO.
FUMI-CHAN-SENSEI SHALL BE WITH US, BUT THOU WOULDST STILL BE LONELY, YES?
OH, THANKS.
I'LL ASK KAHO.
WHAT'RE WE DOING AT THE TRAINING CAMP?
WATCHING ANIME, PLAYING GAMES... AND MORE!
AIN'T THAT WHAT WE ALWAYS DO? SOUNDS MORE LIKE A SLEEPOVER THAN A TRAINING CAMP.
YEAH...
WHAT-EVER, IT'S FINE!
NOT LIKE WE CAN EXPECT MORE FROM OKUTA!
FLIRT
FLIRT
CHATTER
CHATTER

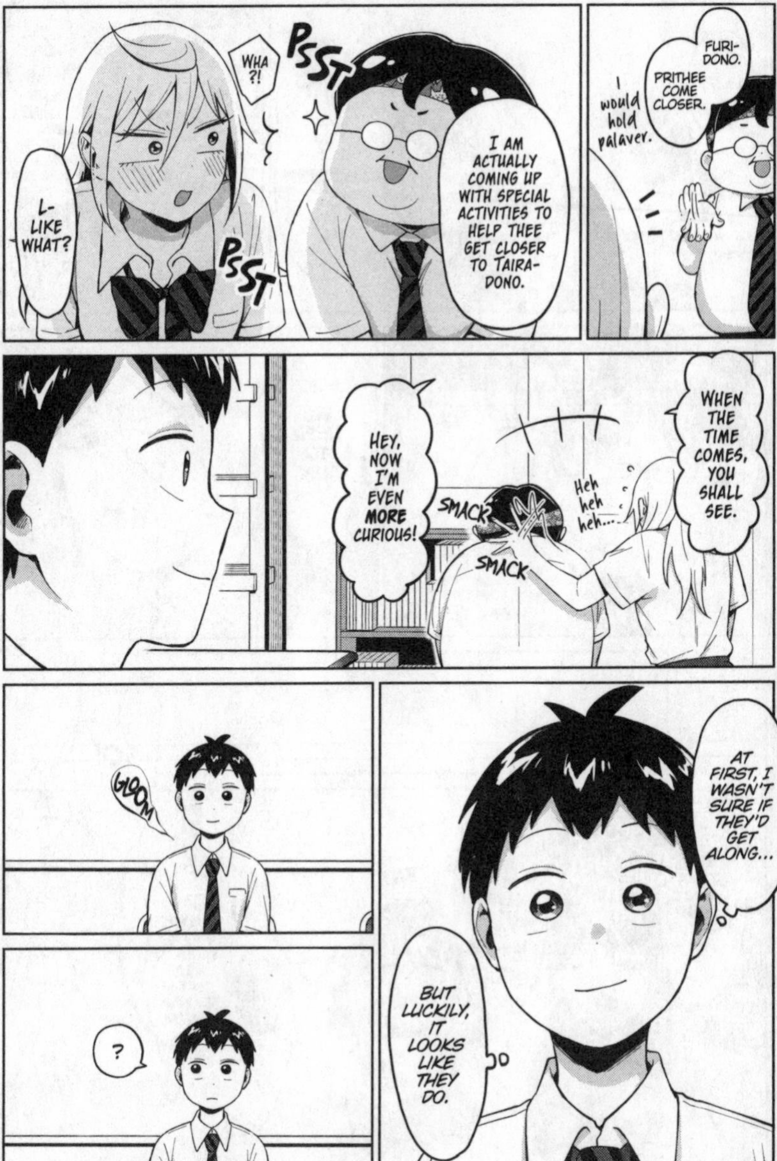
FURI-DONO. PRITHEE COME CLOSER.
I would hold palaver.
PSST
WHA?!
I AM ACTUALLY COMING UP WITH SPECIAL ACTIVITIES TO HELP THEE GET CLOSER TO TAIRA-DONO.
L-LIKE WHAT?
PSST
WHEN THE TIME COMES, YOU SHALL SEE.
Heh heh heh...
SMACK
HEY, NOW I'M EVEN MORE CURIOUS!
SMACK
AT FIRST, I WASN'T SURE IF THEY'D GET ALONG...
BUT LUCKILY, IT LOOKS LIKE THEY DO.
GLOOM
?

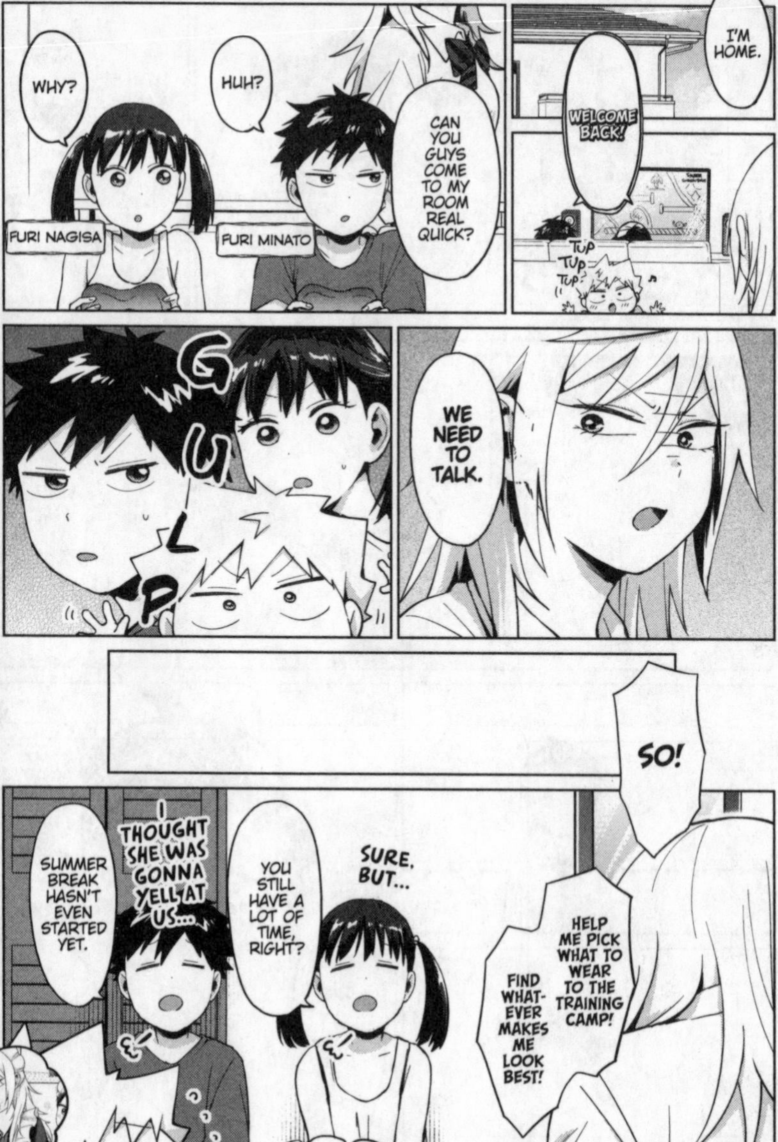
I'M HOME.
WELCOME BACK!
TUP TUP TUP
CAN YOU GUYS COME TO MY ROOM REAL QUICK?
HUH?
FURI MINATO
WHY?
FURI NAGISA
WE NEED TO TALK.
GULP
SO!
HELP ME PICK WHAT TO WEAR TO THE TRAINING CAMP!
FIND WHAT-EVER MAKES ME LOOK BEST!
SURE. BUT...
YOU STILL HAVE A LOT OF TIME, RIGHT?
I THOUGHT SHE WAS GONNA YELL AT US...
SUMMER BREAK HASN'T EVEN STARTED YET.

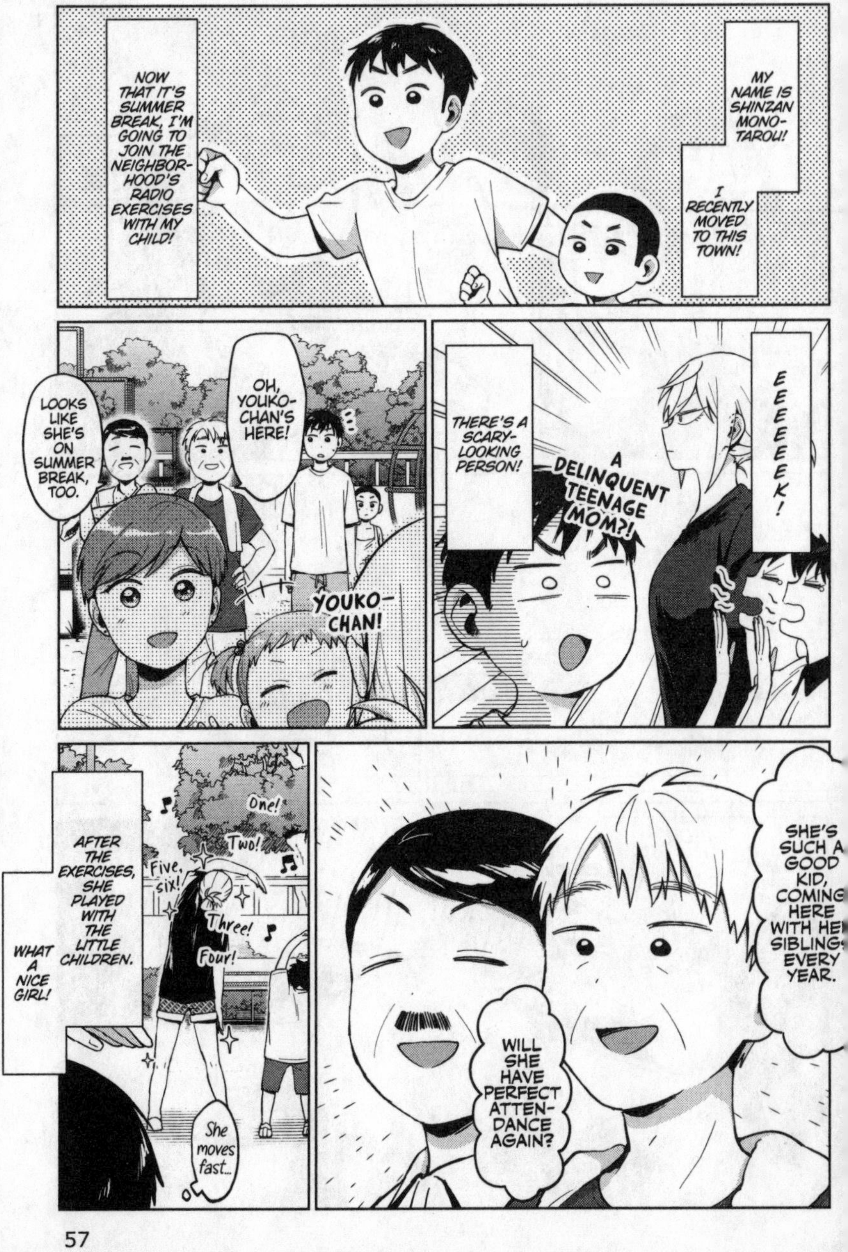
MY NAME IS SHINZAN MONOTAROU!
I RECENTLY MOVED TO THIS TOWN!
NOW THAT IT'S SUMMER BREAK, I'M GOING TO JOIN THE NEIGHBORHOOD'S RADIO EXERCISES WITH MY CHILD!
EEEEEEK!
A DELINQUENT TEENAGE MOM?!
THERE'S A SCARY-LOOKING PERSON!
OH, YOUKO-CHAN'S HERE!
LOOKS LIKE SHE'S ON SUMMER BREAK, TOO.
YOUKO-CHAN!
SHE'S SUCH A GOOD KID, COMING HERE WITH HE SIBLING EVERY YEAR.
WILL SHE HAVE PERFECT ATTENDANCE AGAIN?
AFTER THE EXERCISES, SHE PLAYED WITH THE LITTLE CHILDREN.
One!
Two!
Five, six!
Three!
Four!
WHAT A NICE GIRL!
She moves fast...

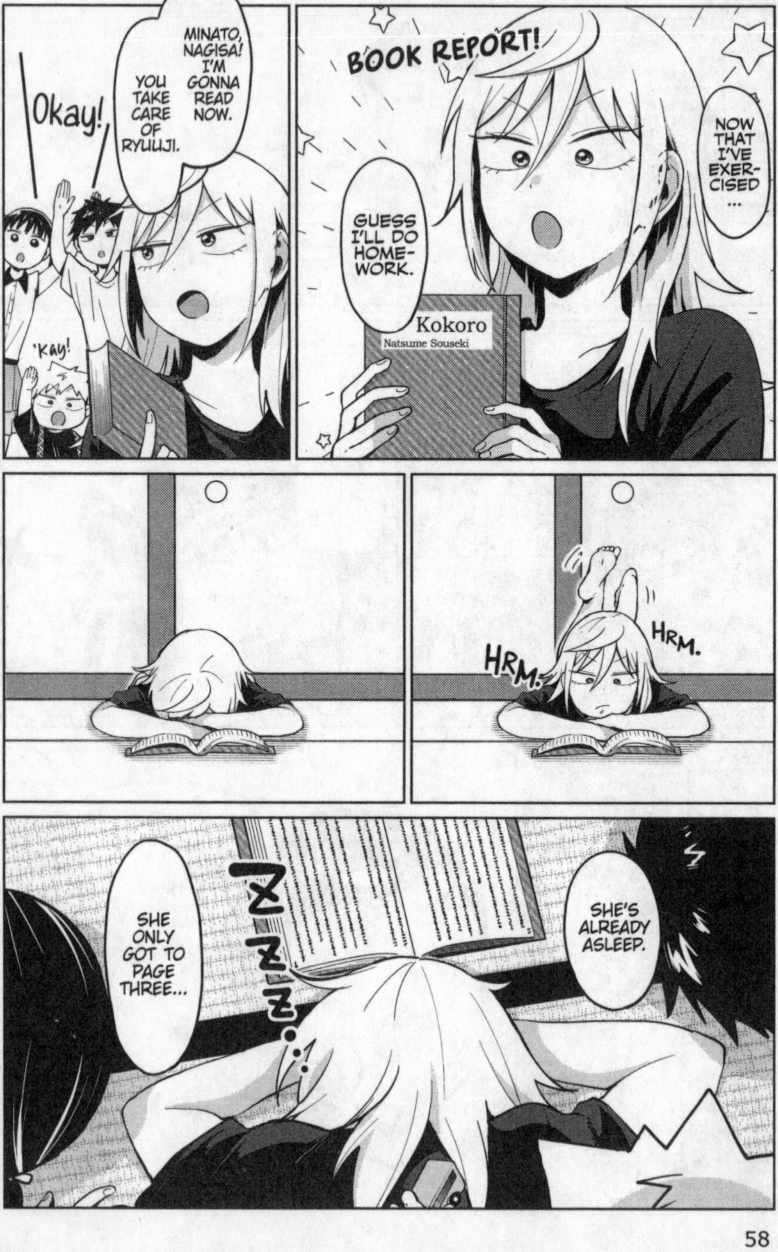
NOW THAT I'VE EXERCISED...
BOOK REPORT!
GUESS I'LL DO HOMEWORK.
Kokoro
Natsume Souseki
MINATO, NAGISA! I'M GONNA READ NOW.
YOU TAKE CARE OF RYUUJI.
Okay!
'Kay!
HRM.
HRM.
SHE'S ALREADY ASLEEP.
ZZZ...
SHE ONLY GOT TO PAGE THREE...

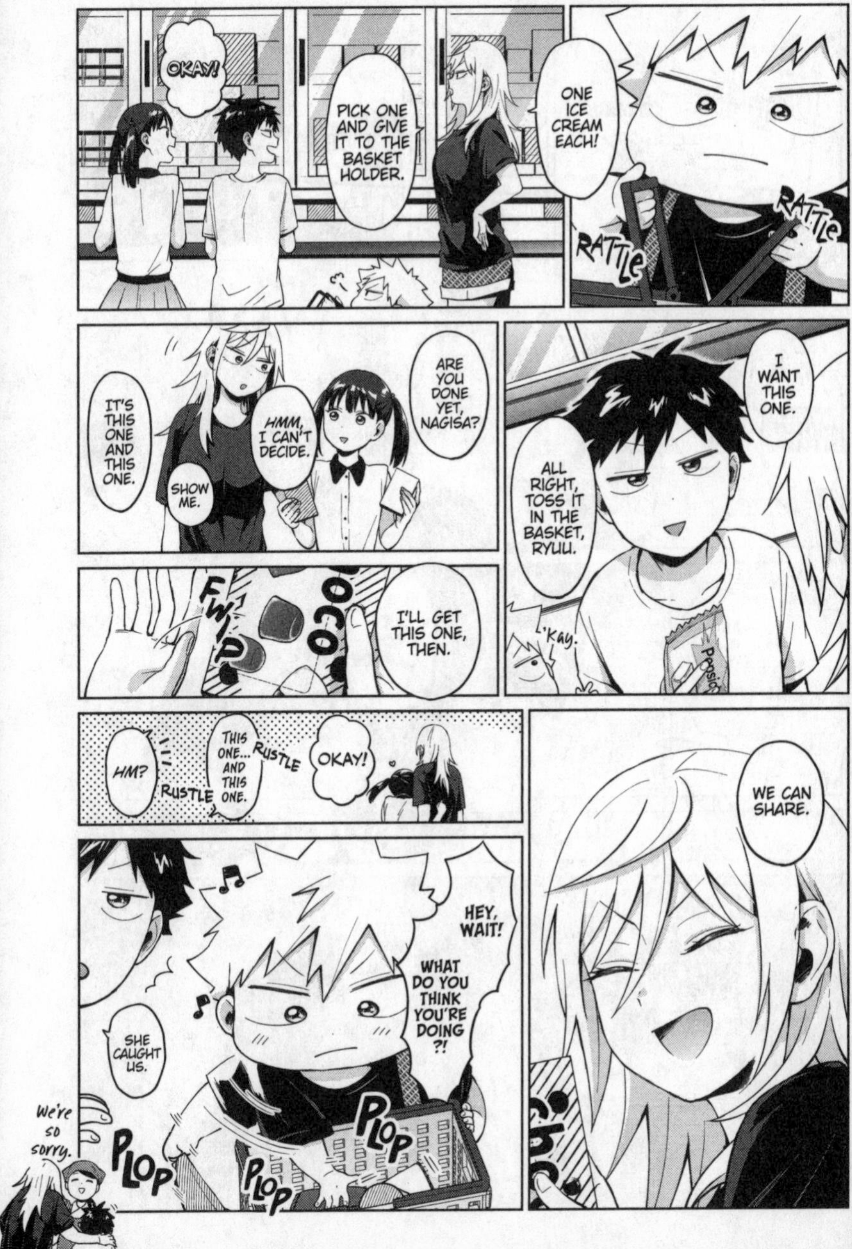
ONE ICE CREAM EACH!
RATTLE
RATTLE
PICK ONE AND GIVE IT TO THE BASKET HOLDER.
OKAY!
I WANT THIS ONE.
ALL RIGHT, TOSS IT IN THE BASKET, RYUU.
'Kay.
ARE YOU DONE YET, NAGISA?
HMM, I CAN'T DECIDE.
IT'S THIS ONE AND THIS ONE.
SHOW ME.
I'LL GET THIS ONE, THEN.
FWIP
WE CAN SHARE.
OKAY!
RUSTLE
THIS ONE... AND THIS ONE.
RUSTLE
HM?
HEY, WAIT!
WHAT DO YOU THINK YOU'RE DOING?!
SHE CAUGHT US.
PLOP
PLOP
PLOP
We're so sorry.

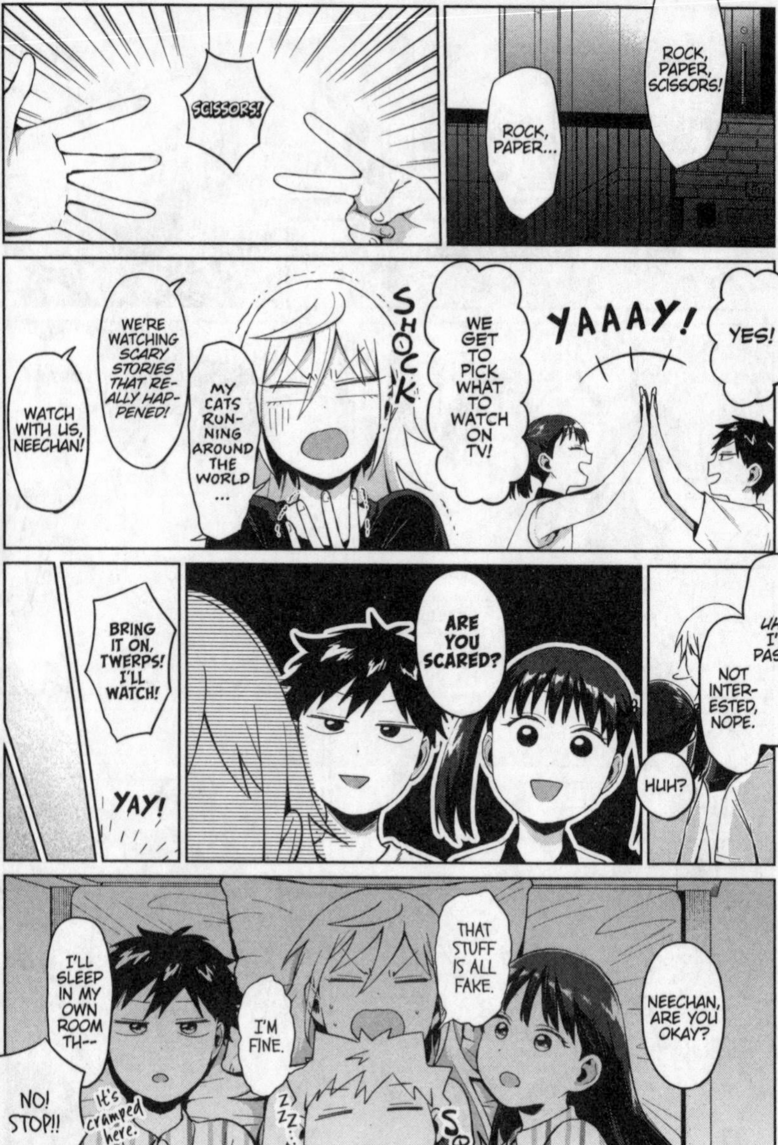
ROCK, PAPER, SCISSORS!
ROCK, PAPER...
SCISSORS!
YES!
YAAAY!
WE GET TO PICK WHAT TO WATCH ON TV!
SHOCK
MY CATS RUNNING AROUND THE WORLD ...
WE'RE WATCHING SCARY STORIES THAT REALLY HAPPENED!
WATCH WITH US, NEECHAN!
UH... I'LL PASS...
NOT INTERESTED, NOPE.
HUH?
ARE YOU SCARED?
BRING IT ON, TWERPS! I'LL WATCH!
YAY!
NEECHAN, ARE YOU OKAY?
THAT STUFF IS ALL FAKE.
I'M FINE.
SQUEEZE
ZZZ...
I'LL SLEEP IN MY OWN ROOM TH--
It's cramped here.
NO! STOP!!

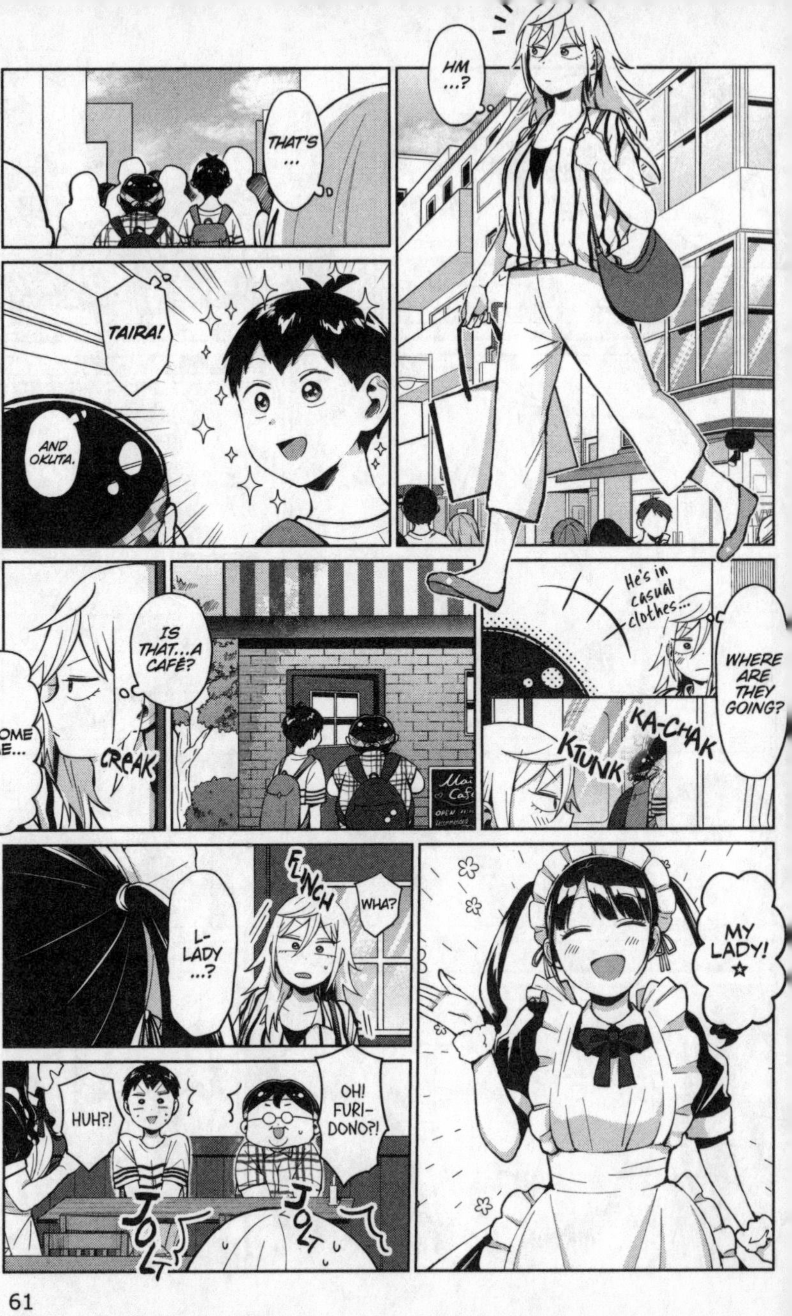
HM ...?
THAT'S ...
TAIRA!
AND OKUTA.
He's in casual clothes...
WHERE ARE THEY GOING?
KA-CHAK
KTUNK
IS THAT...A CAFÉ?
WELCOME HOME...
CREAK
MY LADY! ☆
FLINCH
WHA?
L-LADY ...?
OH! FURI-DONO?!
HUH?!
JOLT
JOLT

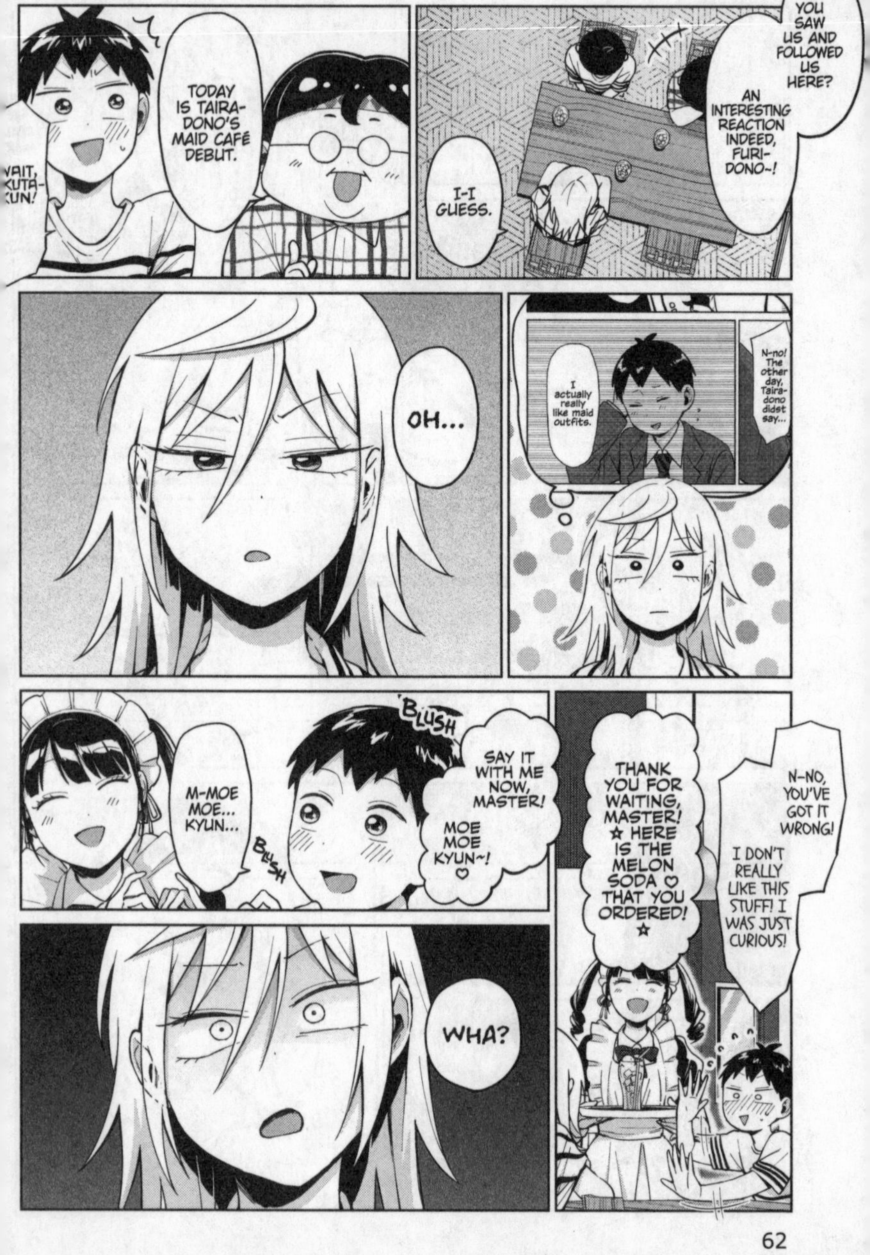
YOU SAW US AND FOLLOWED US HERE?
AN INTERESTING REACTION INDEED, FURI-DONO~!
I-I GUESS.
TODAY IS TAIRA-DONO'S MAID CAFÉ DEBUT.
WAIT, KUTA-KUN!
N-no! The other day, Taira-dono didst say...
I actually really like maid outfits.
OH...
N-NO, YOU'VE GOT IT WRONG!
I DON'T REALLY LIKE THIS STUFF! I WAS JUST CURIOUS!
THANK YOU FOR WAITING, MASTER! ☆ HERE IS THE MELON SODA ♡ THAT YOU ORDERED! ☆
BLUSH
SAY IT WITH ME NOW, MASTER!
MOE MOE KYUN~! ♡
M-MOE MOE... KYUN...
BLUSH
WHA?

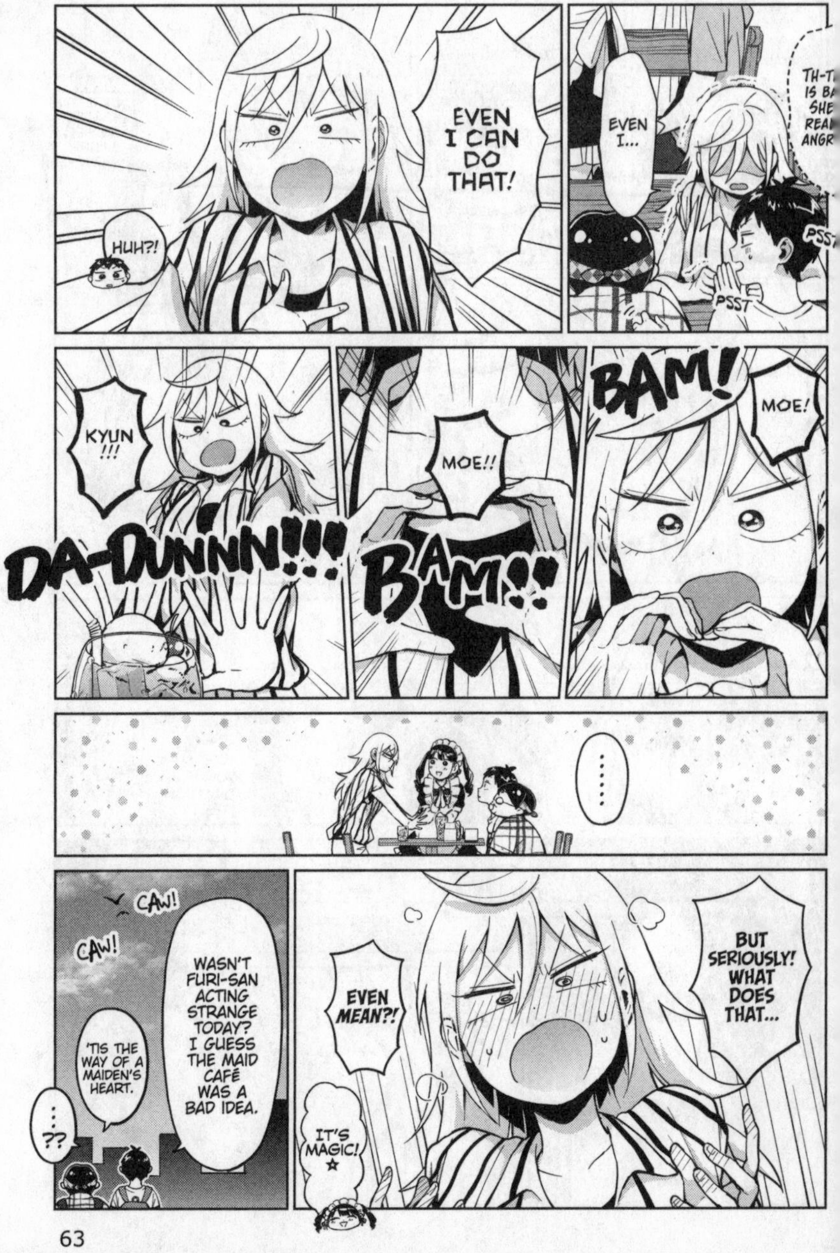
EVEN I...
TH-T IS BA SHE REAL ANGR
PSST
PSST
EVEN I CAN DO THAT!
HUH?!
BAM!
MOE!
MOE!!
BAM!!
KYUN!!!
DA-DUNNN!!!
......
BUT SERIOUSLY! WHAT DOES THAT...
EVEN MEAN?!
IT'S MAGIC! ☆
CAW!
CAW!
WASN'T FURI-SAN ACTING STRANGE TODAY? I GUESS THE MAID CAFÉ WAS A BAD IDEA.
'TIS THE WAY OF A MAIDEN'S HEART.
...??

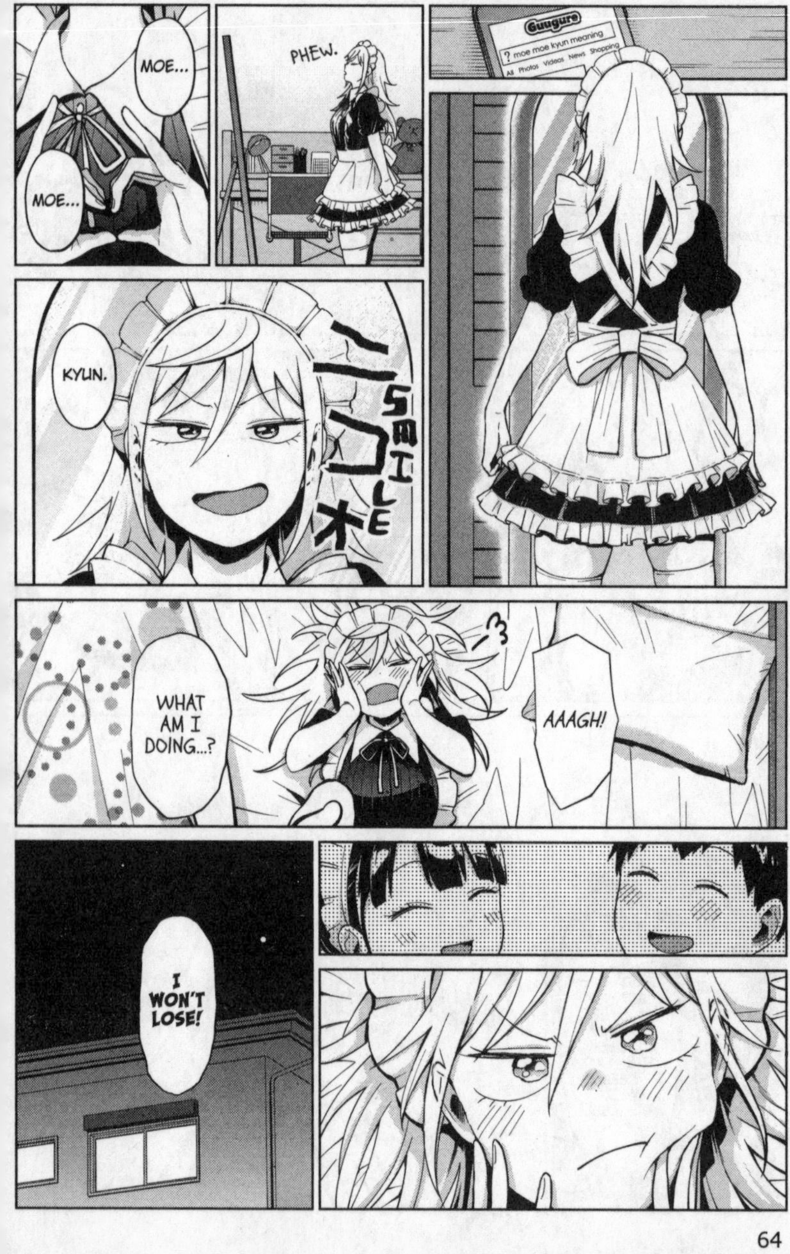
Guugure
moe moe kyun meaning
All Photos Videos News Shopping
PHEW.
MOE...
MOE...
KYUN.
SMILE
AAAGH!
WHAT AM I DOING...?
I WON'T LOSE!

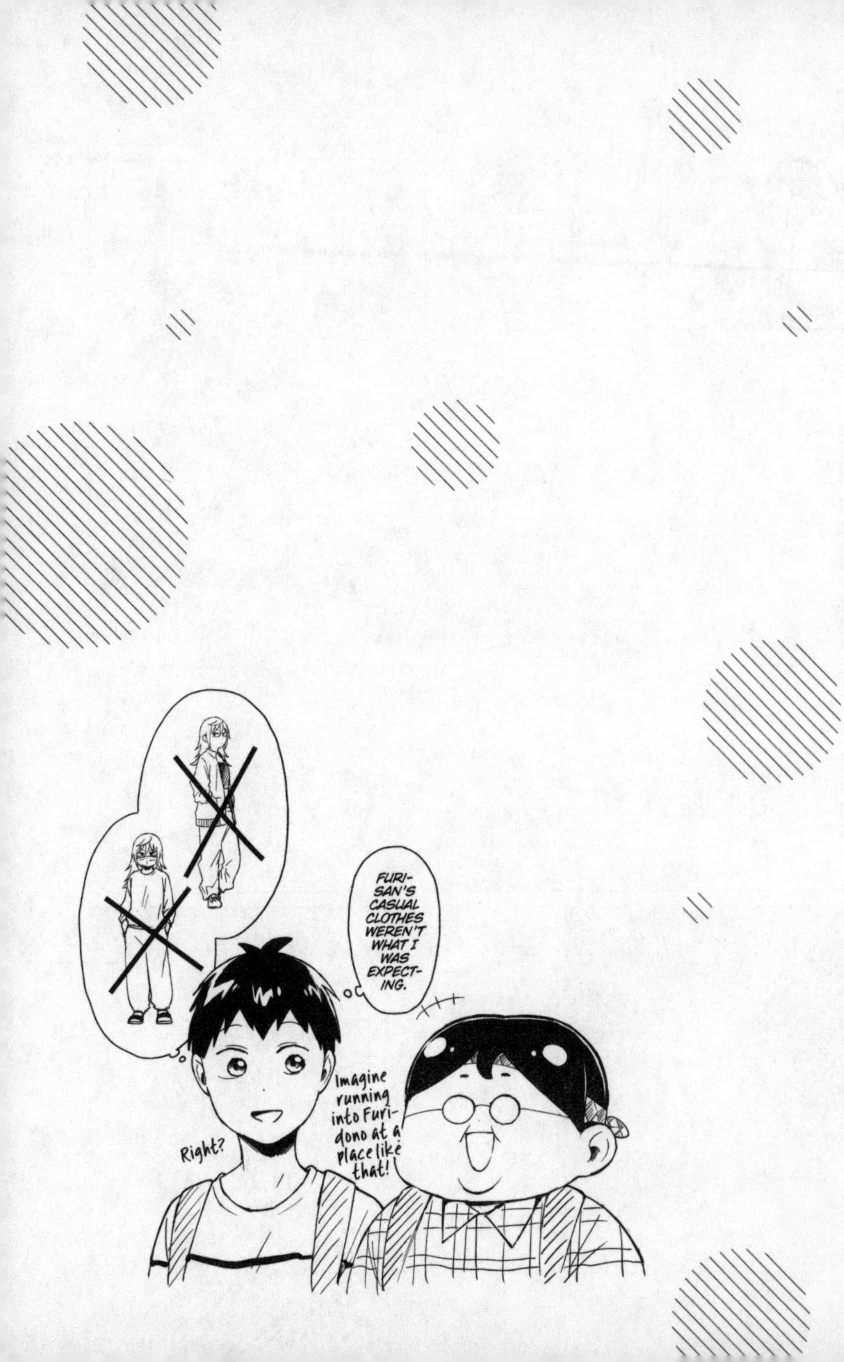
FURI-SAN'S CASUAL CLOTHES WEREN'T WHAT I WAS EXPECTING.
Imagine running into Furi-dono at a place like that!
Right?

Chapter 14

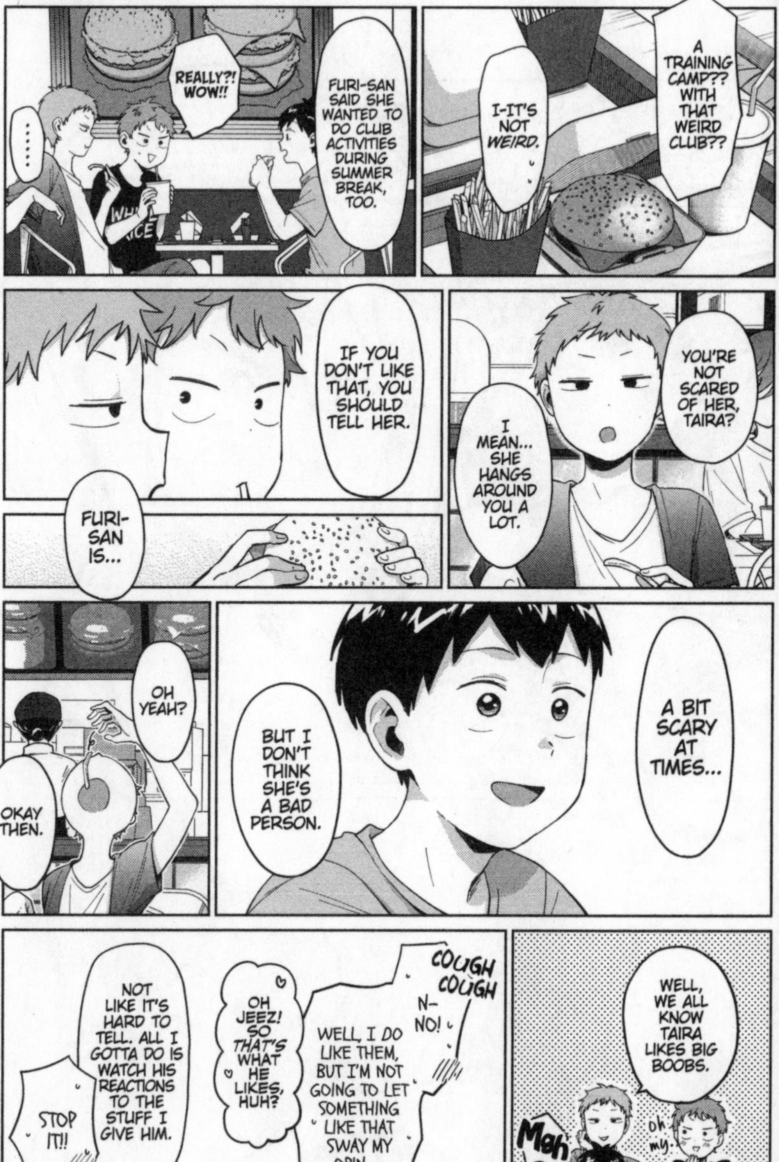
A TRAINING CAMP?? WITH THAT WEIRD CLUB??
I-IT'S NOT *WEIRD.*
FURI-SAN SAID SHE WANTED TO DO CLUB ACTIVITIES DURING SUMMER BREAK, TOO.
REALLY?! WOW!!
......
YOU'RE NOT SCARED OF HER, TAIRA?
I MEAN... SHE HANGS AROUND YOU A LOT.
IF YOU DON'T LIKE THAT, YOU SHOULD TELL HER.
FURI-SAN IS...
A BIT SCARY AT TIMES...
BUT I DON'T THINK SHE'S A BAD PERSON.
OH YEAH?
OKAY THEN.
WELL, WE ALL KNOW TAIRA LIKES BIG BOOBS.
oh my.
Mgh?!!
COUGH COUGH
N-NO!
WELL, I *DO* LIKE THEM, BUT I'M NOT GOING TO LET SOMETHING LIKE THAT SWAY MY OPIN--
OH JEEZ! SO *THAT'S* WHAT HE LIKES, HUH?
NOT LIKE IT'S HARD TO TELL. ALL I GOTTA DO IS WATCH HIS REACTIONS TO THE STUFF I GIVE HIM.
STOP IT!!

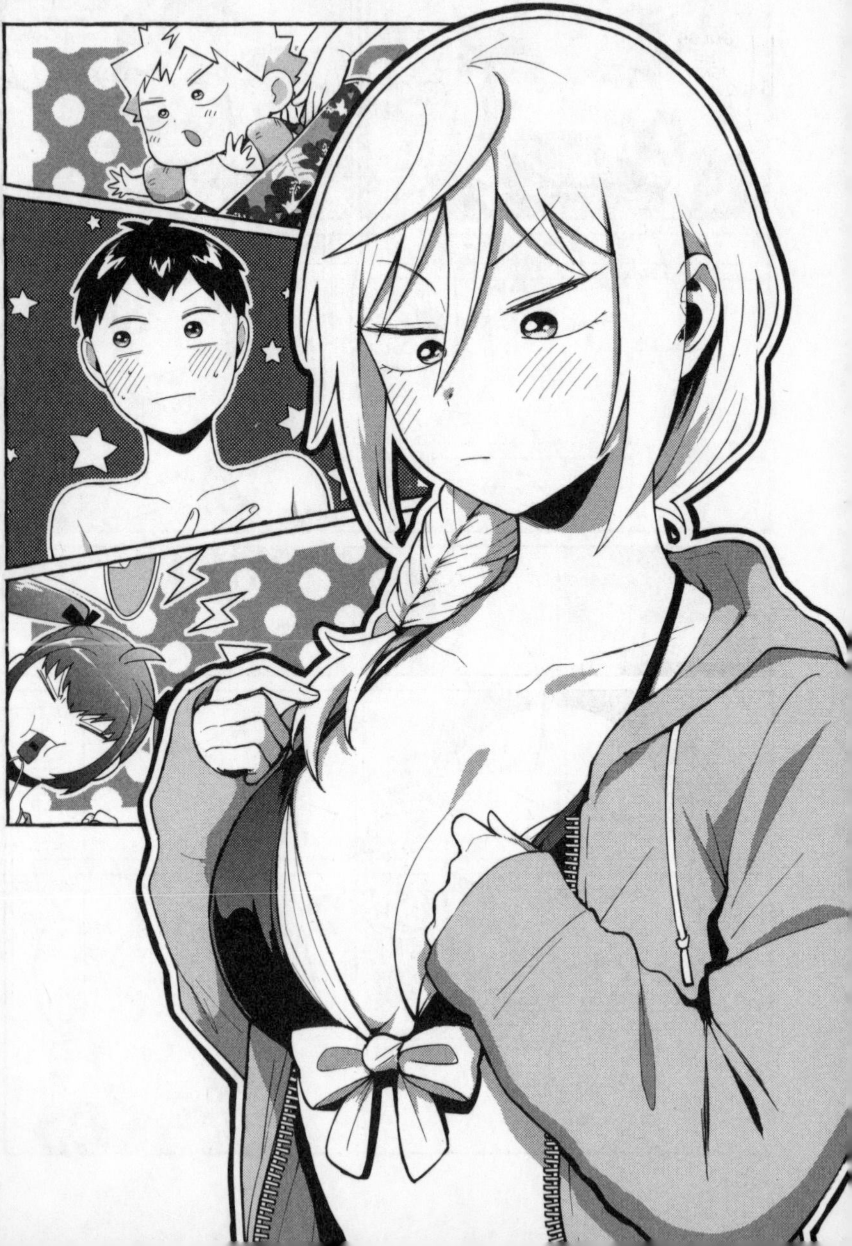

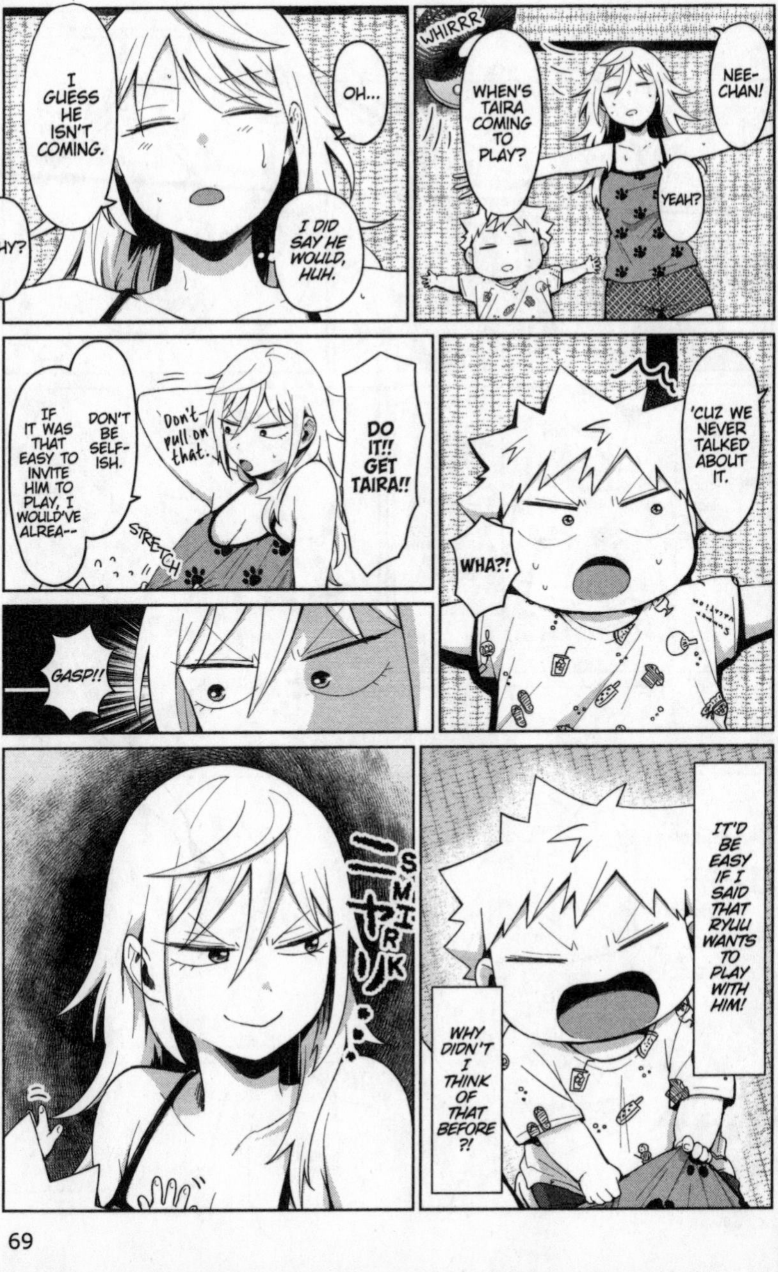
WHIRRR
NEE-CHAN!
YEAH?
WHEN'S TAIRA COMING TO PLAY?
OH...
I DID SAY HE WOULD, HUH.
I GUESS HE ISN'T COMING.
WHY?
'CUZ WE NEVER TALKED ABOUT IT.
WHA?!
DO IT!! GET TAIRA!!
Don't pull on that.
DON'T BE SELF-ISH.
IF IT WAS THAT EASY TO INVITE HIM TO PLAY, I WOULD'VE ALREA--
STRETCH
GASP!!
IT'D BE EASY IF I SAID THAT RYUU WANTS TO PLAY WITH HIM!
WHY DIDN'T I THINK OF THAT BEFORE?!
SMIRK

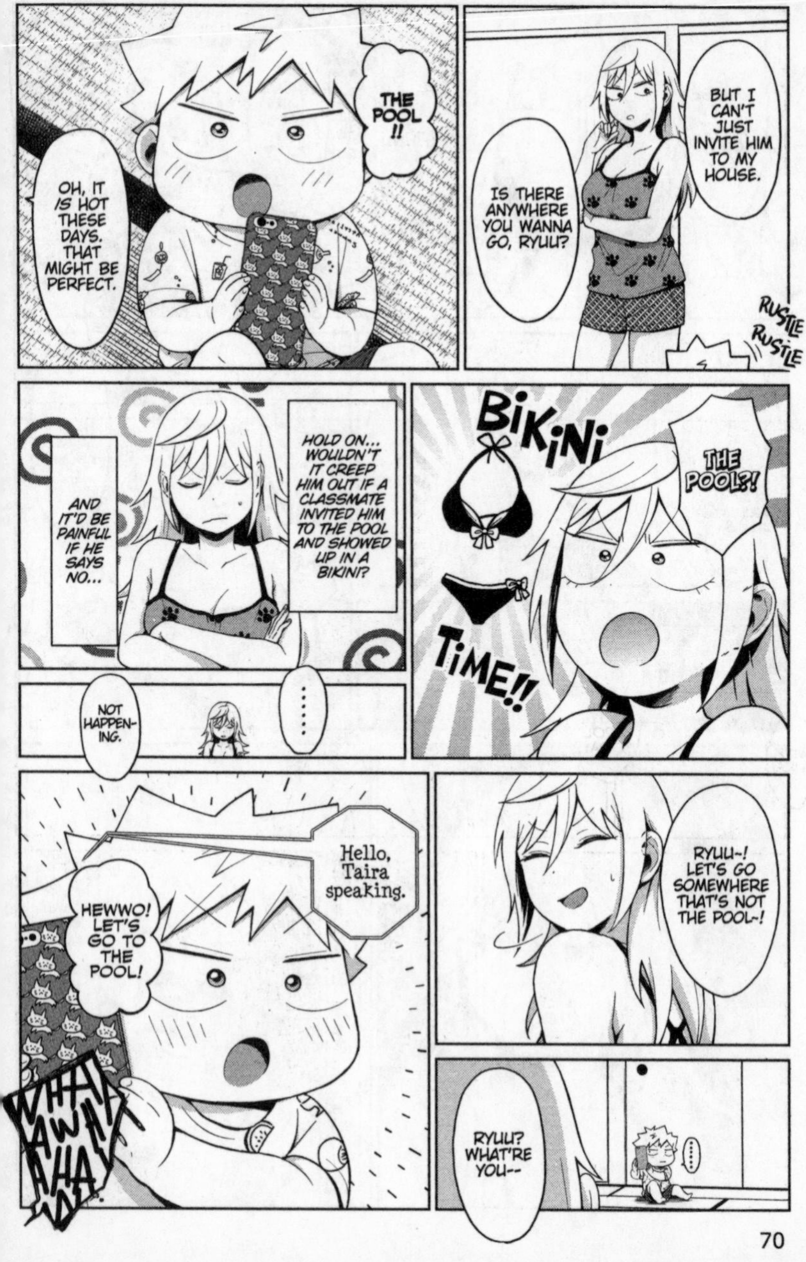
BUT I CAN'T JUST INVITE HIM TO MY HOUSE.
IS THERE ANYWHERE YOU WANNA GO, RYUU?
RUSTLE RUSTLE
THE POOL !!
OH, IT IS HOT THESE DAYS. THAT MIGHT BE PERFECT.
THE POOL?!
BIKINI TIME!!
HOLD ON... WOULDN'T IT CREEP HIM OUT IF A CLASSMATE INVITED HIM TO THE POOL AND SHOWED UP IN A BIKINI?
AND IT'D BE PAINFUL IF HE SAYS NO...
......
NOT HAPPEN-ING.
RYUU~! LET'S GO SOMEWHERE THAT'S NOT THE POOL~!
RYUU? WHAT'RE YOU--
......
Hello, Taira speaking.
HEWWO! LET'S GO TO THE POOL!

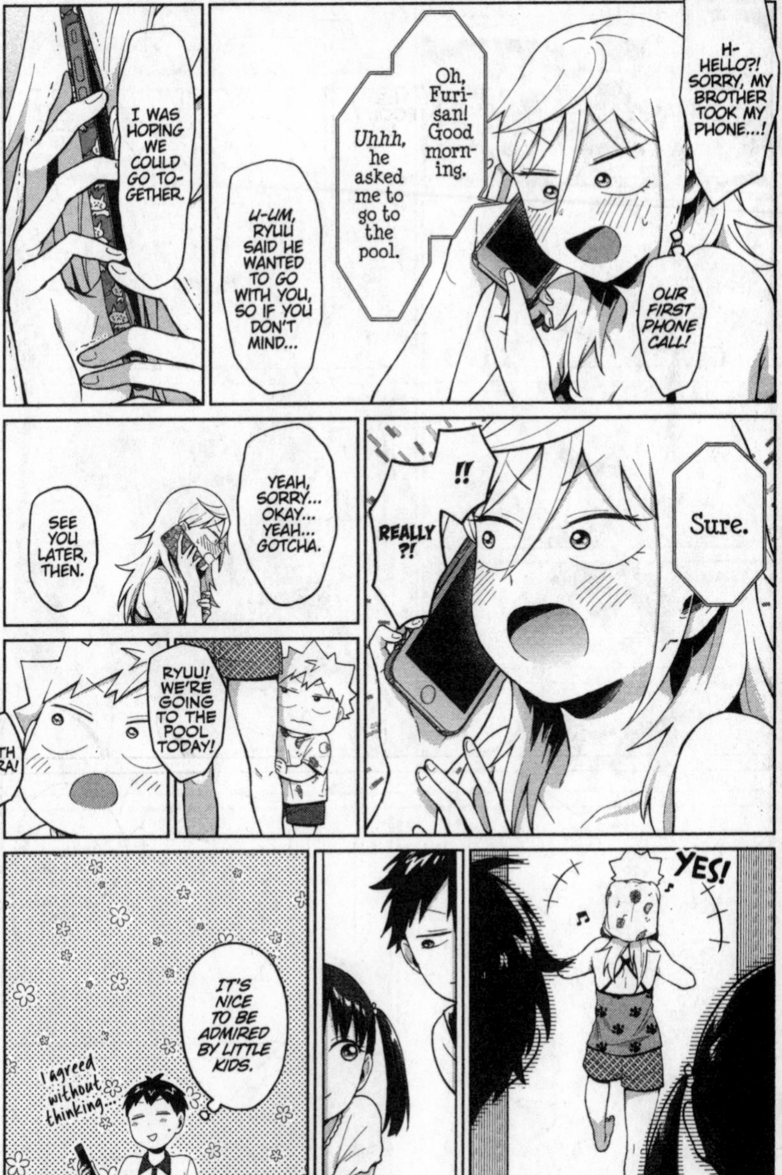
H-HELLO?! SORRY, MY BROTHER TOOK MY PHONE...!
OUR FIRST PHONE CALL!
Oh, Furi-san! Good morning.
Uhhh, he asked me to go to the pool.
U-UM, RYUU SAID HE WANTED TO GO WITH YOU, SO IF YOU DON'T MIND...
I WAS HOPING WE COULD GO TO-GETHER.
Sure.
!!
REALLY ?!
YEAH, SORRY... OKAY... YEAH... GOTCHA.
SEE YOU LATER, THEN.
RYUU! WE'RE GOING TO THE POOL TODAY!
WITH TAIRA!
YES!
IT'S NICE TO BE ADMIRED BY LITTLE KIDS.
I agreed without thinking...

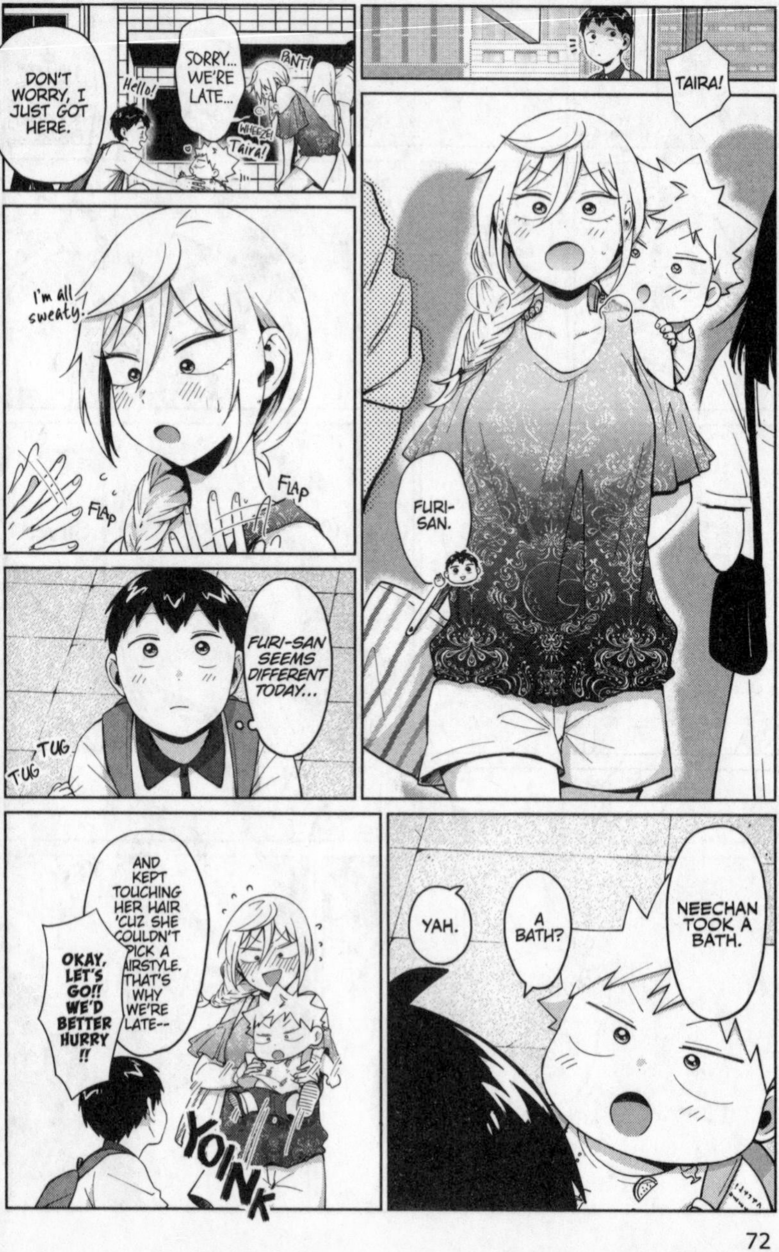
TAIRA!
FURI-SAN.
PANT!
SORRY... WE'RE LATE...
WHEEZE!
Taira!
Hello!
DON'T WORRY, I JUST GOT HERE.
I'm all sweaty!
FLAP
FLAP
FURI-SAN SEEMS DIFFERENT TODAY...
TUG
TUG
NEECHAN TOOK A BATH.
A BATH?
YAH.
AND KEPT TOUCHING HER HAIR 'CUZ SHE COULDN'T PICK A HAIRSTYLE. THAT'S WHY WE'RE LATE--
OKAY, LET'S GO!! WE'D BETTER HURRY!!
YOINK

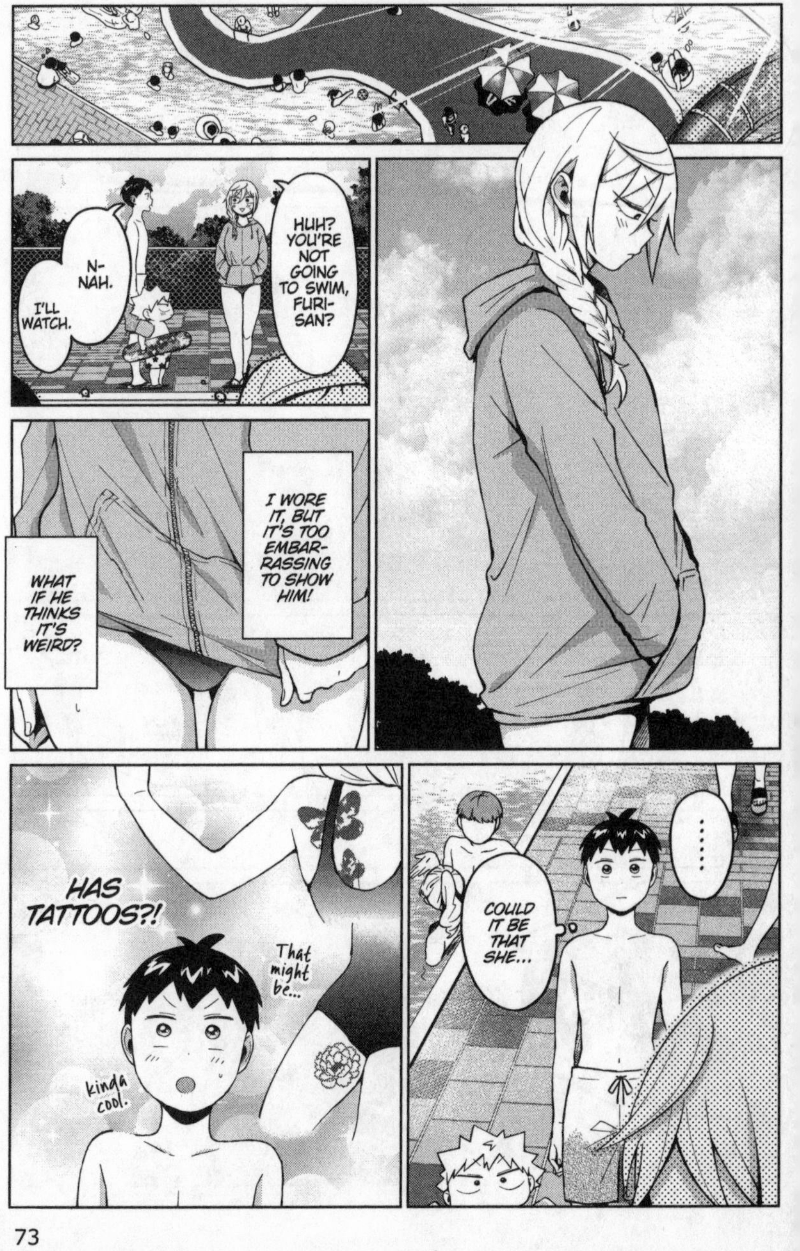
HUH? YOU'RE NOT GOING TO SWIM, FURI-SAN?
N-NAH. I'LL WATCH.
I WORE IT, BUT IT'S TOO EMBARRASSING TO SHOW HIM!
WHAT IF HE THINKS IT'S WEIRD?
......
COULD IT BE THAT SHE...
HAS TATTOOS?!
That might be...
kinda cool.

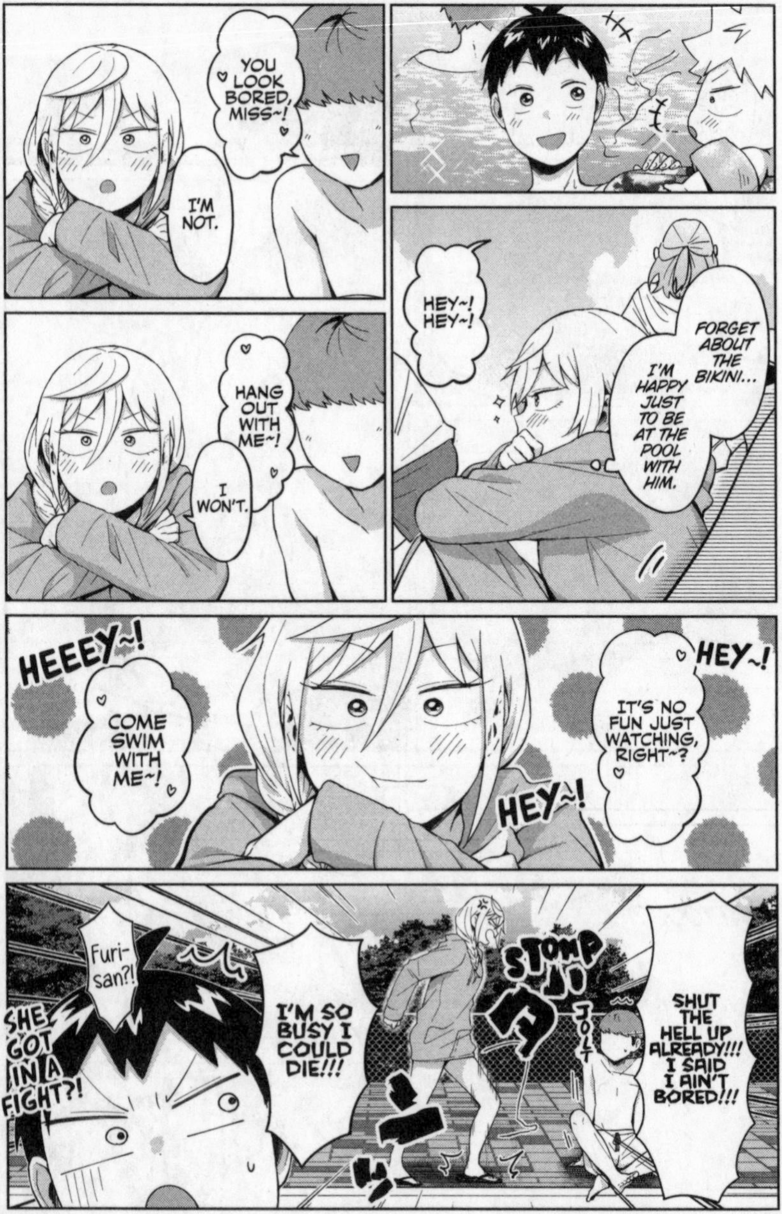
YOU LOOK BORED, MISS~!
I'M NOT.
FORGET ABOUT THE BIKINI...
I'M HAPPY JUST TO BE AT THE POOL WITH HIM.
HEY~! HEY~!
HANG OUT WITH ME~!
I WON'T.
HEY~!
IT'S NO FUN JUST WATCHING, RIGHT~?
HEY~!
HEEEY~!
COME SWIM WITH ME~!
SHUT THE HELL UP ALREADY!!! I SAID I AIN'T BORED!!!
JOLT
STOMP
I'M SO BUSY I COULD DIE!!!
Furi-san?!
SHE GOT IN A FIGHT?!

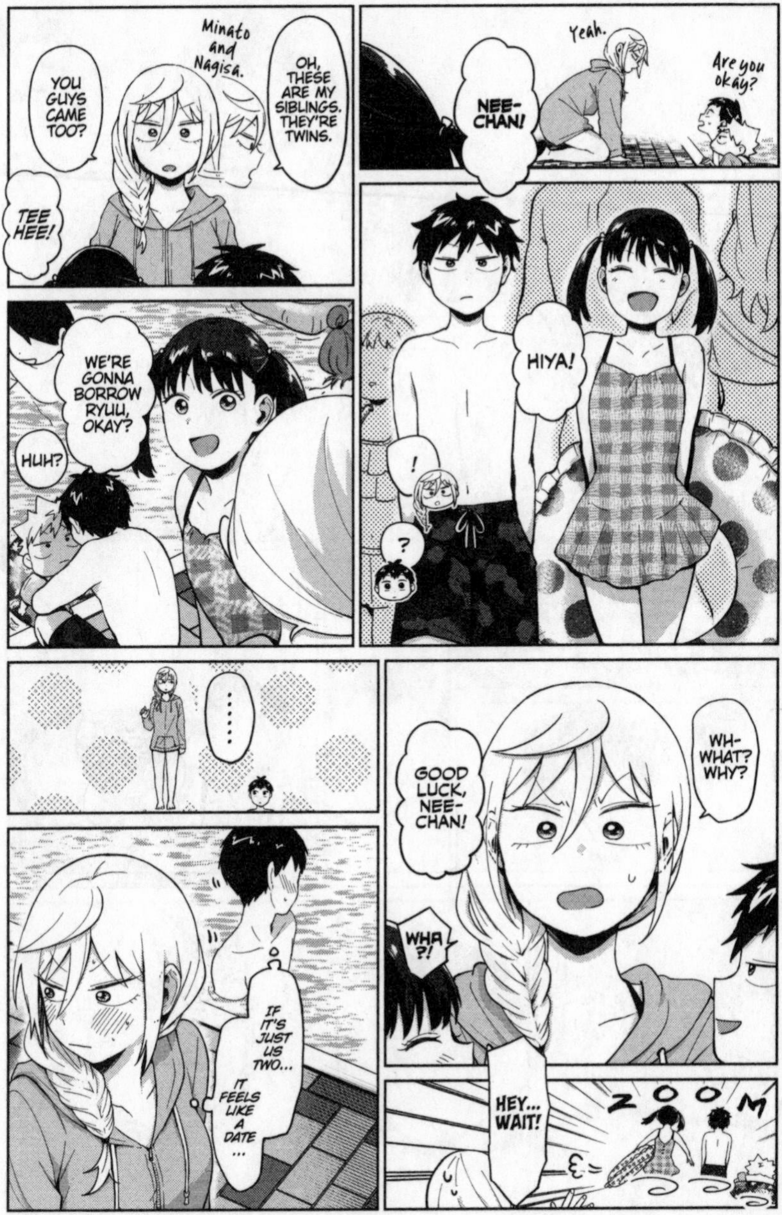

Are you okay?
Yeah.
NEE-CHAN!
Minato and Nagisa.
OH, THESE ARE MY SIBLINGS. THEY'RE TWINS.
YOU GUYS CAME TOO?
TEE HEE!
HIYA!
!
?
WE'RE GONNA BORROW RYUU, OKAY?
HUH?
WH-WHAT? WHY?
GOOD LUCK, NEE-CHAN!
WHA?!
ZOOM
HEY... WAIT!
......
IF IT'S JUST US TWO...
IT FEELS LIKE A DATE...

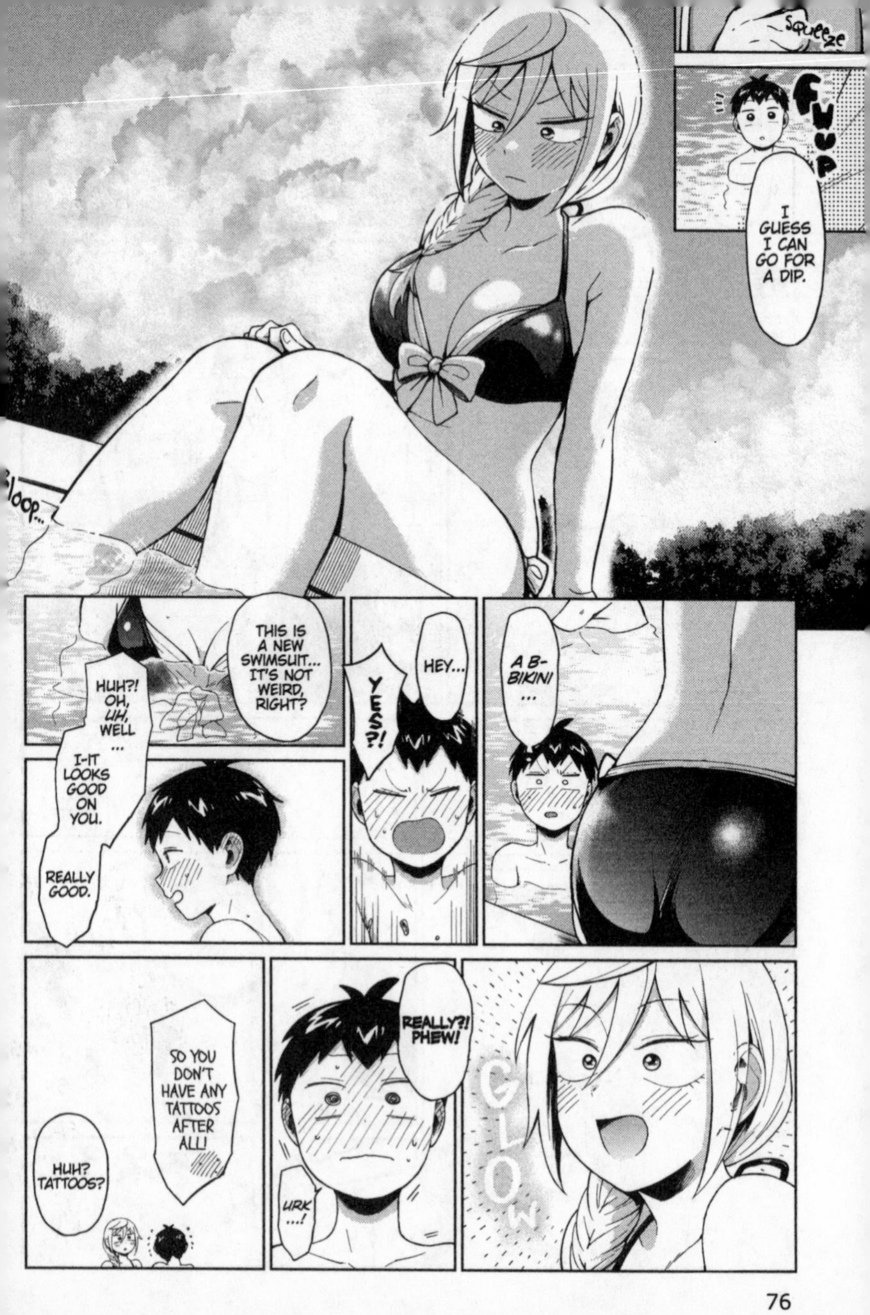
Squeeze
FWUP
I GUESS I CAN GO FOR A DIP.
Sloop...
A B-BIKINI...
HEY...
YES?!
THIS IS A NEW SWIMSUIT... IT'S NOT WEIRD, RIGHT?
HUH?! OH, UH, WELL...
I-IT LOOKS GOOD ON YOU.
REALLY GOOD.
GLOW
REALLY?! PHEW!
URK...!
SO YOU DON'T HAVE ANY TATTOOS AFTER ALL!
HUH? TATTOOS?

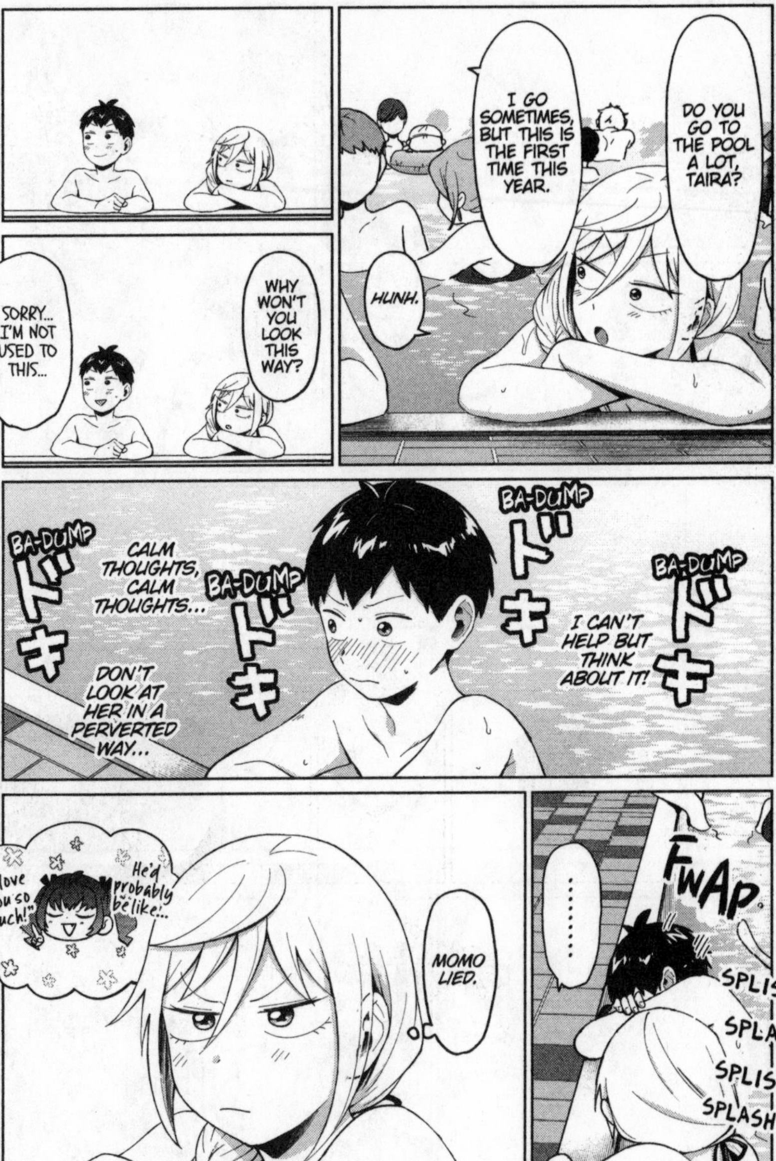
DO YOU GO TO THE POOL A LOT, TAIRA?
I GO SOMETIMES, BUT THIS IS THE FIRST TIME THIS YEAR.
HUNH.
WHY WON'T YOU LOOK THIS WAY?
SORRY... I'M NOT USED TO THIS...
BA-DUMP ドキ
BA-DUMP ドキ
I CAN'T HELP BUT THINK ABOUT IT!
BA-DUMP ドキ
CALM THOUGHTS, CALM THOUGHTS...
DON'T LOOK AT HER IN A PERVERTED WAY...
BA-DUMP ドキ
FWAP
......
SPLISH
SPLASH
SPLISH
SPLASH
MOMO LIED.
He'd probably be like...
"I love you so much!"

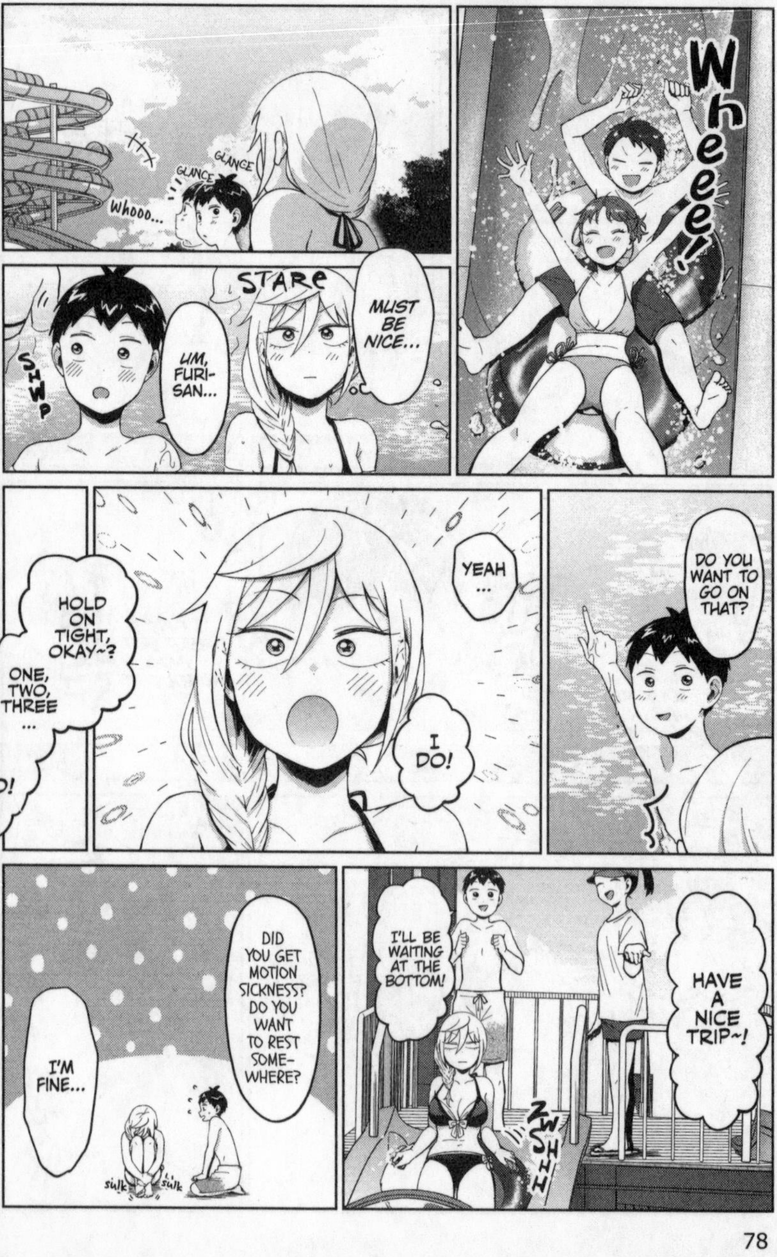
Wheeee!
GLANCE
GLANCE
Whooo...
STARE
MUST BE NICE...
UM, FURI-SAN...
SHWP
DO YOU WANT TO GO ON THAT?
YEAH ...
I DO!
HOLD ON TIGHT, OKAY~?
ONE, TWO, THREE ...
GO!
HAVE A NICE TRIP~!
I'LL BE WAITING AT THE BOTTOM!
ZWSHHH
DID YOU GET MOTION SICKNESS? DO YOU WANT TO REST SOME-WHERE?
I'M FINE...
sulk
sulk

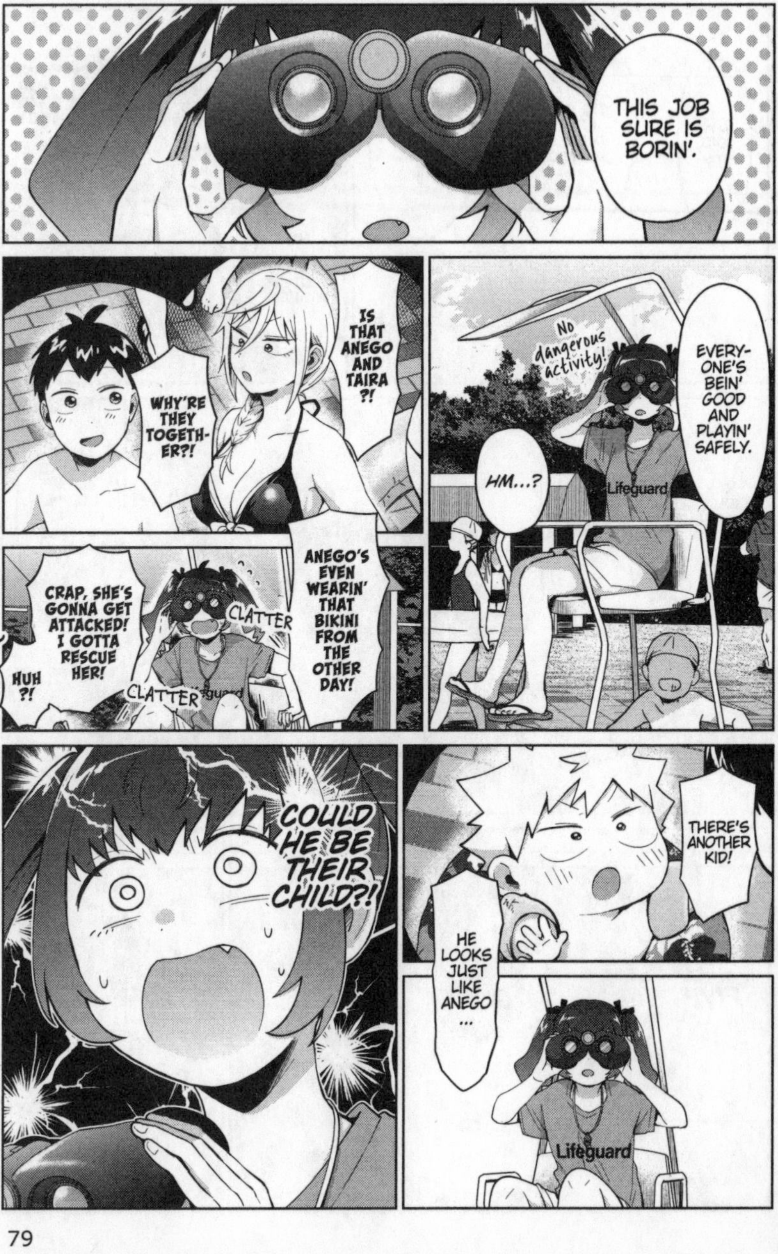
THIS JOB SURE IS BORIN'.
EVERY-ONE'S BEIN' GOOD AND PLAYIN' SAFELY.
No dangerous activity!
Lifeguard
HM...?
IS THAT ANEGO AND TAIRA?!
WHY'RE THEY TOGETH-ER?!
ANEGO'S EVEN WEARIN' THAT BIKINI FROM THE OTHER DAY!
CLATTER
CRAP, SHE'S GONNA GET ATTACKED! I GOTTA RESCUE HER!
CLATTER
HUH?!
THERE'S ANOTHER KID!
HE LOOKS JUST LIKE ANEGO...
Lifeguard
COULD HE BE THEIR CHILD?!

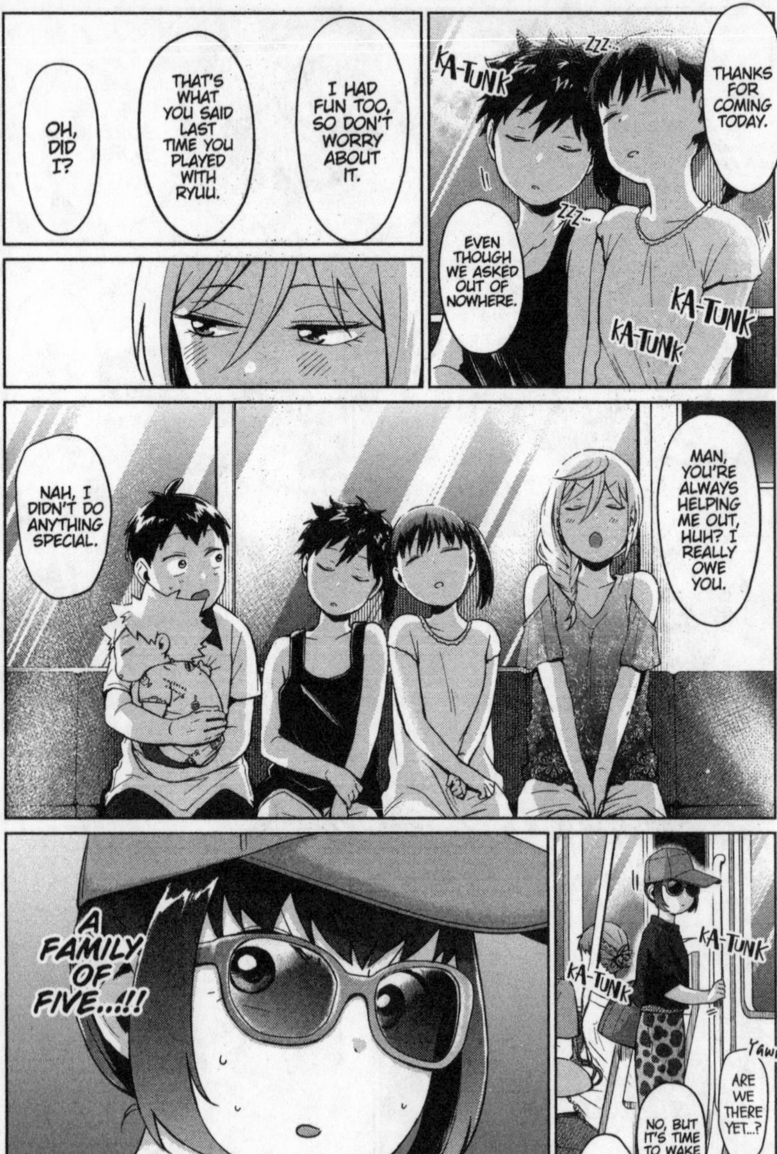
THANKS FOR COMING TODAY.
ZZZ...
KA-TUNK
ZZZ...
EVEN THOUGH WE ASKED OUT OF NOWHERE.
KA-TUNK
KA-TUNK
I HAD FUN TOO, SO DON'T WORRY ABOUT IT.
THAT'S WHAT YOU SAID LAST TIME YOU PLAYED WITH RYUU.
OH, DID I?
MAN, YOU'RE ALWAYS HELPING ME OUT, HUH? I REALLY OWE YOU.
NAH, I DIDN'T DO ANYTHING SPECIAL.
KA-TUNK
KA-TUNK
Yawn...
ARE WE THERE YET...?
NO, BUT IT'S TIME TO WAKE UP.
'KAAAY...
A FAMILY OF FIVE...!!!

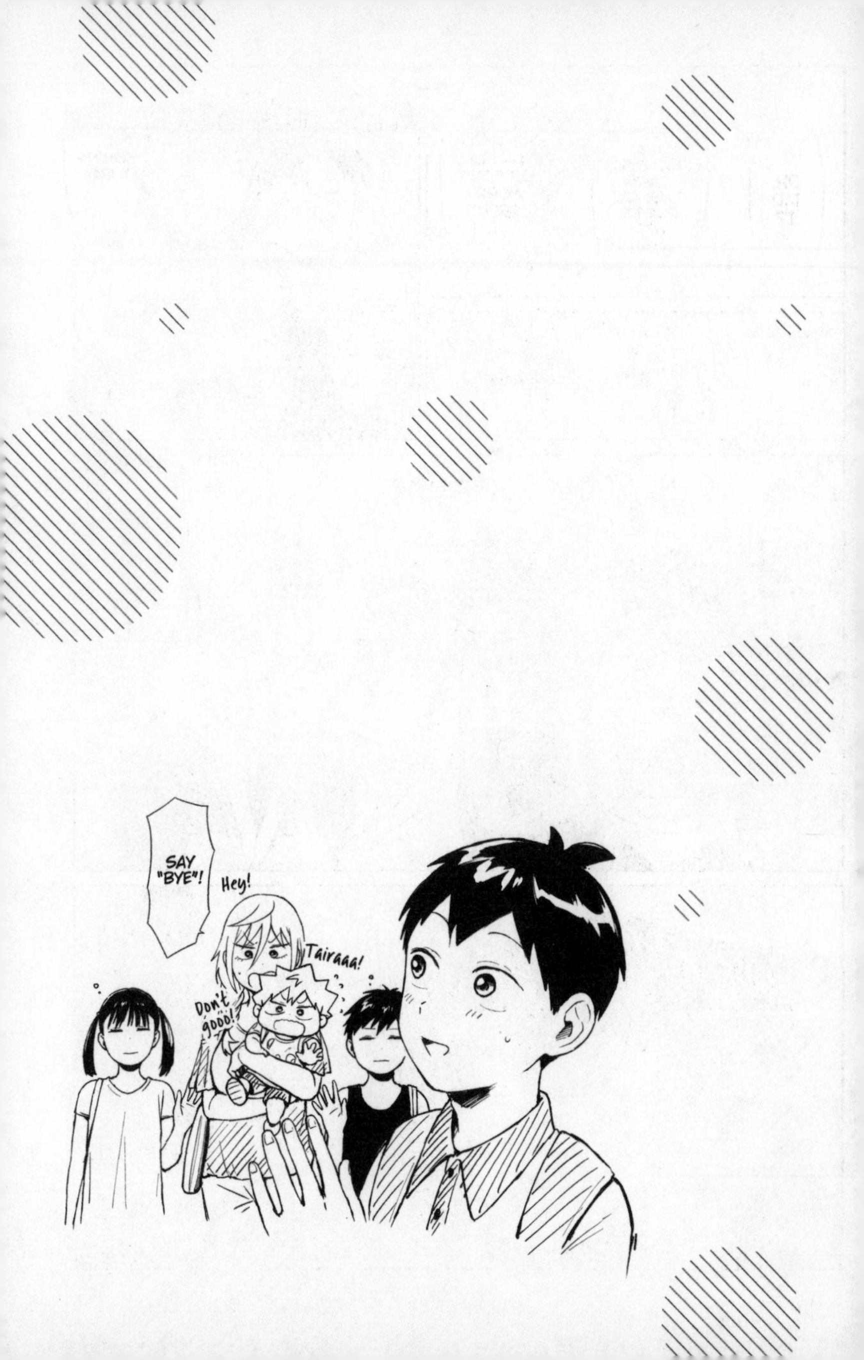
Hey!
SAY "BYE"!
Tairaaa!
Don't gooo!

Chapter 15

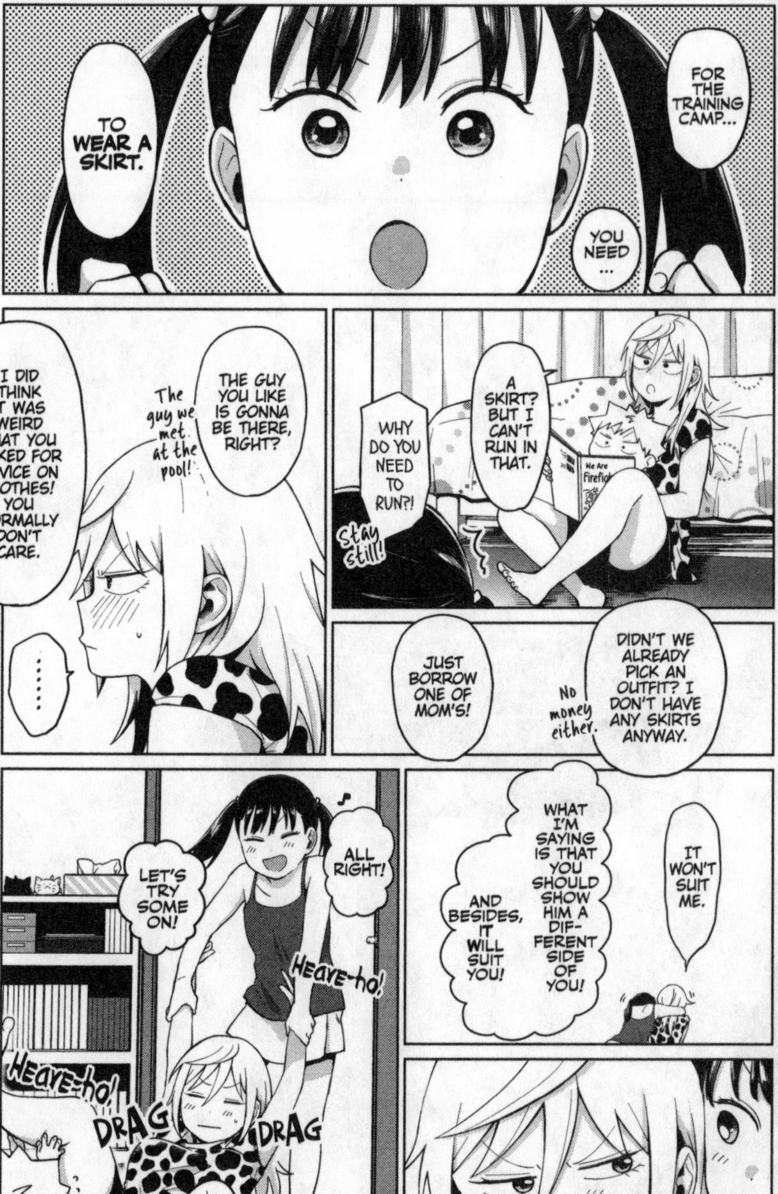
FOR THE TRAINING CAMP...
YOU NEED ...
TO WEAR A SKIRT.
A SKIRT? BUT I CAN'T RUN IN THAT.
WHY DO YOU NEED TO RUN?!
Stay still!
DIDN'T WE ALREADY PICK AN OUTFIT? I DON'T HAVE ANY SKIRTS ANYWAY.
No money either.
JUST BORROW ONE OF MOM'S!
THE GUY YOU LIKE IS GONNA BE THERE, RIGHT?
The guy we met at the pool!
I DID THINK IT WAS WEIRD THAT YOU ASKED FOR ADVICE ON CLOTHES! YOU NORMALLY DON'T CARE.
......
IT WON'T SUIT ME.
WHAT I'M SAYING IS THAT YOU SHOULD SHOW HIM A DIF-FERENT SIDE OF YOU!
AND BESIDES, IT WILL SUIT YOU!
ALL RIGHT!
LET'S TRY SOME ON!
Heave-ho!
Heave-ho!
DRAG
DRAG

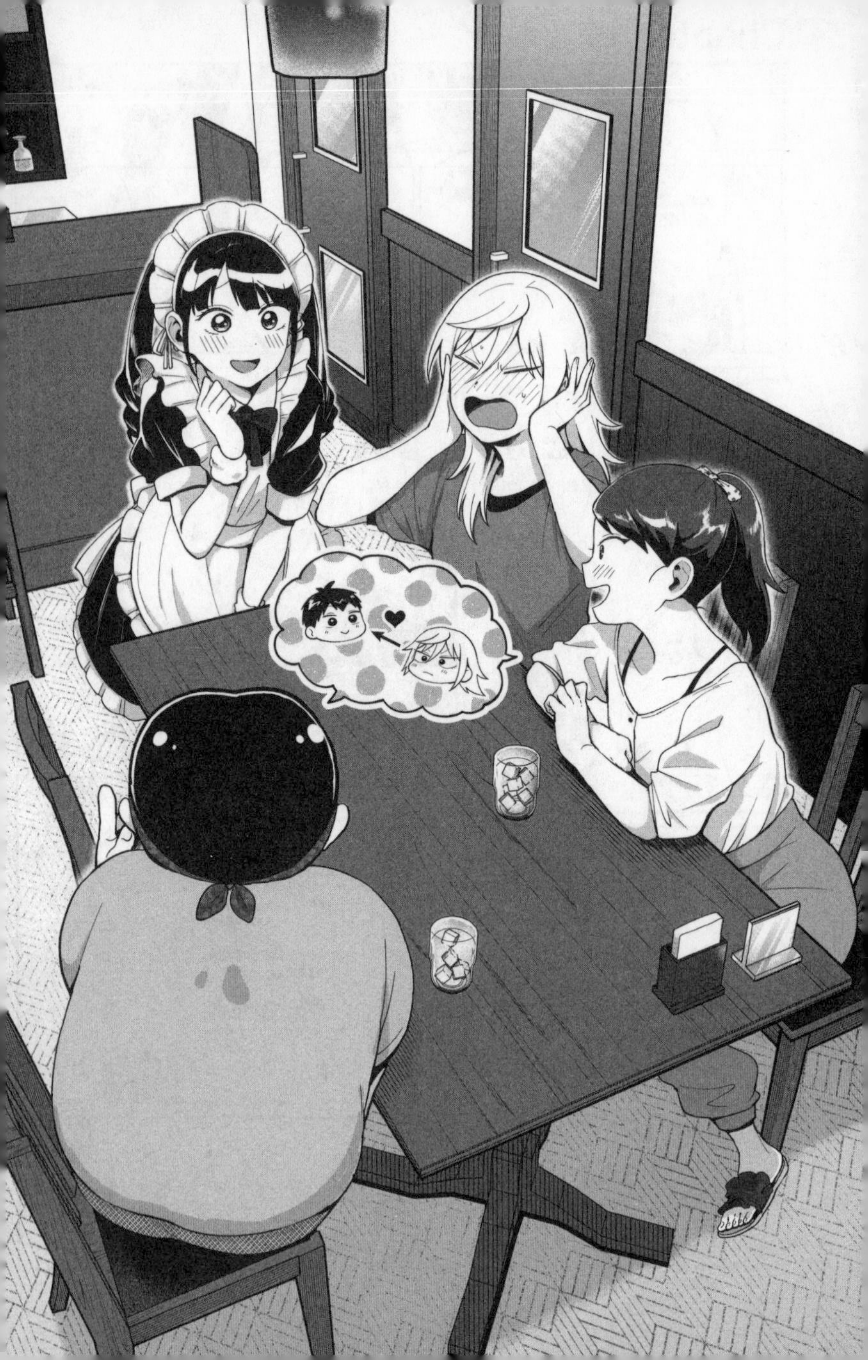

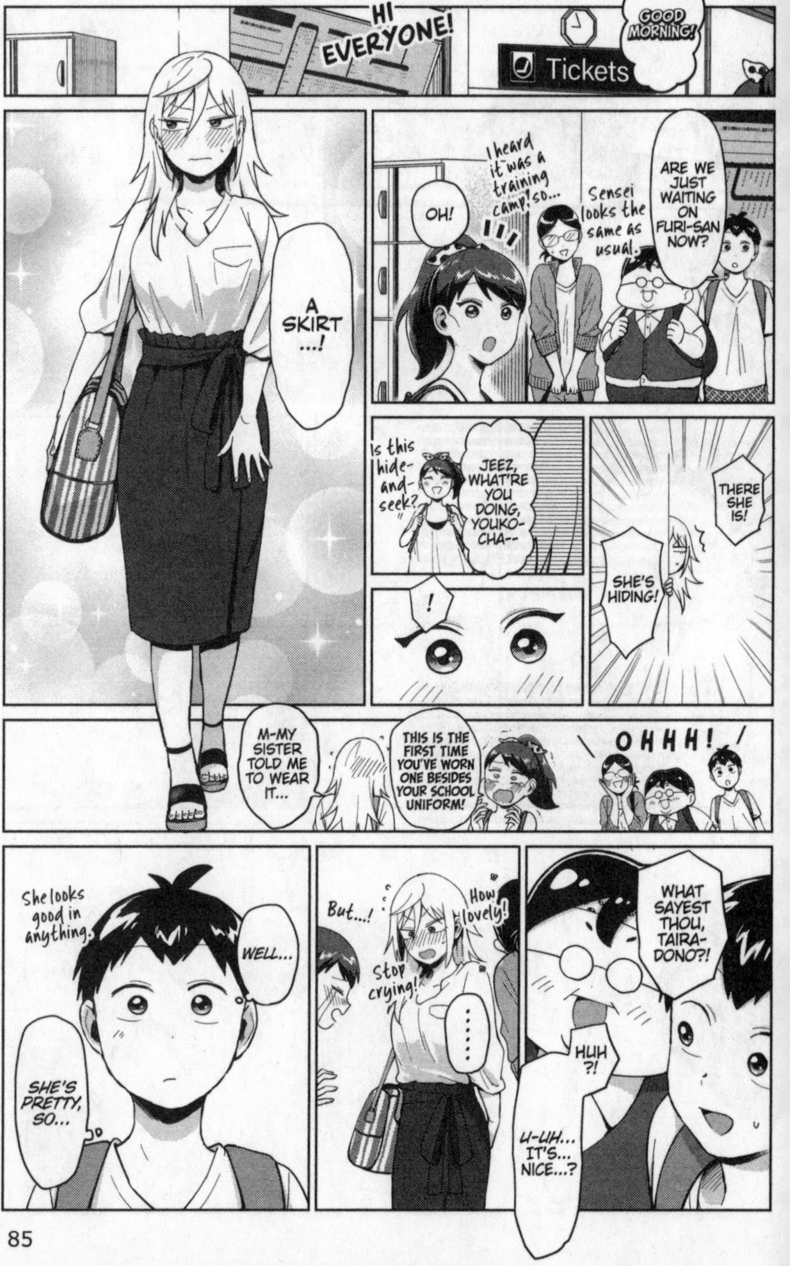
GOOD MORNING!
Tickets
HI EVERYONE!
ARE WE JUST WAITING ON FURI-SAN NOW?
Sensei looks the same as usual.
I heard it was a training camp, so...
OH!
THERE SHE IS!
SHE'S HIDING!
JEEZ, WHAT'RE YOU DOING, YOUKO-CHA--
Is this hide-and-seek?
!
A SKIRT ...!
OHHHH!
THIS IS THE FIRST TIME YOU'VE WORN ONE BESIDES YOUR SCHOOL UNIFORM!
M-MY SISTER TOLD ME TO WEAR IT...
WHAT SAYEST THOU, TAIRA-DONO?!
HUH?!
U-UH... IT'S... NICE...?
How lovely!
But...!
Stop crying!
......
WELL...
She looks good in anything.
SHE'S PRETTY, SO...

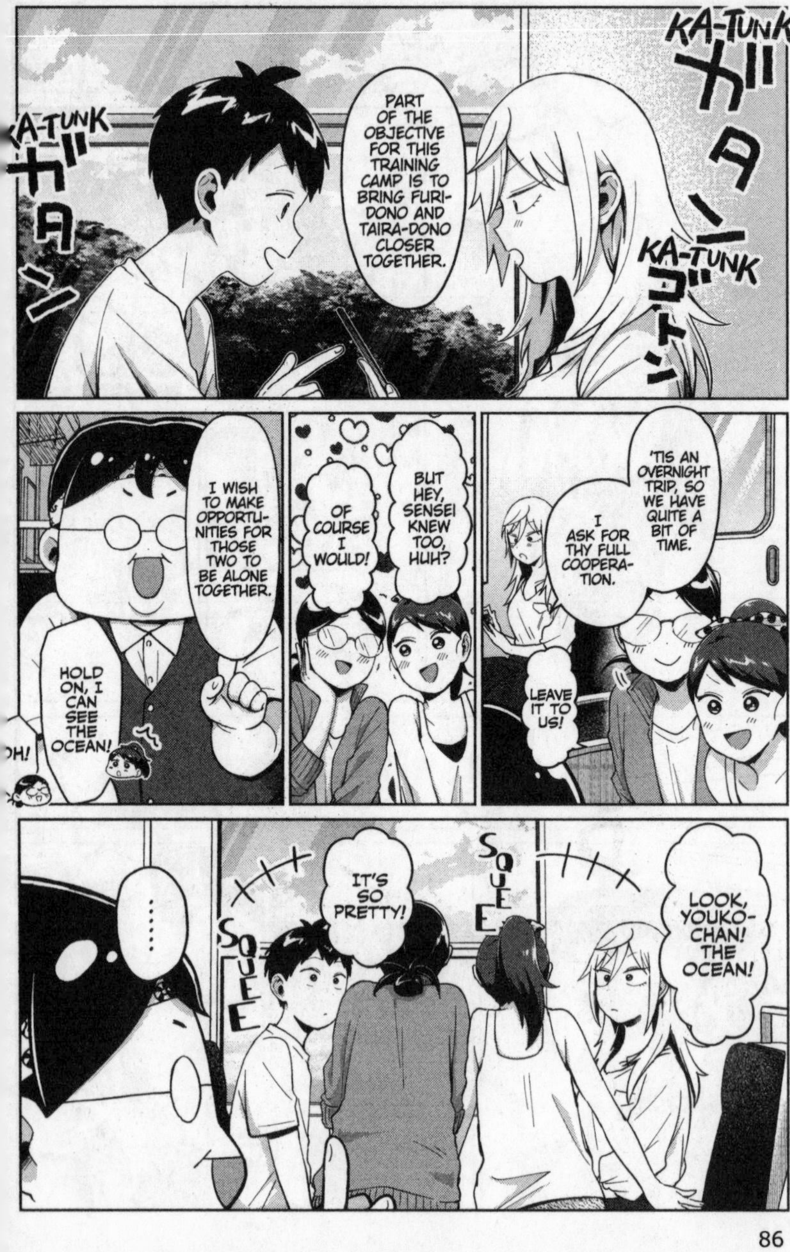
KA-TUNK ガタン
PART OF THE OBJECTIVE FOR THIS TRAINING CAMP IS TO BRING FURI-DONO AND TAIRA-DONO CLOSER TOGETHER.
KA-TUNK ゴトン
KA-TUNK ガタン
'TIS AN OVERNIGHT TRIP, SO WE HAVE QUITE A BIT OF TIME.
I ASK FOR THY FULL COOPERA-TION.
LEAVE IT TO US!
BUT HEY, SENSEI KNEW TOO, HUH?
OF COURSE I WOULD!
I WISH TO MAKE OPPORTU-NITIES FOR THOSE TWO TO BE ALONE TOGETHER.
HOLD ON, I CAN SEE THE OCEAN!
LOOK, YOUKO-CHAN! THE OCEAN!
SQUEE
SQUEE
IT'S SO PRETTY!
......

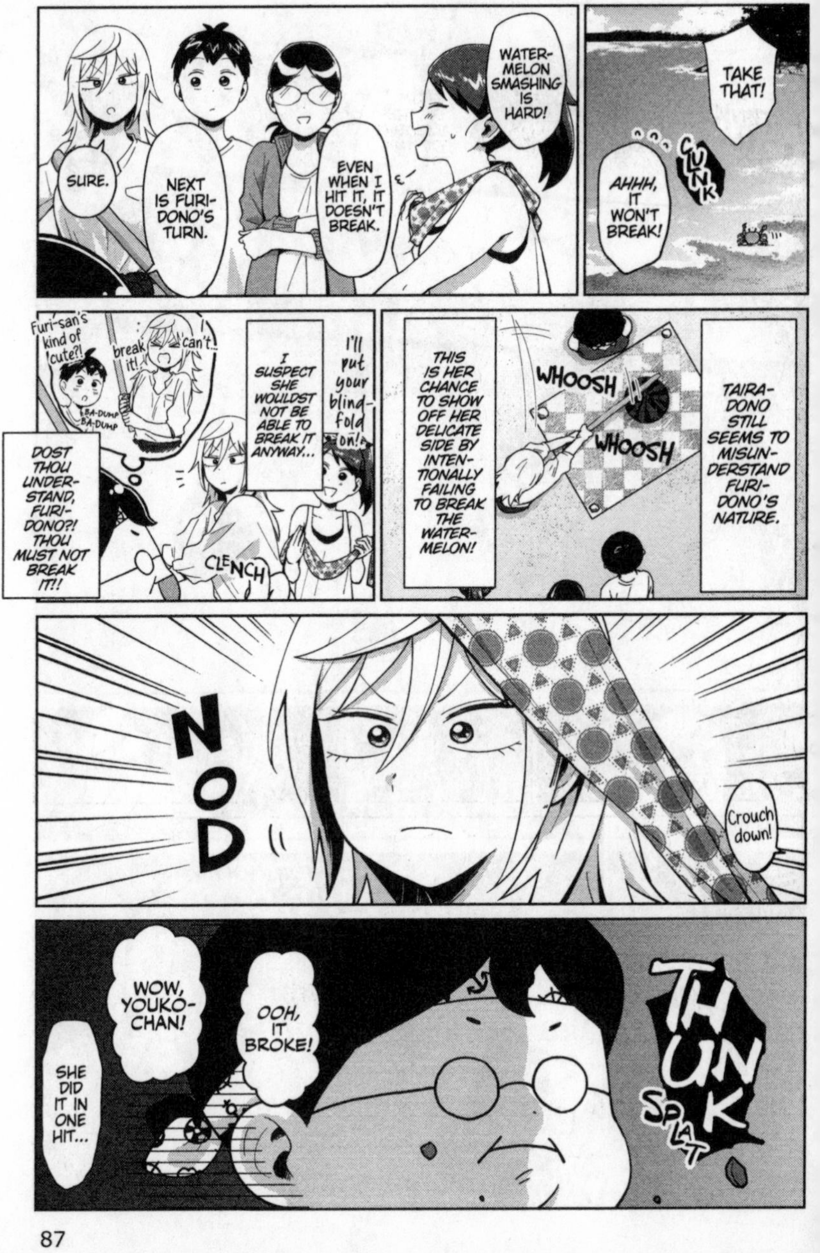

TAKE THAT!
CLUNK
AHHH, IT WON'T BREAK!
WATER-MELON SMASHING IS HARD!
EVEN WHEN I HIT IT, IT DOESN'T BREAK.
NEXT IS FURI-DONO'S TURN.
SURE.
TAIRA-DONO STILL SEEMS TO MISUNDERSTAND FURI-DONO'S NATURE.
WHOOSH
WHOOSH
THIS IS HER CHANCE TO SHOW OFF HER DELICATE SIDE BY INTENTIONALLY FAILING TO BREAK THE WATER-MELON!
I'll put your blind-fold on!
I SUSPECT SHE WOULDST NOT BE ABLE TO BREAK IT ANYWAY...
can't...
break it!
Furi-san's kind of cute?!
BA-DUMP BA-DUMP
DOST THOU UNDER-STAND, FURI-DONO?! THOU MUST NOT BREAK IT!!
CLENCH
Crouch down!
NOD
THUNK
SPLAT
OOH, IT BROKE!
WOW, YOUKO-CHAN!
SHE DID IT IN ONE HIT...

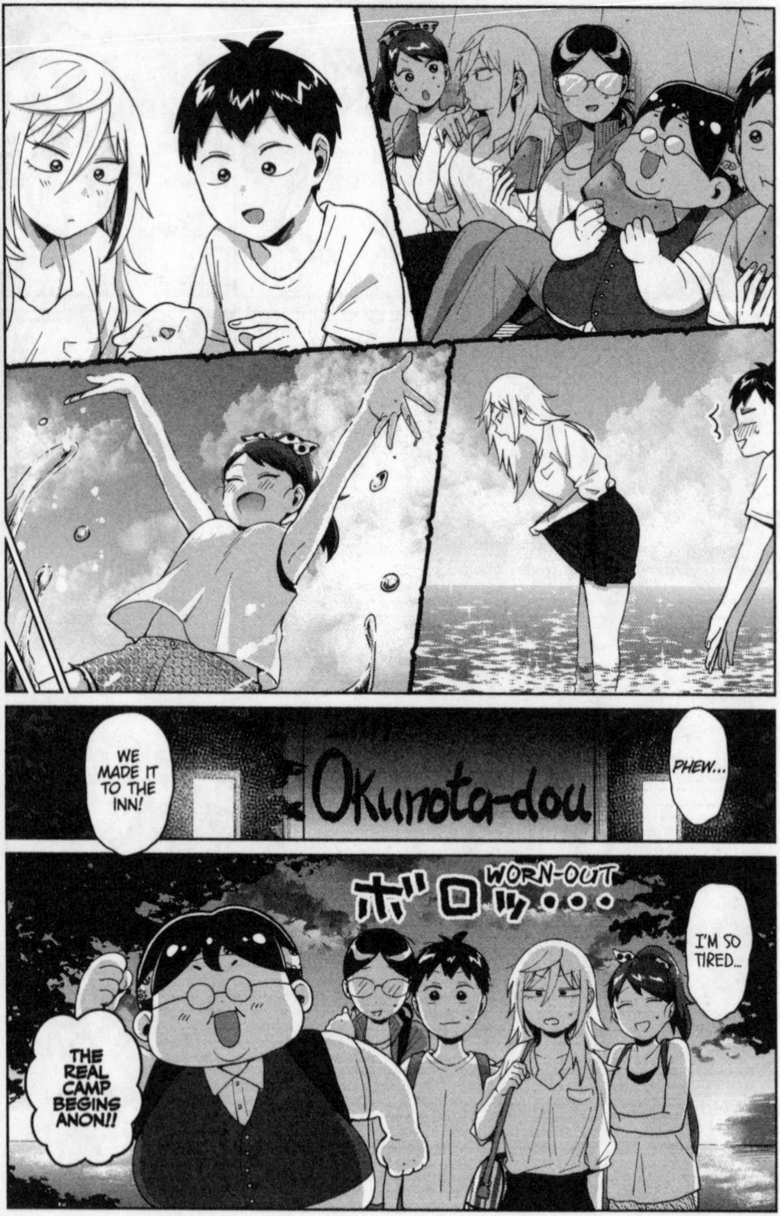
PHEW...
Okunota-dou
WE MADE IT TO THE INN!
ボロッ・・・
WORN-OUT
I'M SO TIRED...
THE REAL CAMP BEGINS ANON!!

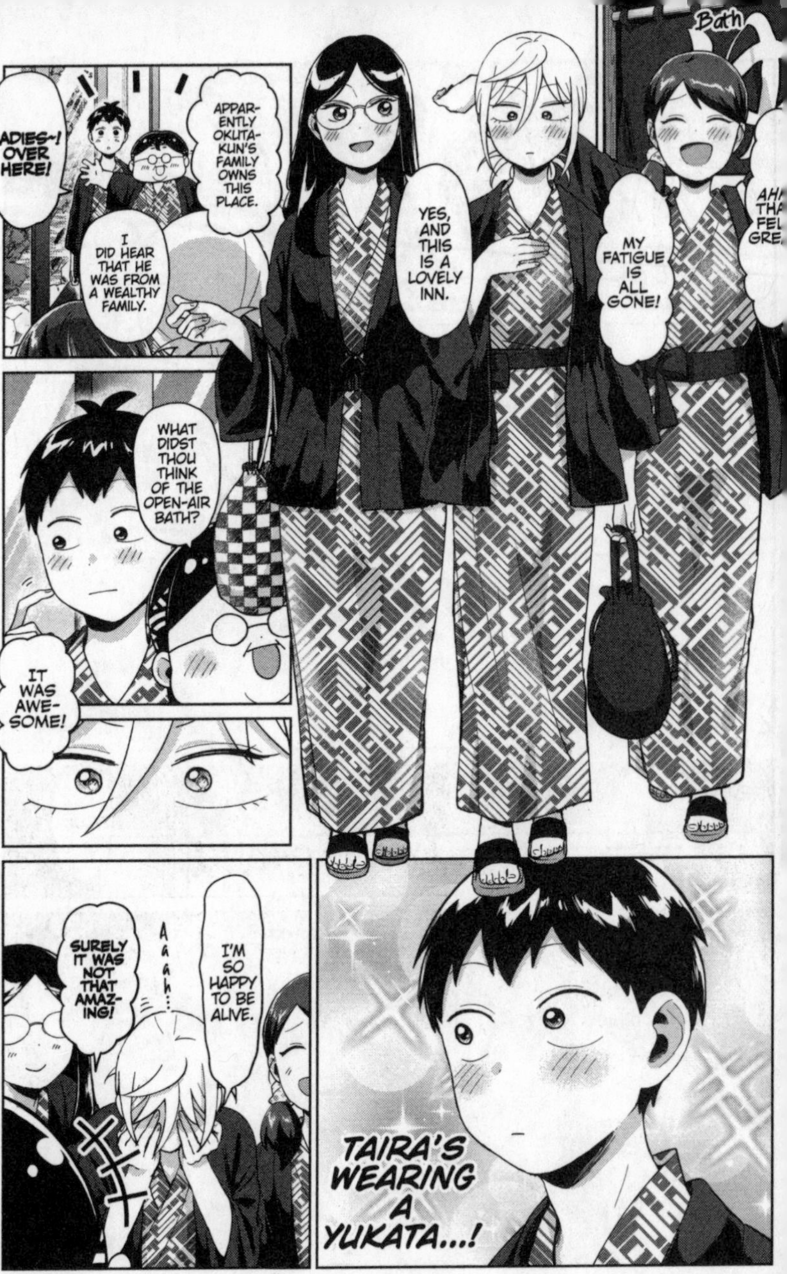
Bath
MY FATIGUE IS ALL GONE!
YES, AND THIS IS A LOVELY INN.
APPARENTLY OKUTA-KUN'S FAMILY OWNS THIS PLACE.
LADIES~! OVER HERE!
I DID HEAR THAT HE WAS FROM A WEALTHY FAMILY.
WHAT DIDST THOU THINK OF THE OPEN-AIR BATH?
IT WAS AWESOME!
TAIRA'S WEARING A YUKATA...!
I'M SO HAPPY TO BE ALIVE.
Aaah...
SURELY IT WAS NOT THAT AMAZING!

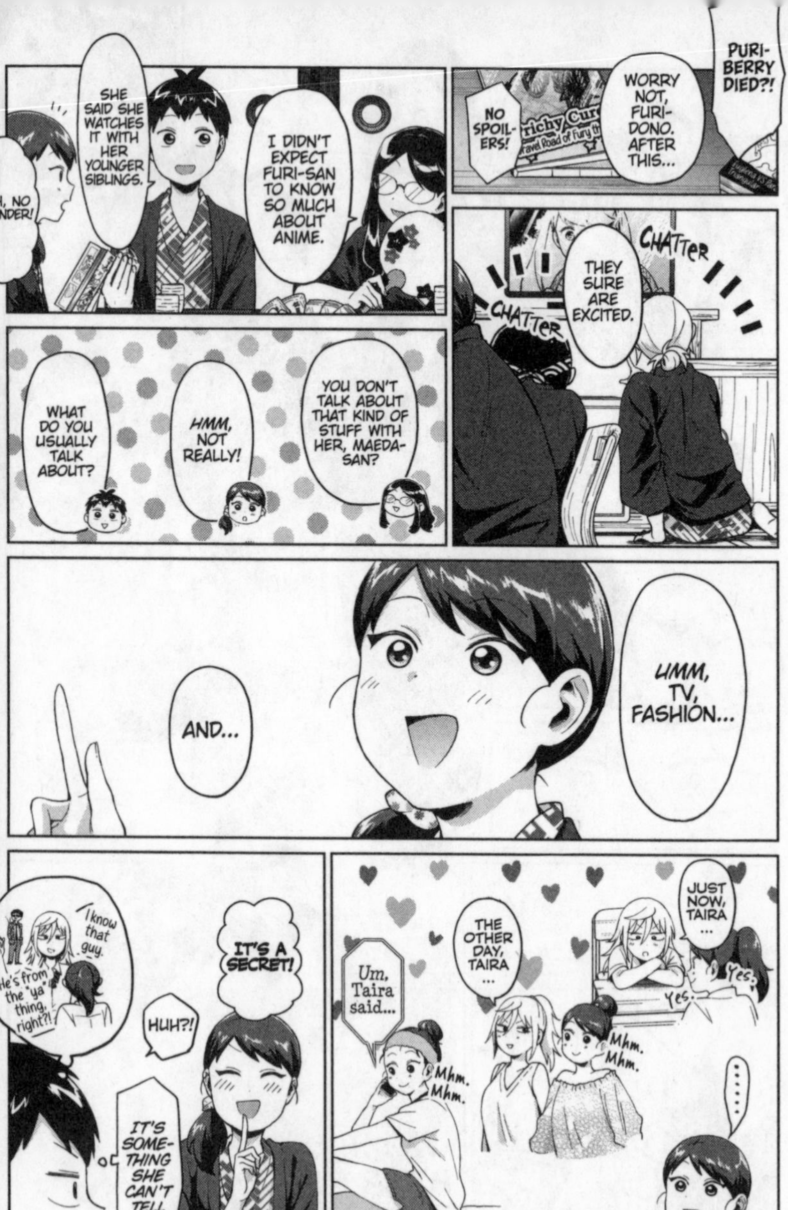
PURI-BERRY DIED?!
WORRY NOT, FURI-DONO. AFTER THIS...
NO SPOILERS!
I DIDN'T EXPECT FURI-SAN TO KNOW SO MUCH ABOUT ANIME.
SHE SAID SHE WATCHES IT WITH HER YOUNGER SIBLINGS.
H, NO NDER!
CHATTER
THEY SURE ARE EXCITED.
CHATTER
YOU DON'T TALK ABOUT THAT KIND OF STUFF WITH HER, MAEDA-SAN?
HMM, NOT REALLY!
WHAT DO YOU USUALLY TALK ABOUT?
UMM, TV, FASHION...
AND...
JUST NOW, TAIRA ...
Yes.
Yes.
THE OTHER DAY, TAIRA ...
Um, Taira said...
Mhm. Mhm.
Mhm. Mhm.
......
IT'S A SECRET!
I know that guy.
He's from the "ya" thing, right?!
HUH?!
IT'S SOMETHING SHE CAN'T TELL US?!

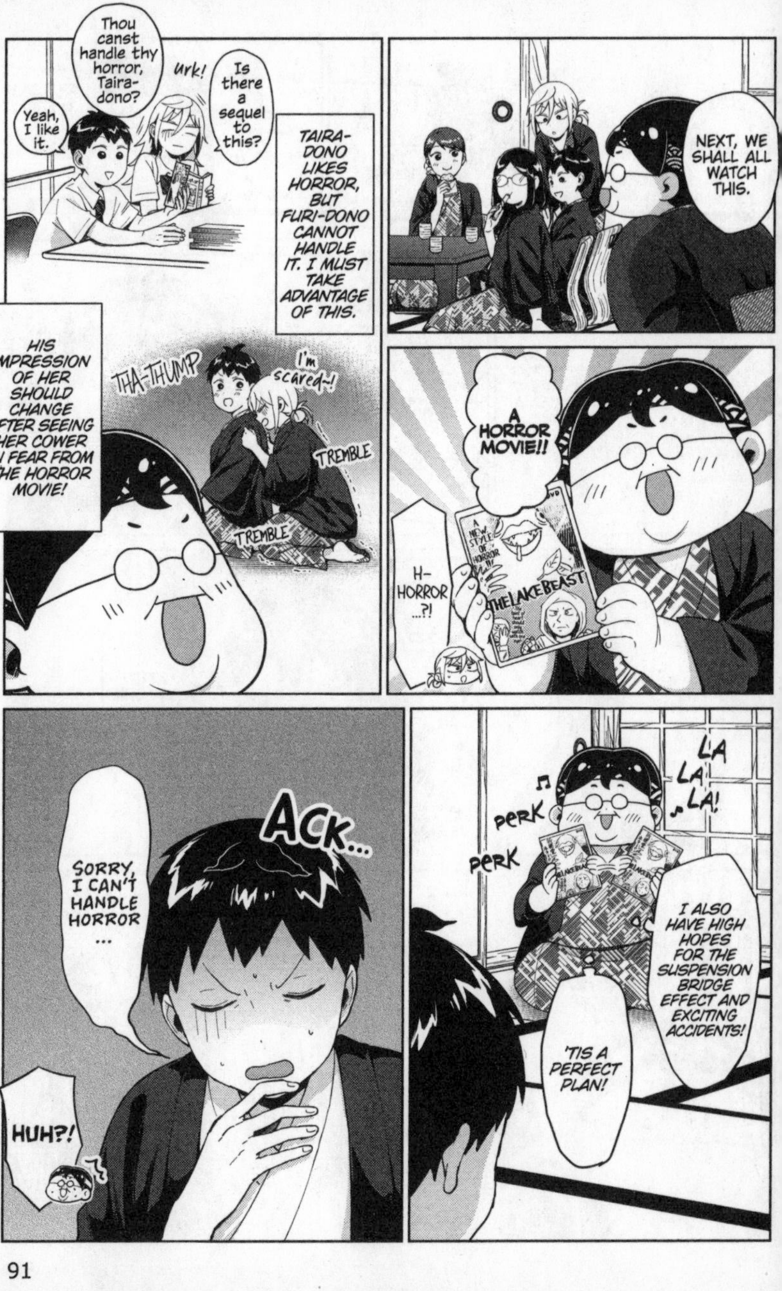
NEXT, WE SHALL ALL WATCH THIS.
TAIRA-DONO LIKES HORROR, BUT FURI-DONO CANNOT HANDLE IT. I MUST TAKE ADVANTAGE OF THIS.
Is there a sequel to this?
Urk!
Thou canst handle thy horror, Taira-dono?
Yeah, I like it.
A HORROR MOVIE!!
A NEW STYLE OF HORROR!!
THE LAKE BEAST
H-HORROR...?!
HIS IMPRESSION OF HER SHOULD CHANGE AFTER SEEING HER COWER IN FEAR FROM THE HORROR MOVIE!
I'm scared~!
THA-THUMP
TREMBLE
TREMBLE
LA LA LA!
PERK
PERK
I ALSO HAVE HIGH HOPES FOR THE SUSPENSION BRIDGE EFFECT AND EXCITING ACCIDENTS!
'TIS A PERFECT PLAN!
ACK...
SORRY, I CAN'T HANDLE HORROR...
HUH?!

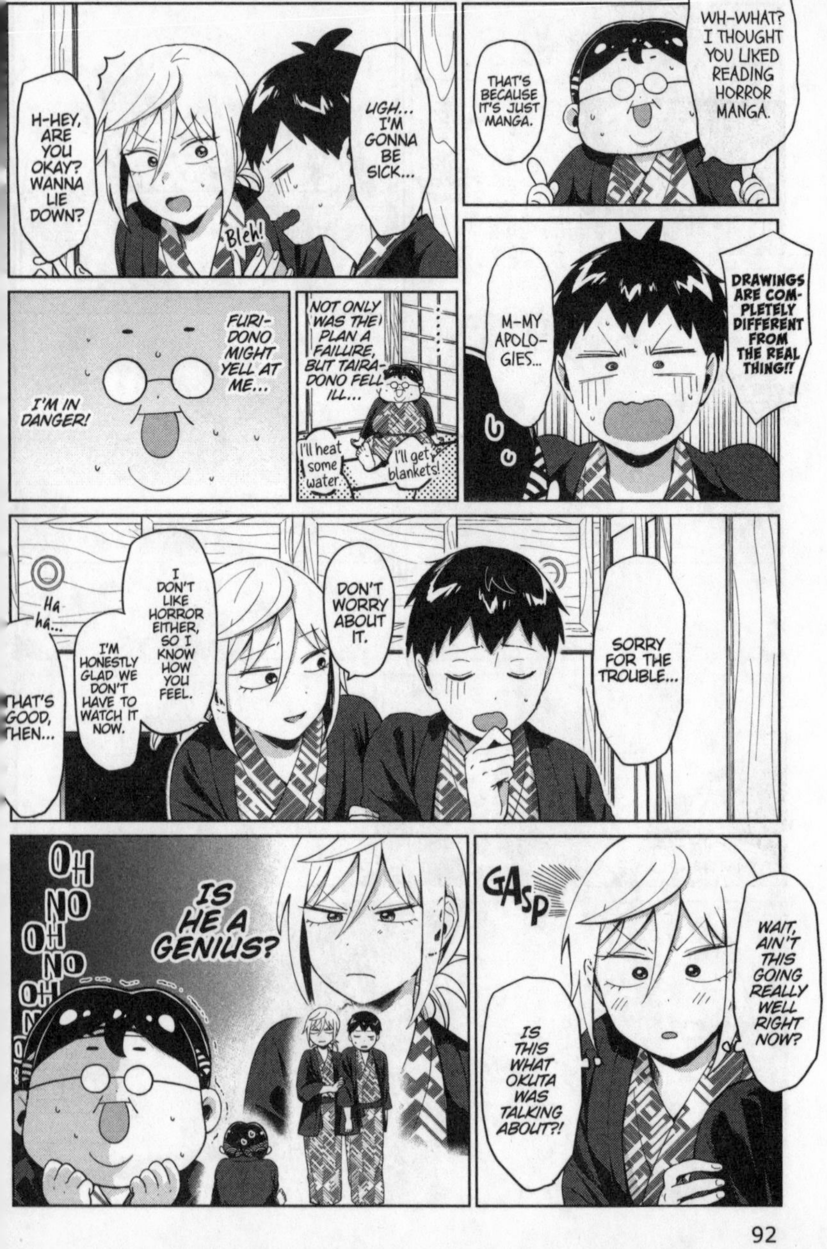
WH-WHAT? I THOUGHT YOU LIKED READING HORROR MANGA.
THAT'S BECAUSE IT'S JUST MANGA.
UGH... I'M GONNA BE SICK...
H-HEY, ARE YOU OKAY? WANNA LIE DOWN?
Bleh!
DRAWINGS ARE COMPLETELY DIFFERENT FROM THE REAL THING!!
M-MY APOLOGIES...
NOT ONLY WAS THE PLAN A FAILURE, BUT TAIRA-DONO FELL ILL...
I'll get blankets!
I'll heat some water.
FURI-DONO MIGHT YELL AT ME...
I'M IN DANGER!
SORRY FOR THE TROUBLE...
DON'T WORRY ABOUT IT.
I DON'T LIKE HORROR EITHER, SO I KNOW HOW YOU FEEL.
I'M HONESTLY GLAD WE DON'T HAVE TO WATCH IT NOW.
Ha ha...
THAT'S GOOD, THEN...
GASP
WAIT, AIN'T THIS GOING REALLY WELL RIGHT NOW?
IS THIS WHAT OKUTA WAS TALKING ABOUT?!
IS HE A GENIUS?
OH NO OH NO

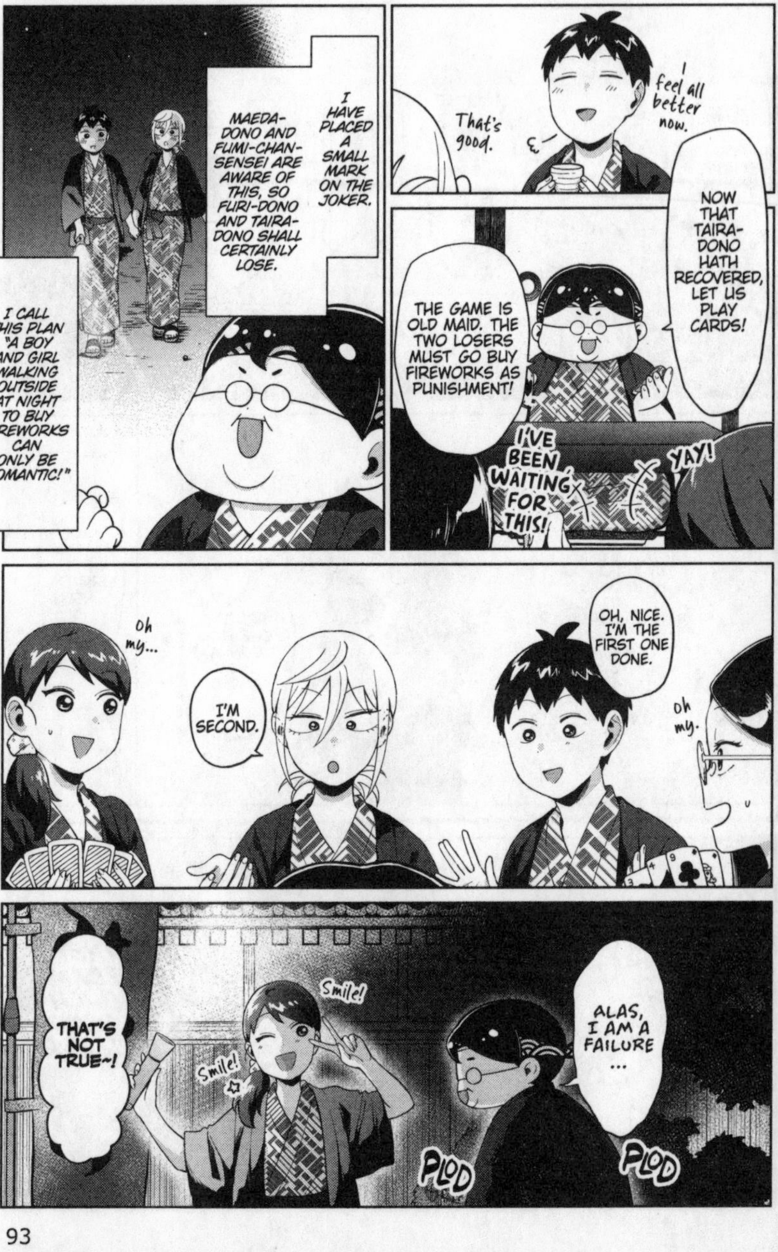
I feel all better now.
That's good.
NOW THAT TAIRA-DONO HATH RECOVERED, LET US PLAY CARDS!
THE GAME IS OLD MAID. THE TWO LOSERS MUST GO BUY FIREWORKS AS PUNISHMENT!
YAY!
I'VE BEEN WAITING FOR THIS!
I HAVE PLACED A SMALL MARK ON THE JOKER.
MAEDA-DONO AND FUMI-CHAN-SENSEI ARE AWARE OF THIS, SO FURI-DONO AND TAIRA-DONO SHALL CERTAINLY LOSE.
I CALL THIS PLAN "A BOY AND GIRL WALKING OUTSIDE AT NIGHT TO BUY FIREWORKS CAN ONLY BE ROMANTIC!"
OH, NICE. I'M THE FIRST ONE DONE.
oh my.
I'M SECOND.
Oh my...
ALAS, I AM A FAILURE ...
PLOD
PLOD
Smile!
Smile!
THAT'S NOT TRUE~!

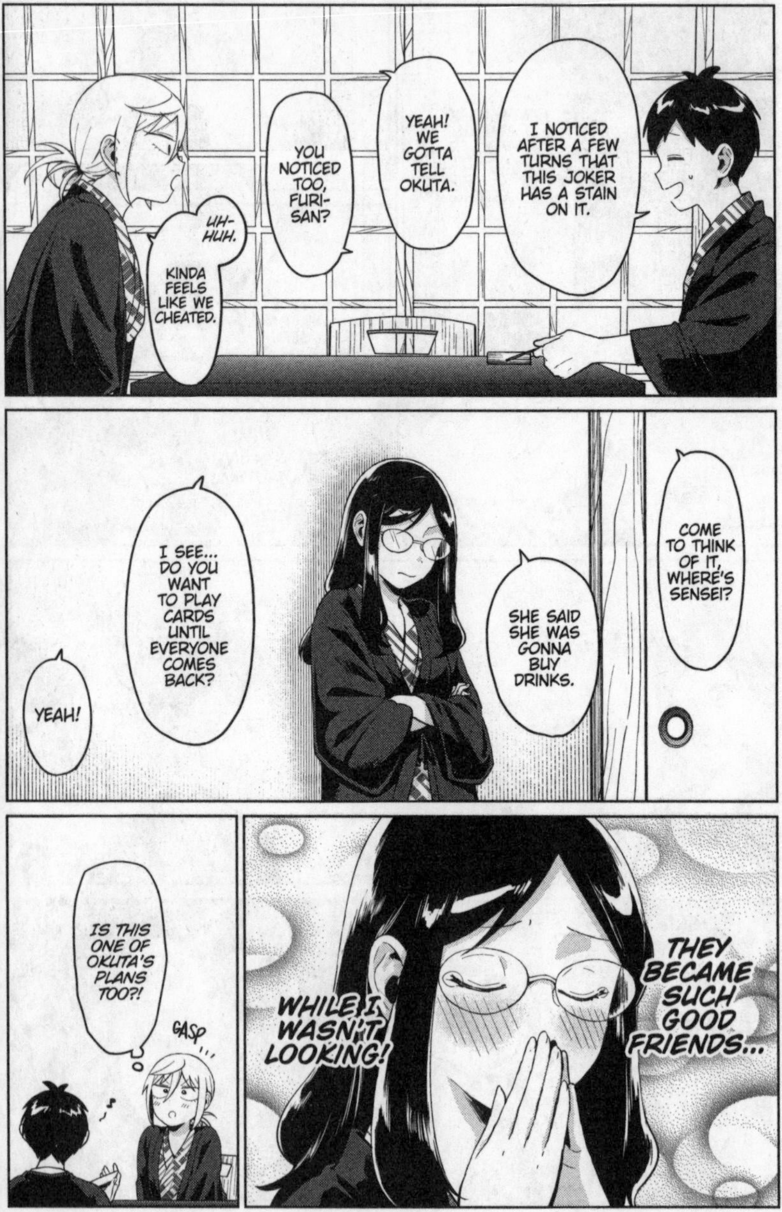
I NOTICED AFTER A FEW TURNS THAT THIS JOKER HAS A STAIN ON IT.
YEAH! WE GOTTA TELL OKUTA.
YOU NOTICED TOO, FURI-SAN?
UH-HUH.
KINDA FEELS LIKE WE CHEATED.
COME TO THINK OF IT, WHERE'S SENSEI?
SHE SAID SHE WAS GONNA BUY DRINKS.
I SEE... DO YOU WANT TO PLAY CARDS UNTIL EVERYONE COMES BACK?
YEAH!
THEY BECAME SUCH GOOD FRIENDS...
WHILE I WASN'T LOOKING!
IS THIS ONE OF OKUTA'S PLANS TOO?!
GASP

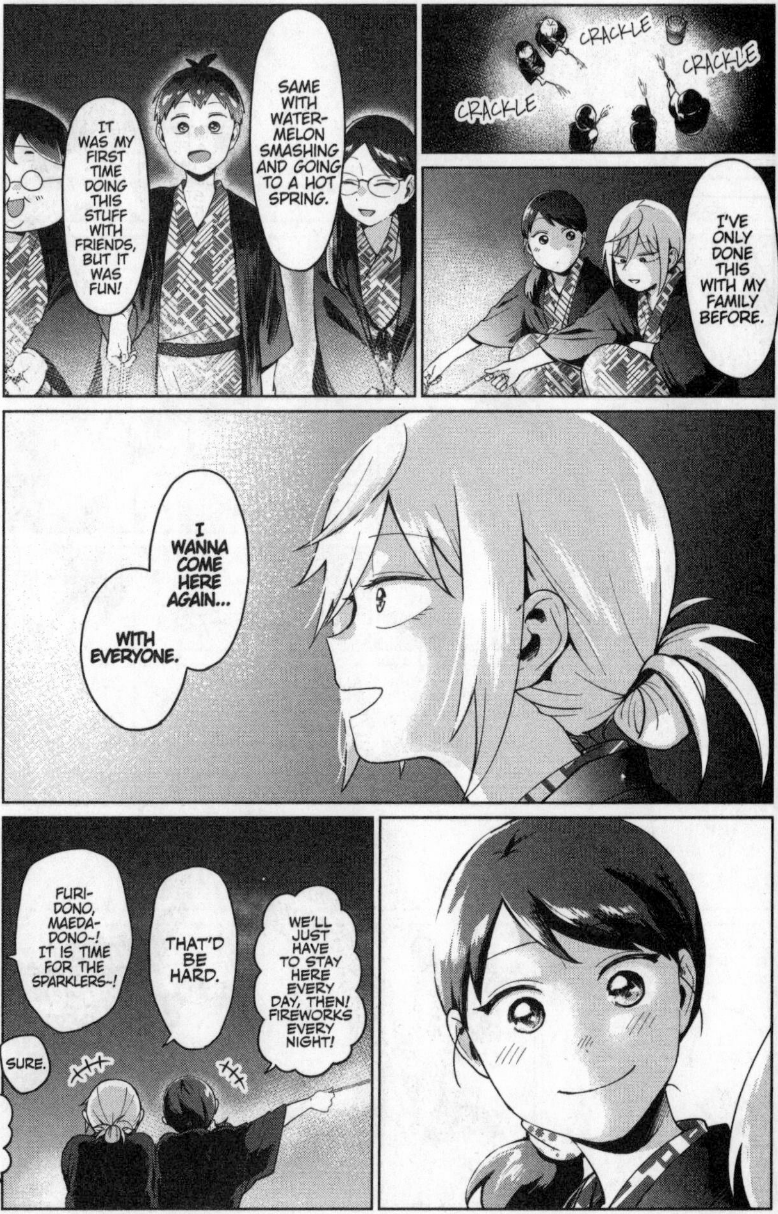
CRACKLE
CRACKLE
CRACKLE
I'VE ONLY DONE THIS WITH MY FAMILY BEFORE.
IT WAS MY FIRST TIME DOING THIS STUFF WITH FRIENDS, BUT IT WAS FUN!
SAME WITH WATER-MELON SMASHING AND GOING TO A HOT SPRING.
I WANNA COME HERE AGAIN...
WITH EVERYONE.
WE'LL JUST HAVE TO STAY HERE EVERY DAY, THEN! FIREWORKS EVERY NIGHT!
THAT'D BE HARD.
FURI-DONO, MAEDA-DONO~! IT IS TIME FOR THE SPARKLERS~!
SURE.
OKAY!

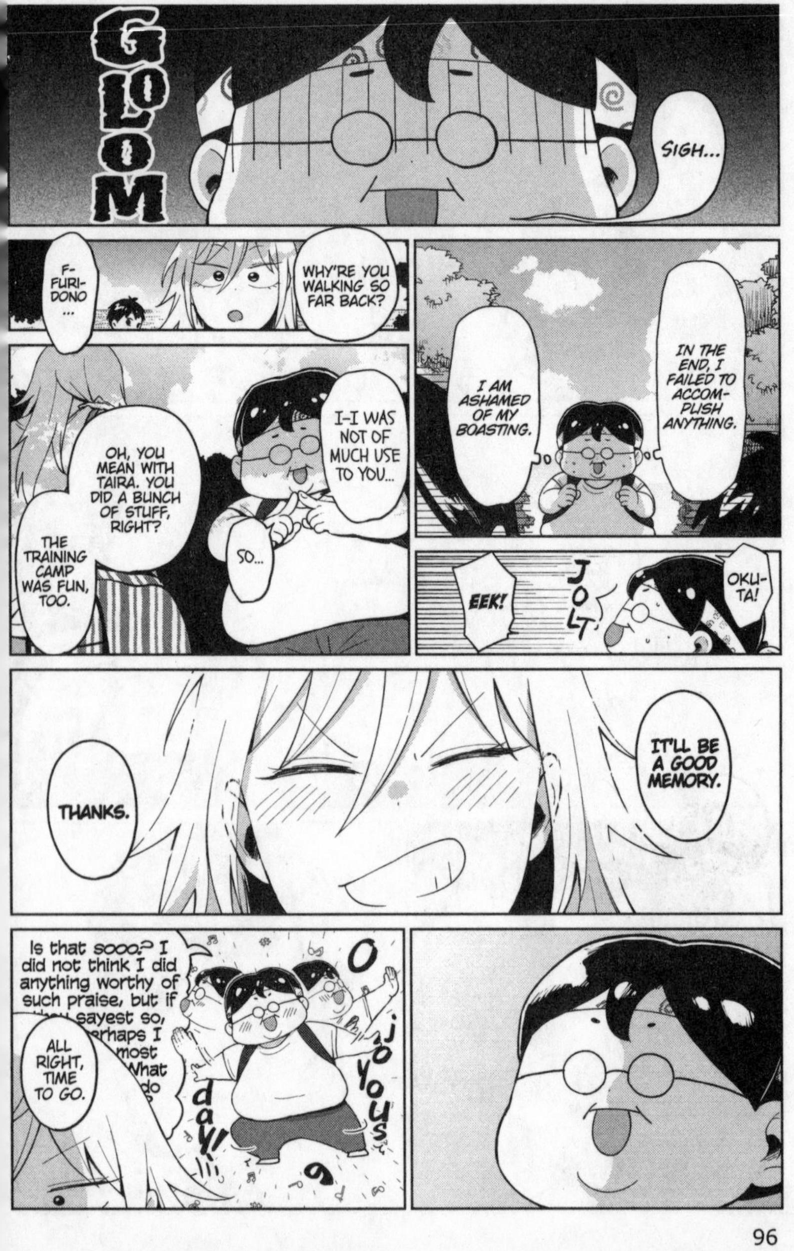
GLOOM
SIGH...
IN THE END, I FAILED TO ACCOM-PLISH ANYTHING.
I AM ASHAMED OF MY BOASTING.
OKU-TA!
JOLT
EEK!
WHY'RE YOU WALKING SO FAR BACK?
F-FURI-DONO ...
I-I WAS NOT OF MUCH USE TO YOU...
SO...
OH, YOU MEAN WITH TAIRA. YOU DID A BUNCH OF STUFF, RIGHT?
THE TRAINING CAMP WAS FUN, TOO.
IT'LL BE A GOOD MEMORY.
THANKS.
Is that sooo? I did not think I did anything worthy of such praise, but if
sayest so,
erhaps I
most
What
do
O
JOYOUS
day!
ALL RIGHT, TIME TO GO.

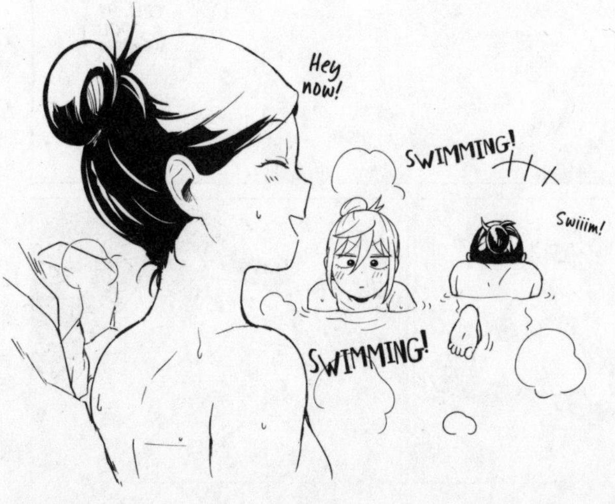
SWIMMING!
Swiiim!
SWIMMING!
Hey now!

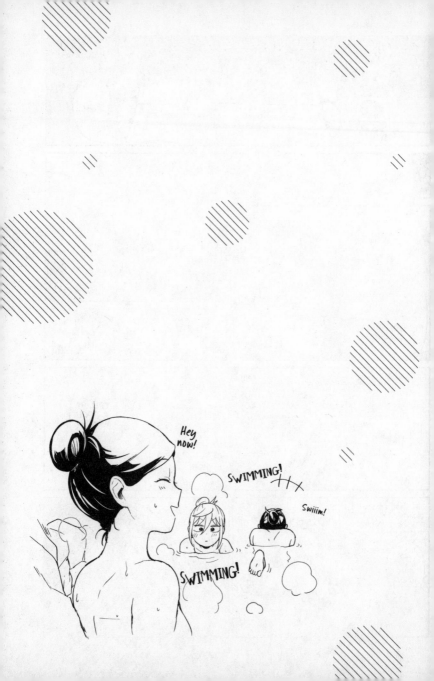

Chapter 16

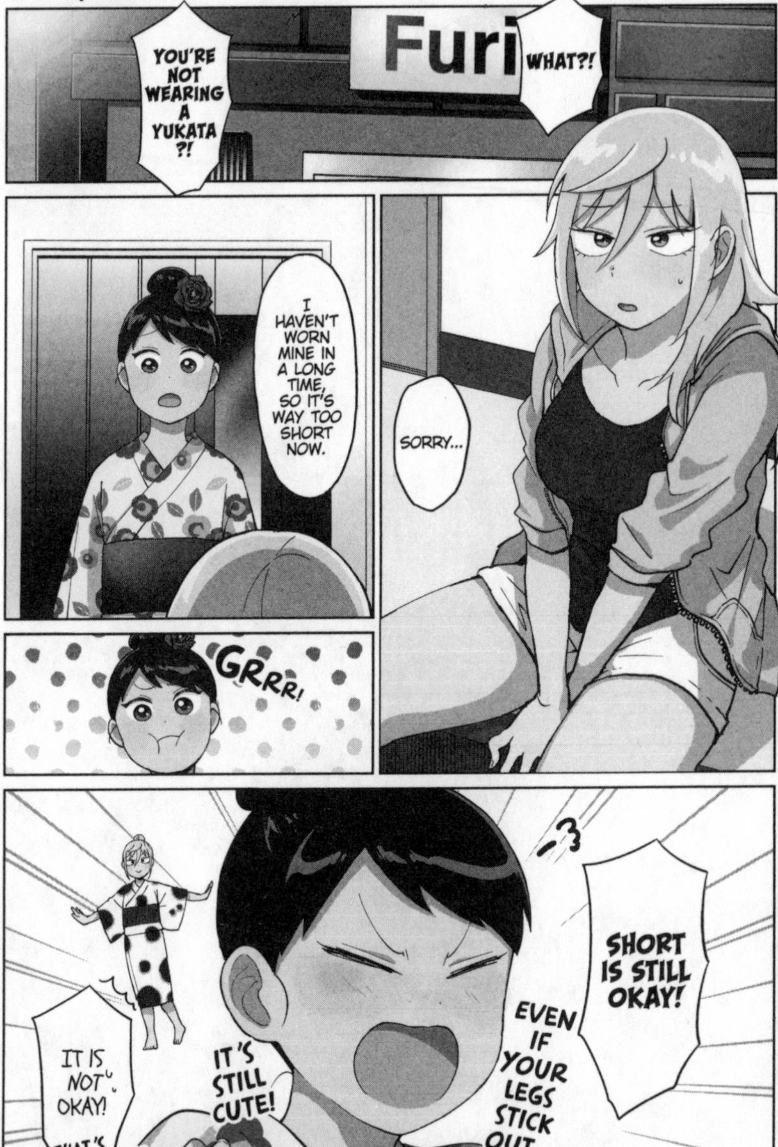
WHAT?!
Furi
YOU'RE NOT WEARING A YUKATA?!
SORRY...
I HAVEN'T WORN MINE IN A LONG TIME, SO IT'S WAY TOO SHORT NOW.
GRRRR!
SHORT IS STILL OKAY!
EVEN IF YOUR LEGS STICK OUT...
IT'S STILL CUTE!
IT IS NOT OKAY!
THAT'S EMBARRASSING!

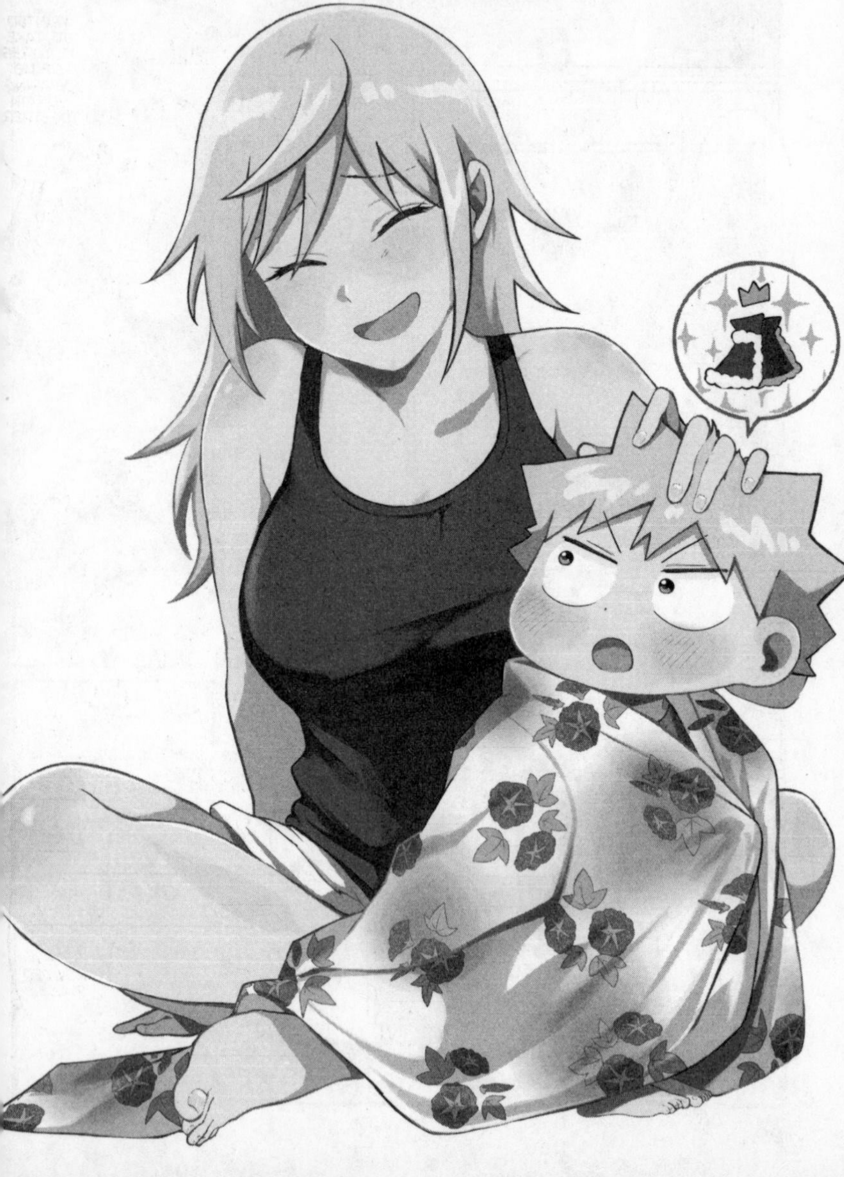

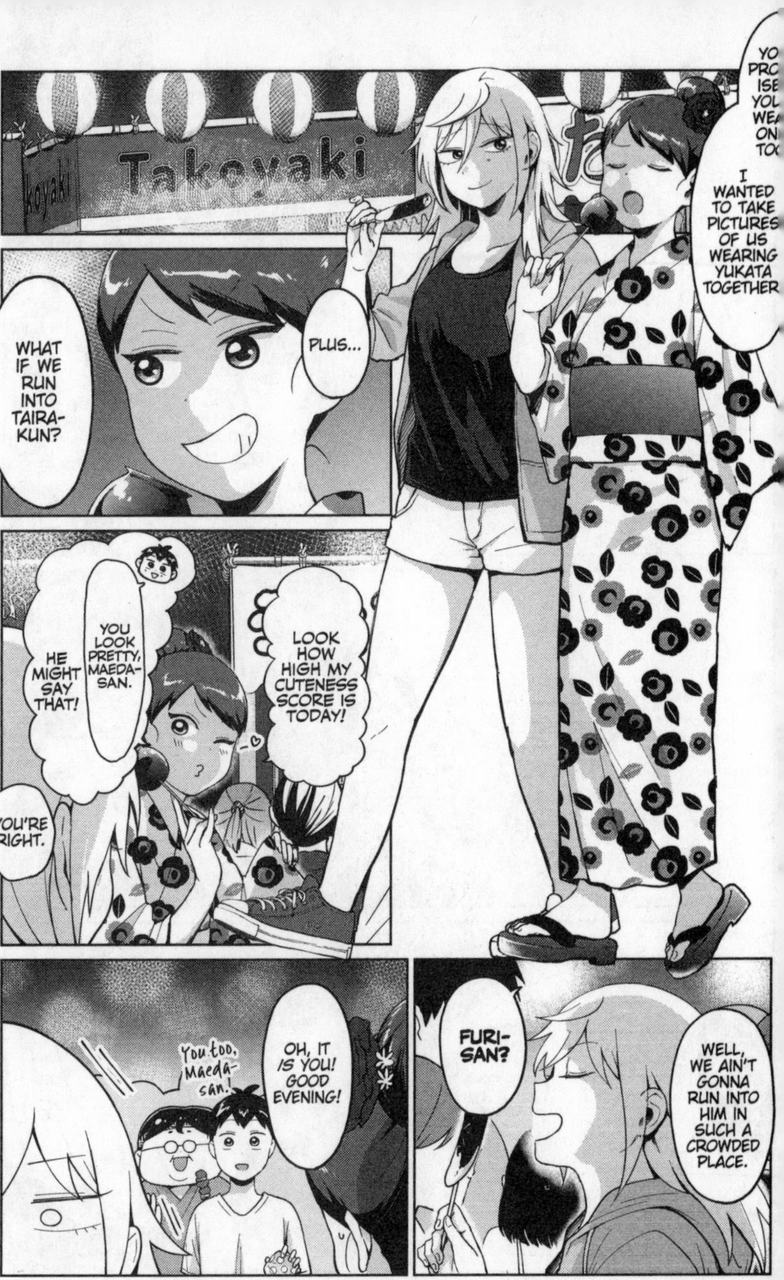
YO PRO ISE YOU WEA ON TOO
I WANTED TO TAKE PICTURES OF US WEARING YUKATA TOGETHER
Takoyaki
PLUS...
WHAT IF WE RUN INTO TAIRA-KUN?
LOOK HOW HIGH MY CUTENESS SCORE IS TODAY!
YOU LOOK PRETTY, MAEDA-SAN.
HE MIGHT SAY THAT!
YOU'RE RIGHT.
WELL, WE AIN'T GONNA RUN INTO HIM IN SUCH A CROWDED PLACE.
FURI-SAN?
OH, IT IS YOU! GOOD EVENING!
You too, Maeda-san!

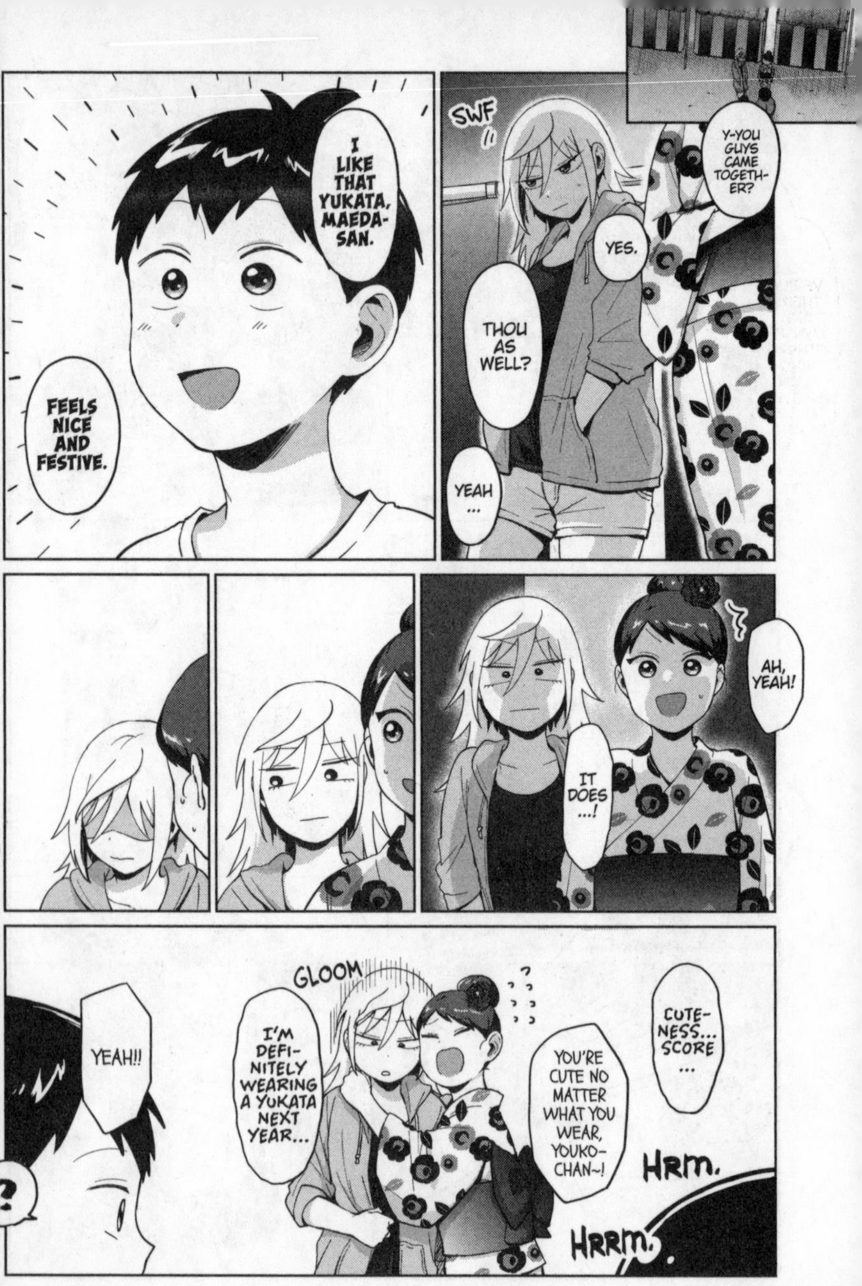
Y-YOU GUYS CAME TOGETHER?
SWF
YES.
THOU AS WELL?
YEAH...
I LIKE THAT YUKATA, MAEDA-SAN.
FEELS NICE AND FESTIVE.
AH, YEAH!
IT DOES...!
CUTENESS... SCORE...
HRM.
HRRM.
YOU'RE CUTE NO MATTER WHAT YOU WEAR, YOUKO-CHAN~!
GLOOM
I'M DEFINITELY WEARING A YUKATA NEXT YEAR...
YEAH!!
?

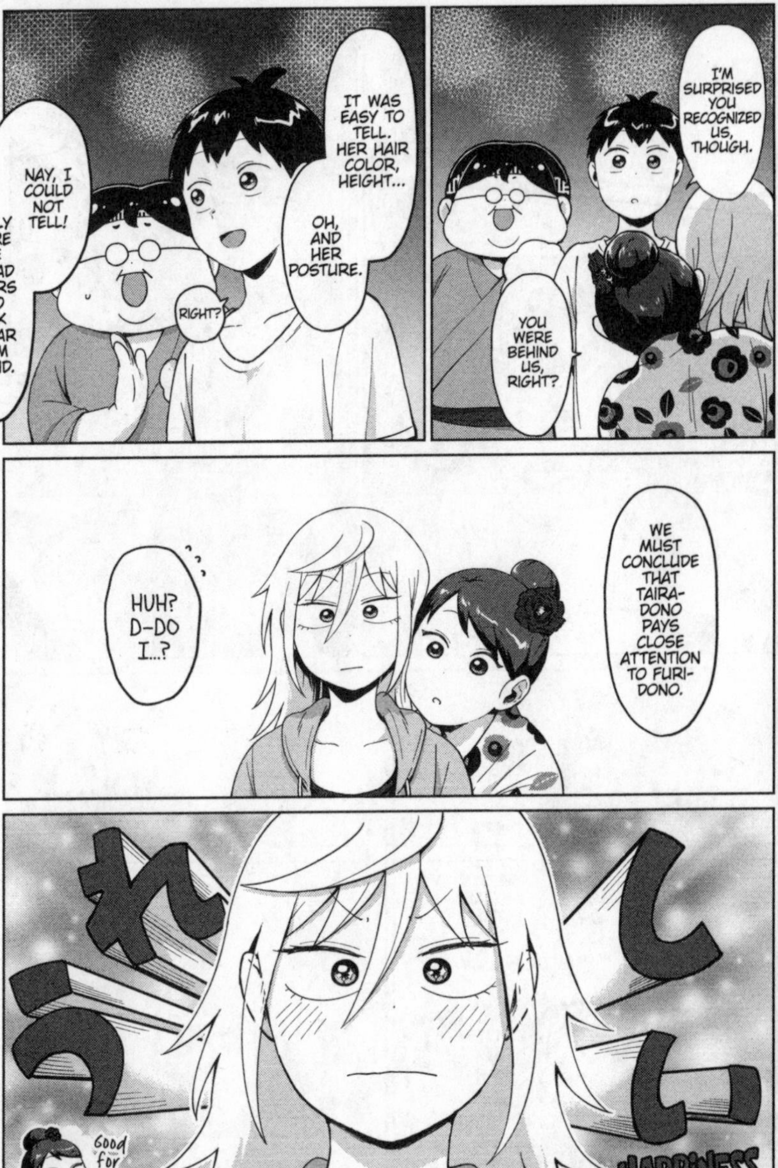
I'M SURPRISED YOU RECOGNIZED US, THOUGH.
YOU WERE BEHIND US, RIGHT?
IT WAS EASY TO TELL. HER HAIR COLOR, HEIGHT...
OH, AND HER POSTURE.
RIGHT?
NAY, I COULD NOT TELL!
VERILY THERE ARE MYRIAD OTHERS WHO LOOK SIMILAR FROM BEHIND.
WE MUST CONCLUDE THAT TAIRA-DONO PAYS CLOSE ATTENTION TO FURI-DONO.
HUH? D-DO I...?
HAPPINESS
Good for you!

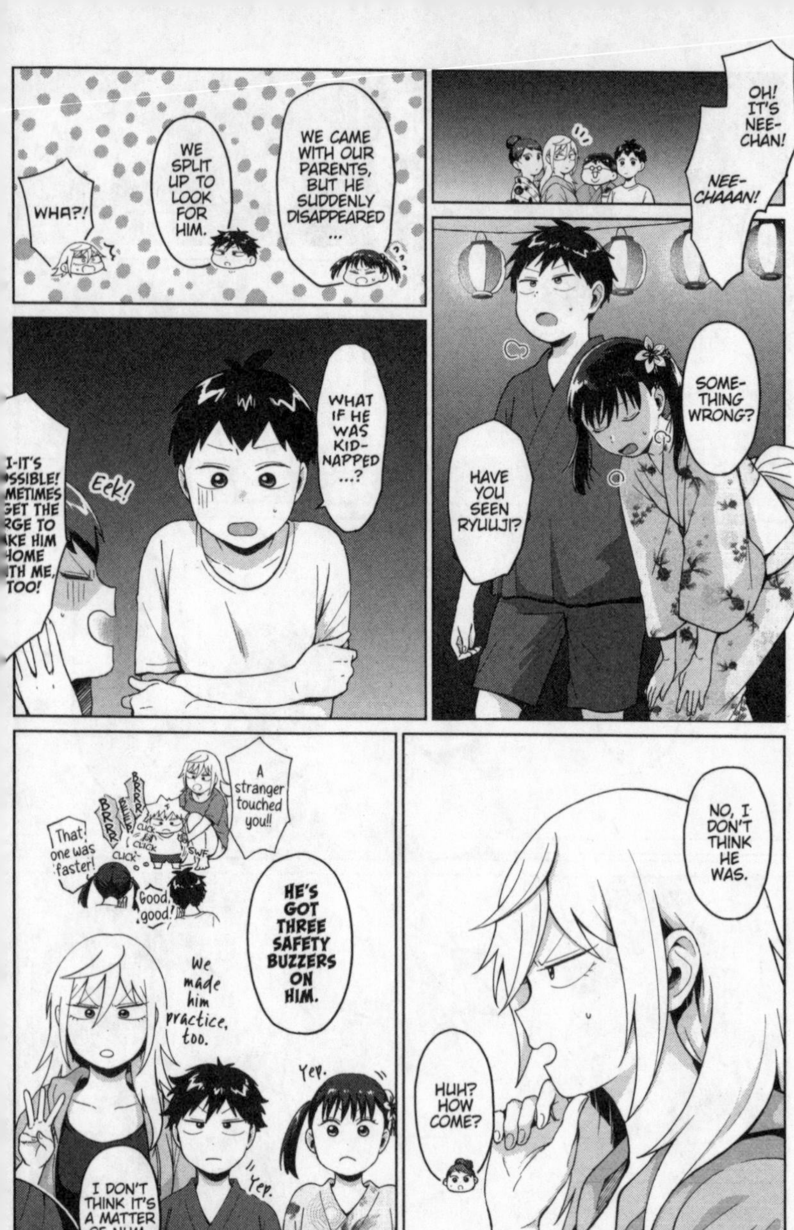

OH! IT'S NEE-CHAN!
NEE-CHAAAN!
SOME-THING WRONG?
HAVE YOU SEEN RYUUJI?
WE CAME WITH OUR PARENTS, BUT HE SUDDENLY DISAPPEARED ...
WE SPLIT UP TO LOOK FOR HIM.
WHA?!
WHAT IF HE WAS KID-NAPPED ...?
Eek!
I-IT'S SSIBLE! METIMES GET THE RGE TO KE HIM HOME TH ME, TOO!
NO, I DON'T THINK HE WAS.
HUH? HOW COME?
HE'S GOT THREE SAFETY BUZZERS ON HIM.
A stranger touched you!!
BRRR
BEEP
BRRR
CLICK
CLICK
CLICK
SWF
That one was faster!
Good, good!
We made him practice, too.
Yep.
Yep.
I DON'T THINK IT'S A MATTER OF NUM-BERS...

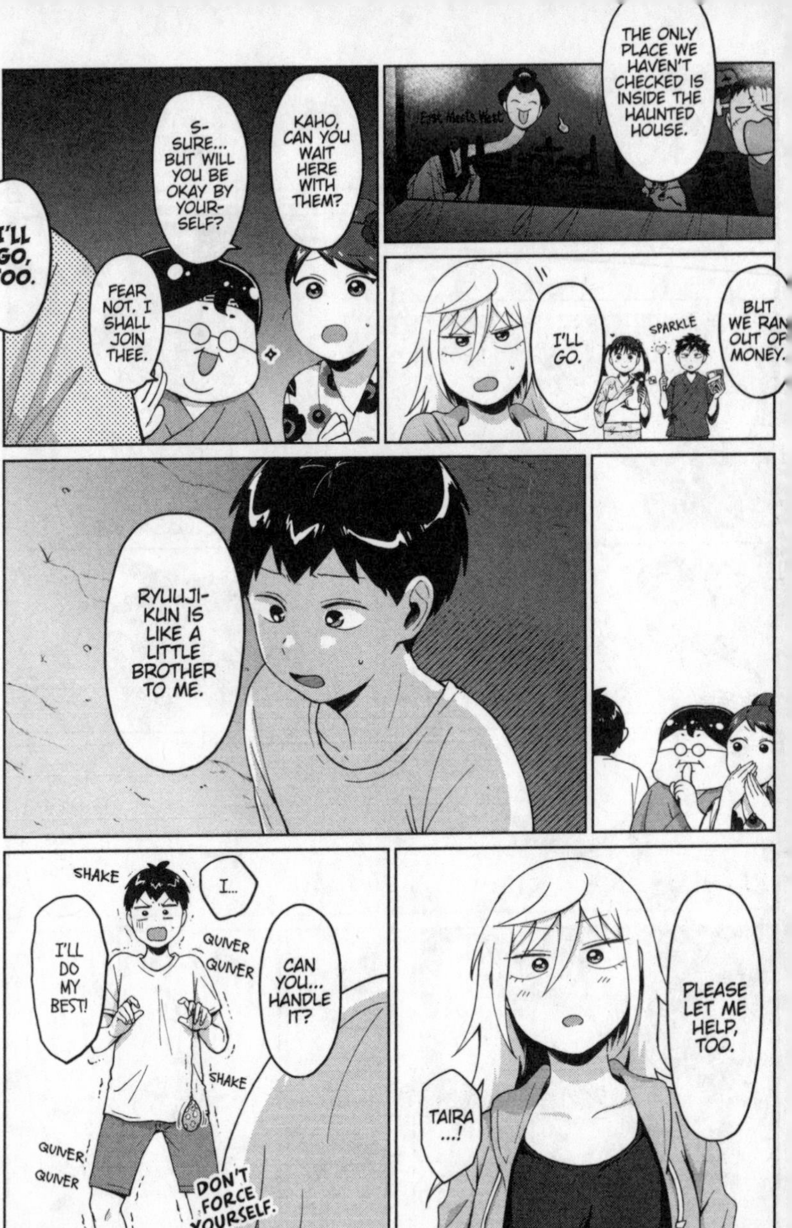
East Meets West
THE ONLY PLACE WE HAVEN'T CHECKED IS INSIDE THE HAUNTED HOUSE.
BUT WE RAN OUT OF MONEY.
SPARKLE
I'LL GO.
KAHO, CAN YOU WAIT HERE WITH THEM?
S-SURE... BUT WILL YOU BE OKAY BY YOURSELF?
FEAR NOT. I SHALL JOIN THEE.
I'LL GO, TOO.
RYUUJI-KUN IS LIKE A LITTLE BROTHER TO ME.
PLEASE LET ME HELP, TOO.
TAIRA...!
I...
CAN YOU... HANDLE IT?
SHAKE
QUIVER QUIVER
I'LL DO MY BEST!
SHAKE
QUIVER QUIVER
DON'T FORCE YOURSELF.

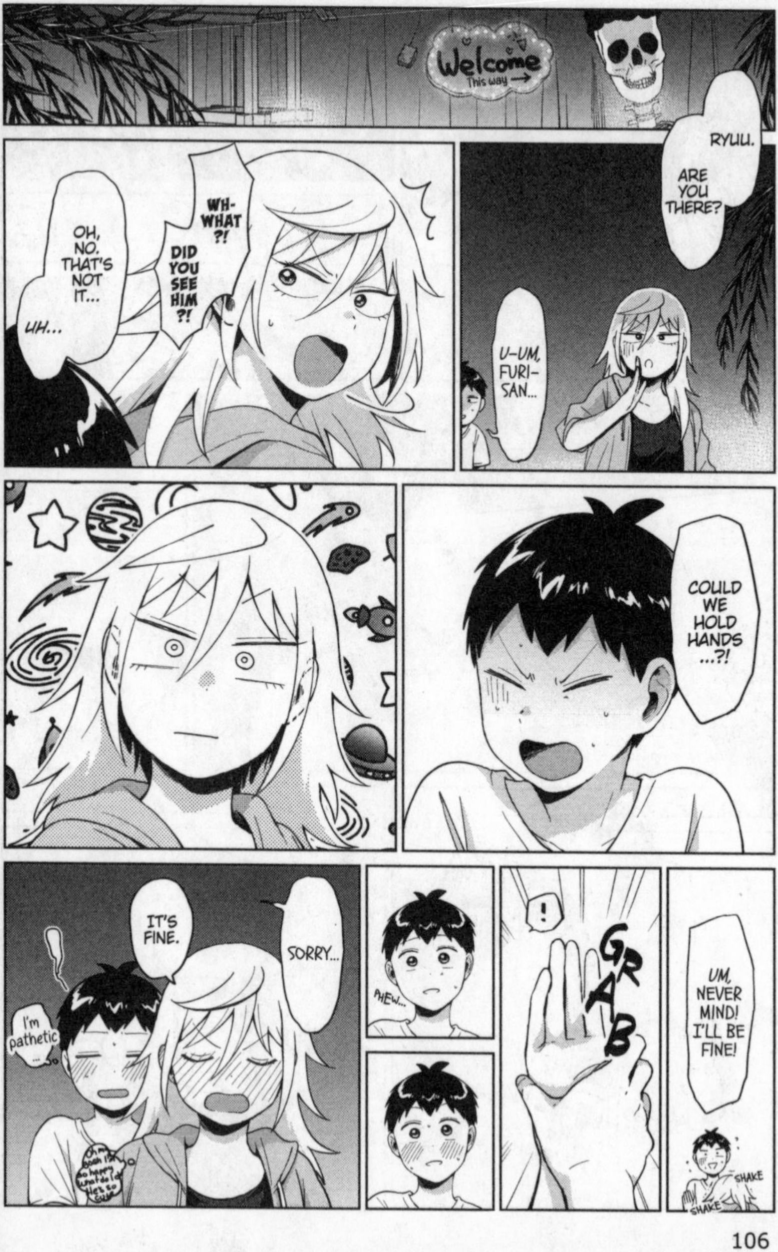
Welcome
This way →
RYUU.
ARE YOU THERE?
U-UM, FURI-SAN...
WH-WHAT?!
DID YOU SEE HIM?!
OH, NO. THAT'S NOT IT...
UH...
COULD WE HOLD HANDS...?!
UM, NEVER MIND! I'LL BE FINE!
SHAKE
SHAKE
!
GRAB
PHEW...
SORRY...
IT'S FINE.
I'm pathetic...

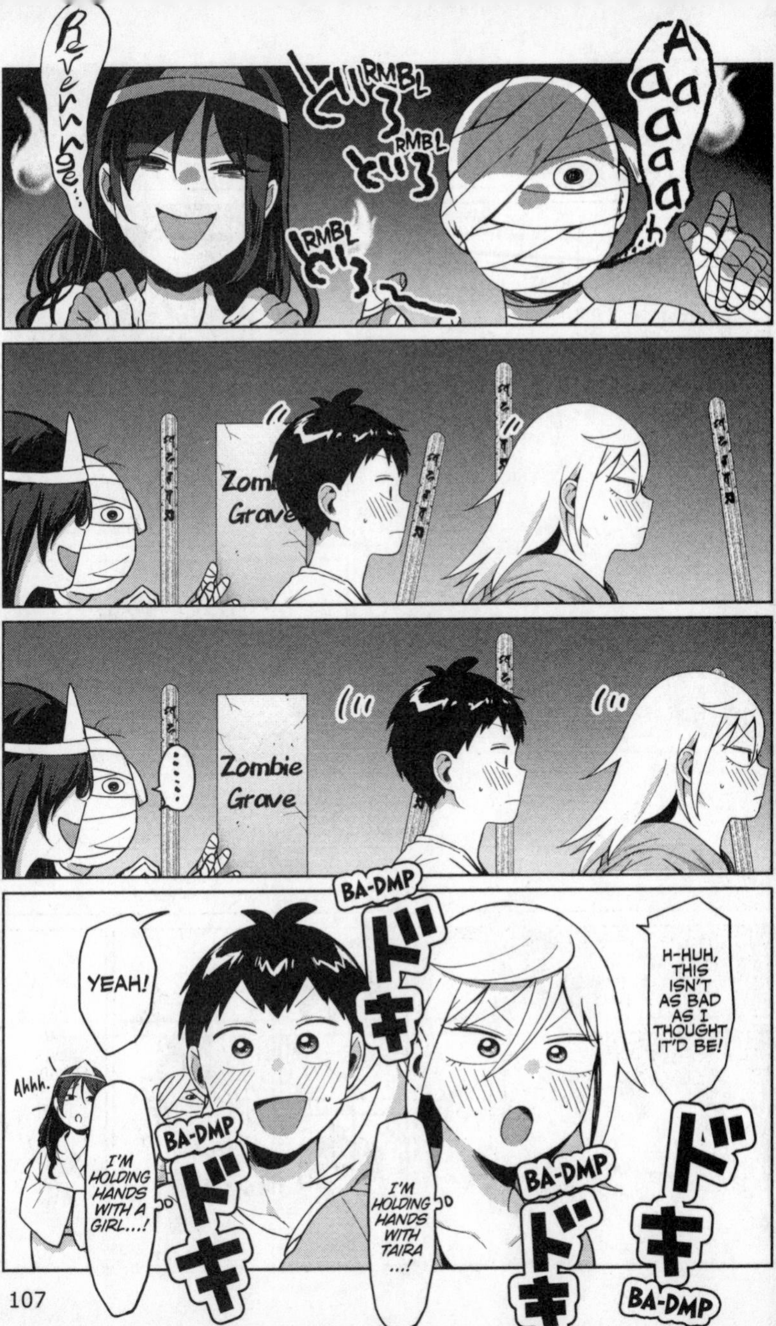
Aaaaaah...
RMBL
RMBL
RMBL
Revennnge...
......
BA-DMP
ドキ
H-HUH, THIS ISN'T AS BAD AS I THOUGHT IT'D BE!
YEAH!
BA-DMP
ドキ
BA-DMP
ドキ
I'M HOLDING HANDS WITH TAIRA...!
BA-DMP
ドキ
I'M HOLDING HANDS WITH A GIRL...!
Ahhh.

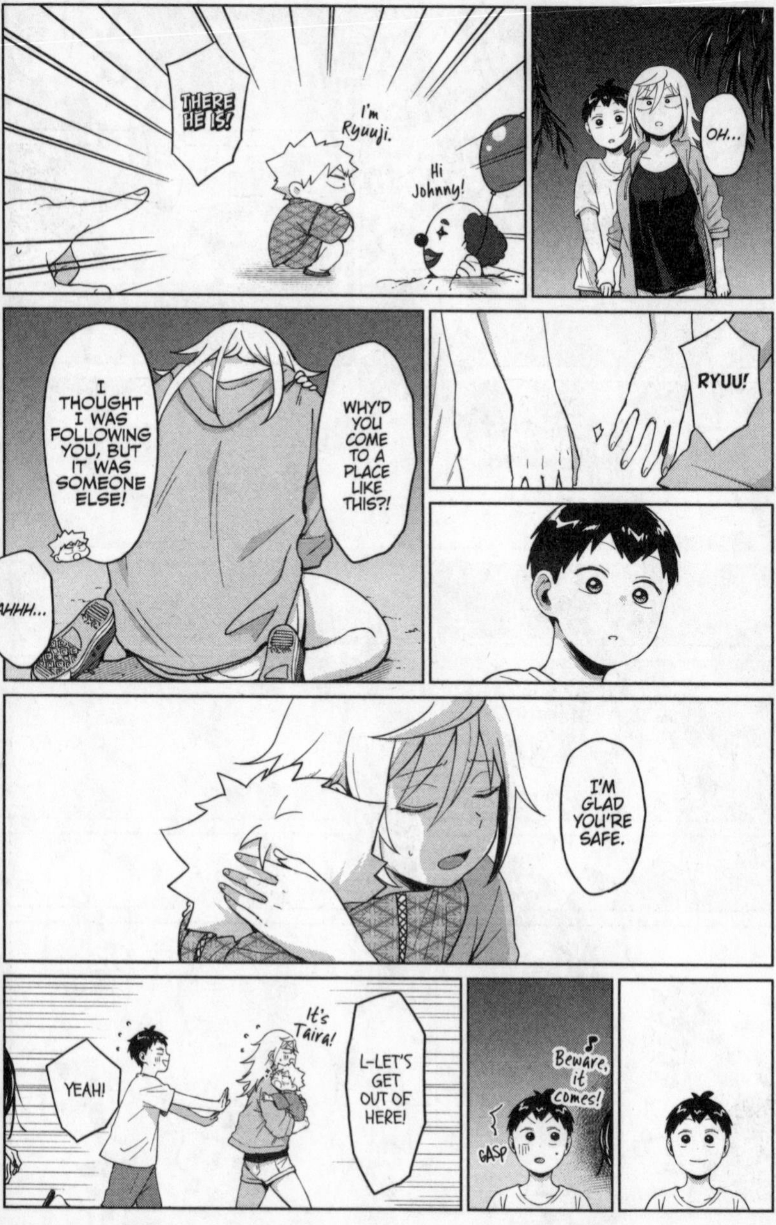
OH...
Hi Johnny!
I'm Ryuuji.
THERE HE IS!
RYUU!
WHY'D YOU COME TO A PLACE LIKE THIS?!
I THOUGHT I WAS FOLLOWING YOU, BUT IT WAS SOMEONE ELSE!
AHHH...
I'M GLAD YOU'RE SAFE.
Beware, it comes!
GASP
L-LET'S GET OUT OF HERE!
It's Taira!
YEAH!

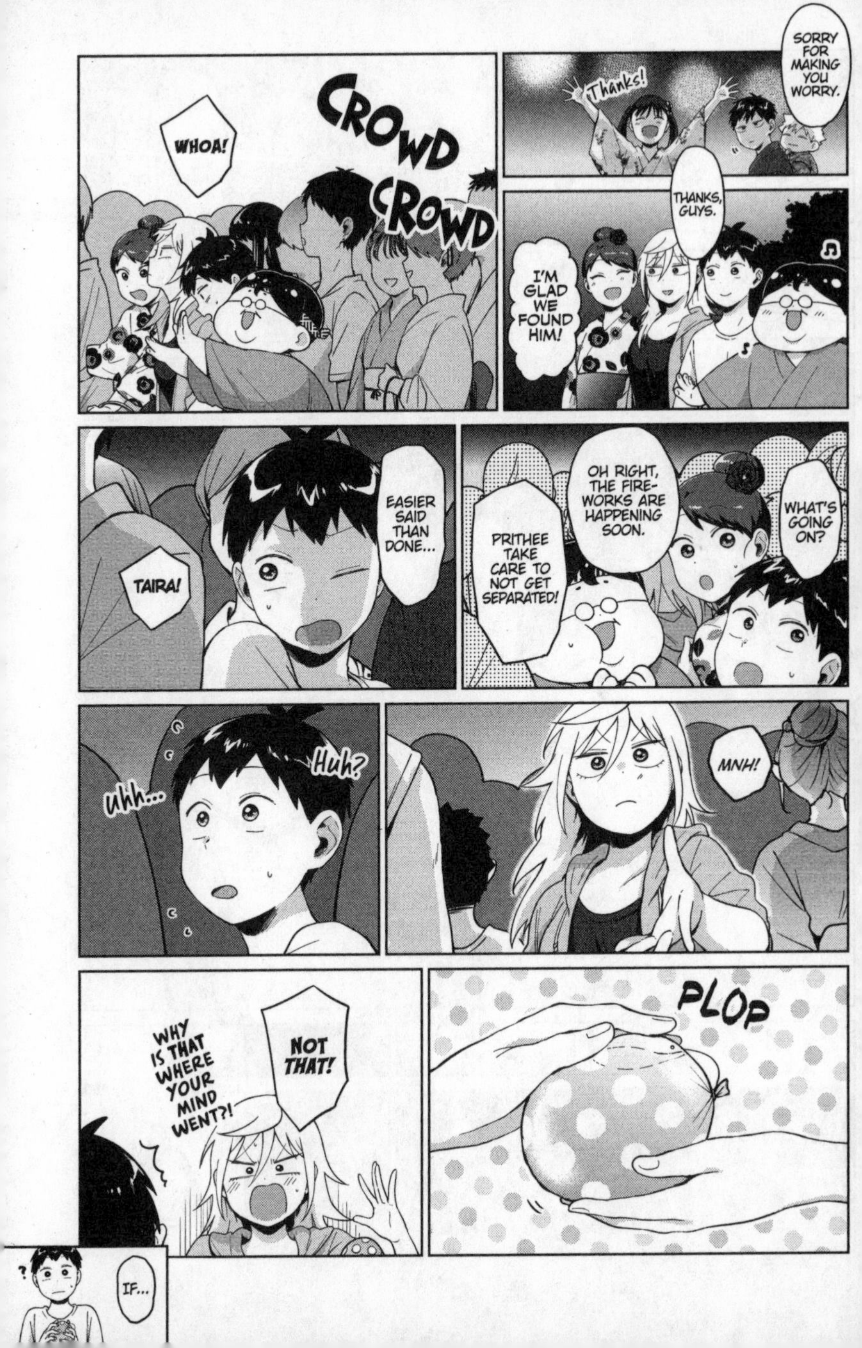
SORRY FOR MAKING YOU WORRY.
Thanks!
THANKS, GUYS.
I'M GLAD WE FOUND HIM!
CROWD
CROWD
WHOA!
WHAT'S GOING ON?
OH RIGHT, THE FIRE-WORKS ARE HAPPENING SOON.
PRITHEE TAKE CARE TO NOT GET SEPARATED!
EASIER SAID THAN DONE...
TAIRA!
MNH!
Huh?
uhh...
PLOP
NOT THAT!
WHY IS THAT WHERE YOUR MIND WENT?!
IF...

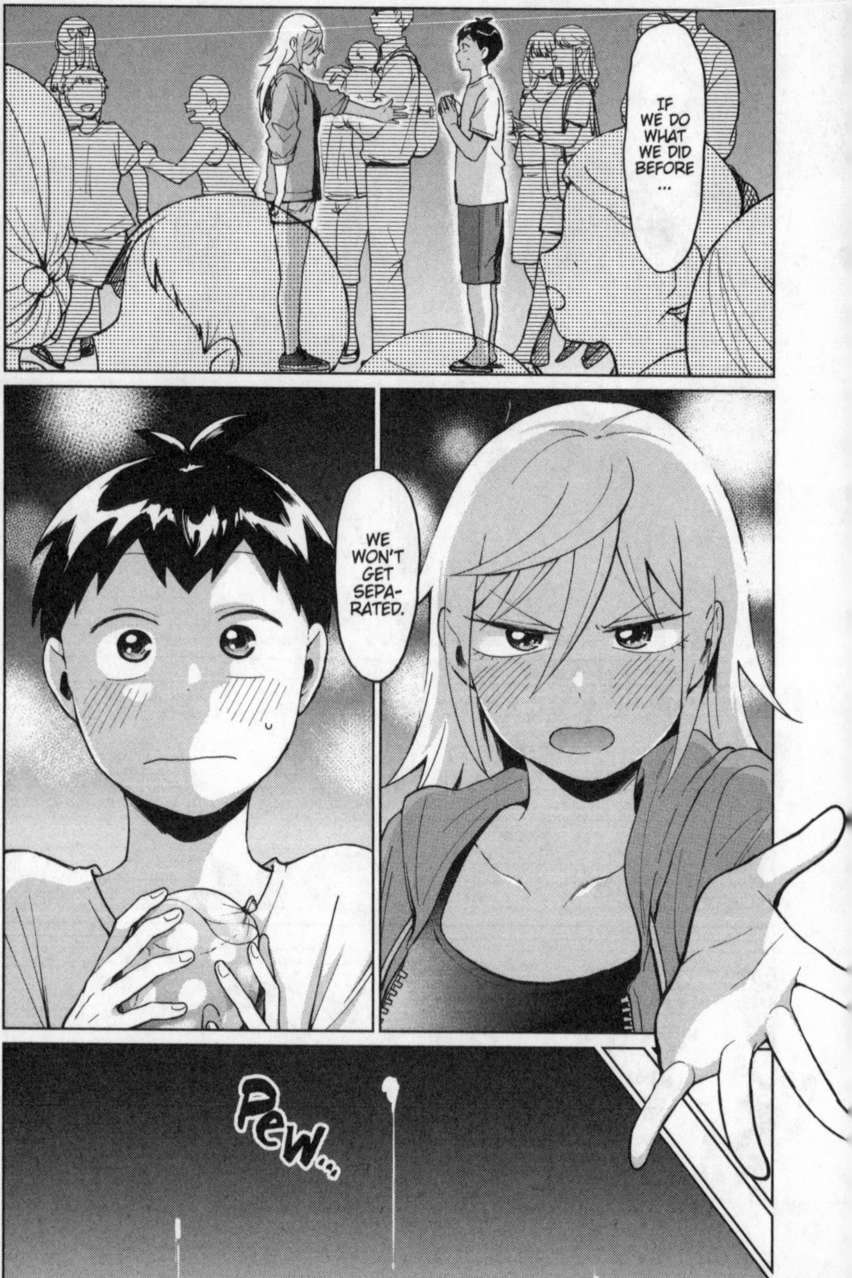
IF WE DO WHAT WE DID BEFORE ...
WE WON'T GET SEPA-RATED.
Pew...

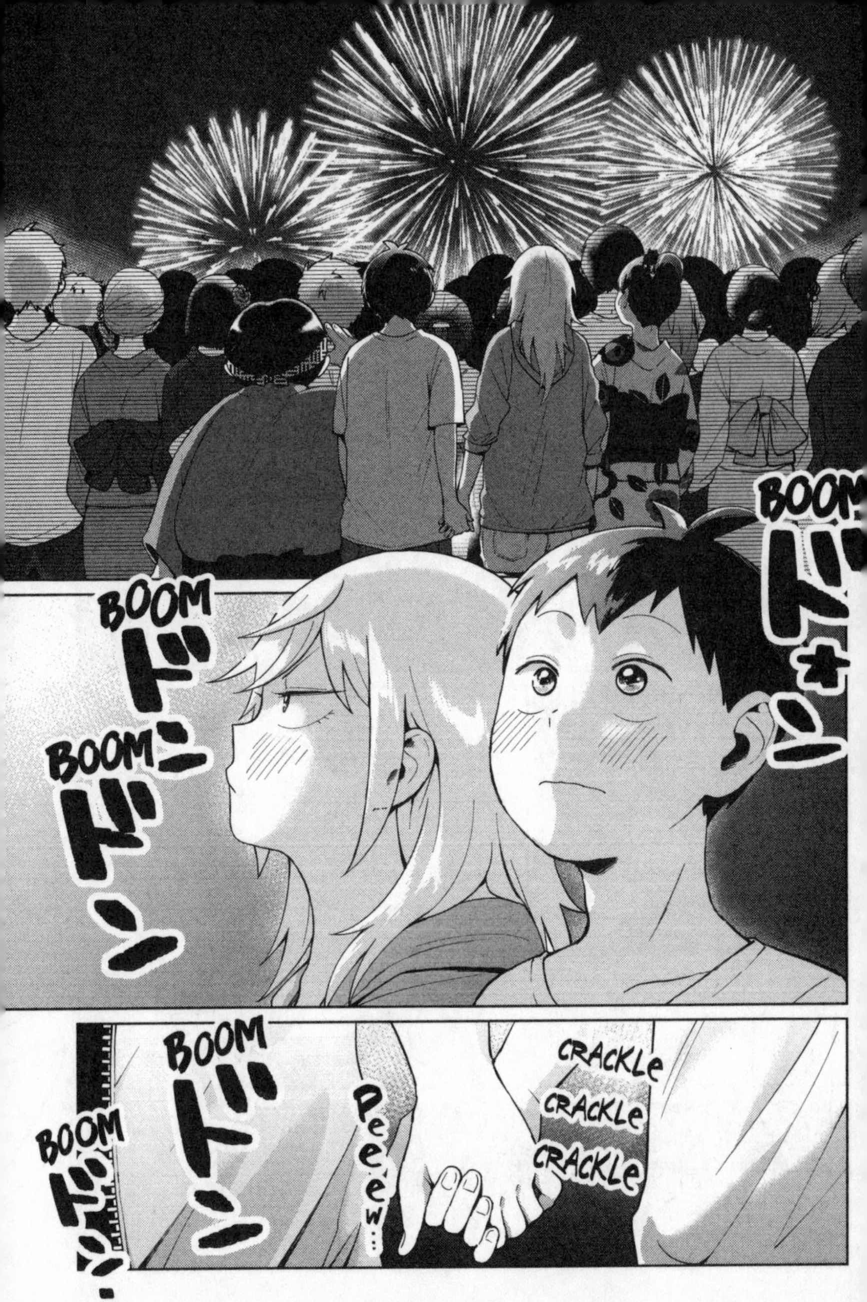
BOOM
ドーン
BOOM
ドン
BOOM
ドーン
CRACKLE
CRACKLE
CRACKLE
Peeew...
BOOM
ドーン
BOOM
ドーン...

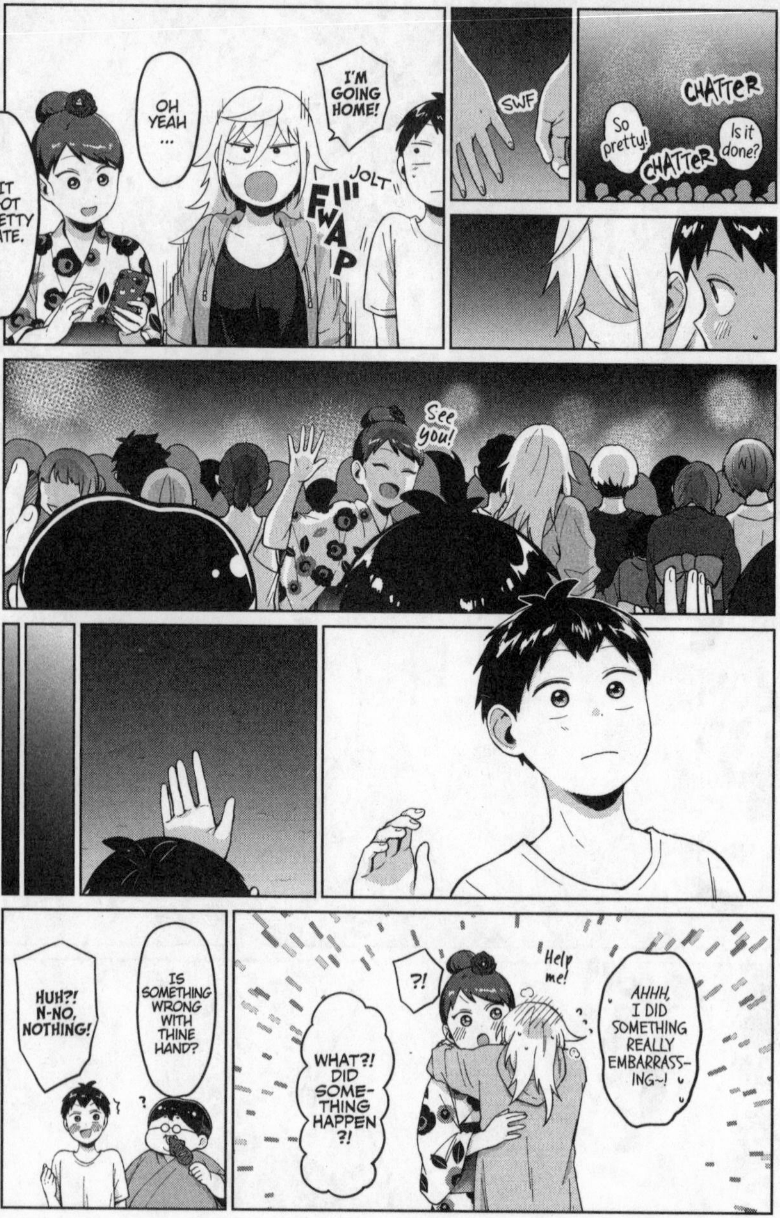
CHATTER
Is it done?
So pretty!
CHATTER
SWF
I'M GOING HOME!
JOLT
FWAP
OH YEAH ...
IT GOT RETTY ATE.
See you!
AHHH, I DID SOMETHING REALLY EMBARRASSING~!
Help me!
?!
WHAT?! DID SOMETHING HAPPEN?!
IS SOMETHING WRONG WITH THINE HAND?
HUH?! N-NO, NOTHING!

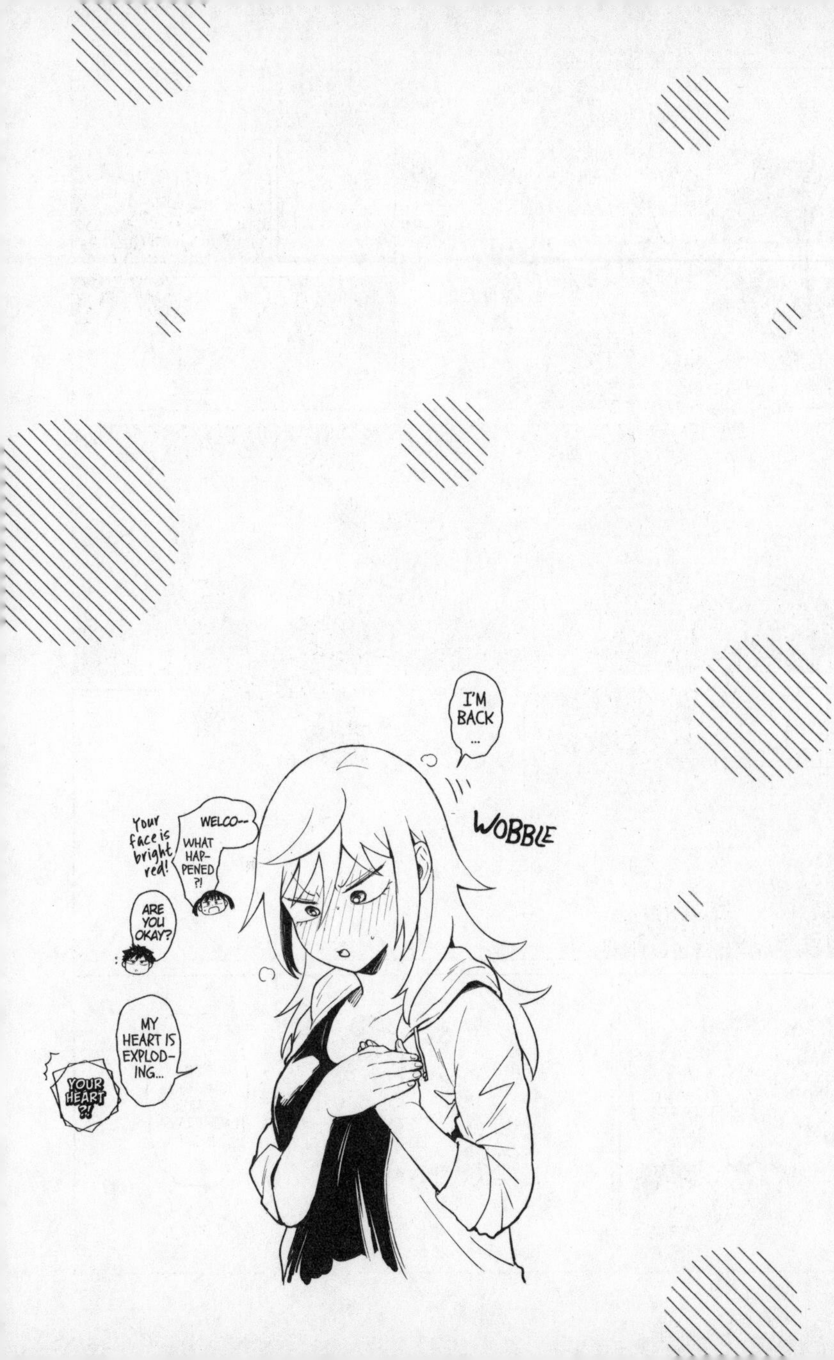
I'M BACK ...
WOBBLE
WELCO-- WHAT HAPPENED?!
Your face is bright red!
ARE YOU OKAY?
MY HEART IS EXPLODING...
YOUR HEART?!

Chapter 17

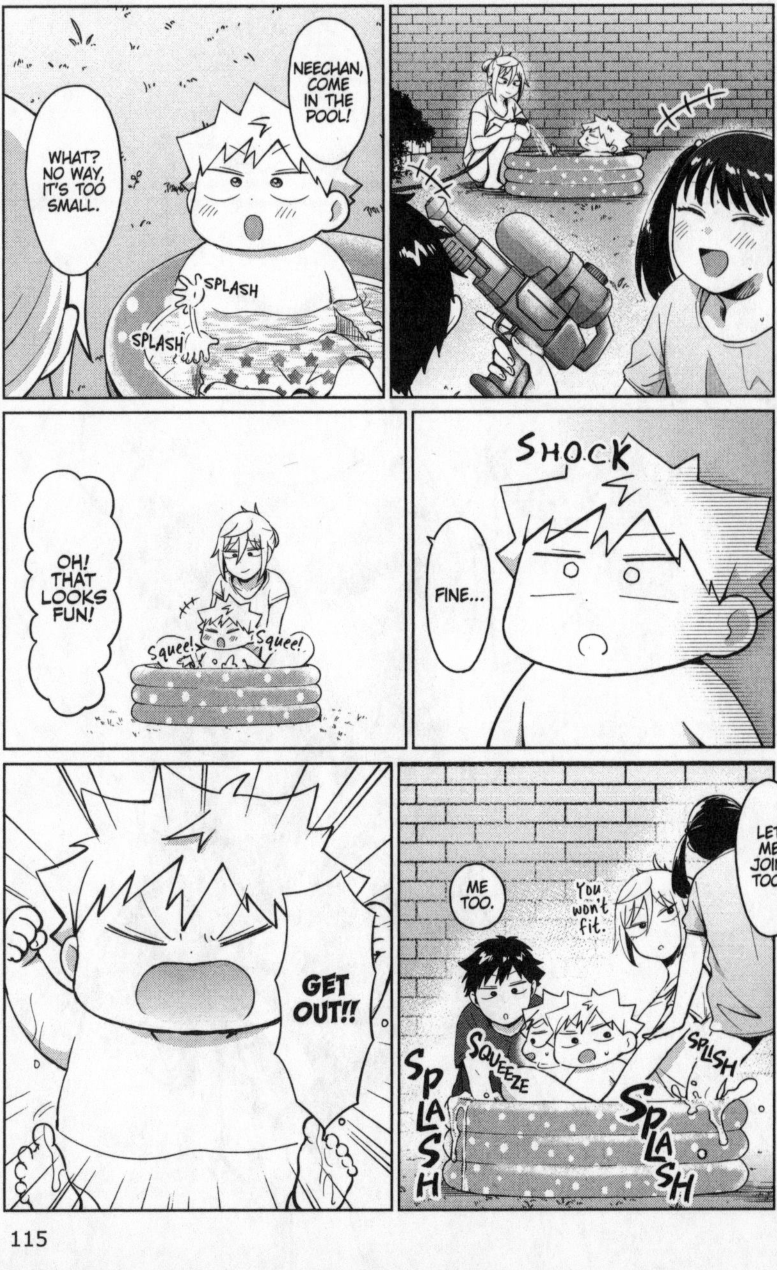
NEECHAN, COME IN THE POOL!
WHAT? NO WAY, IT'S TOO SMALL.
SPLASH
SPLASH
SHOCK
FINE...
OH! THAT LOOKS FUN!
Squee!
Squee!
LET ME JOIN TOO!
You won't fit.
ME TOO.
SPLISH
SPLASH
SQUEEZE
SPLASH
GET OUT!!

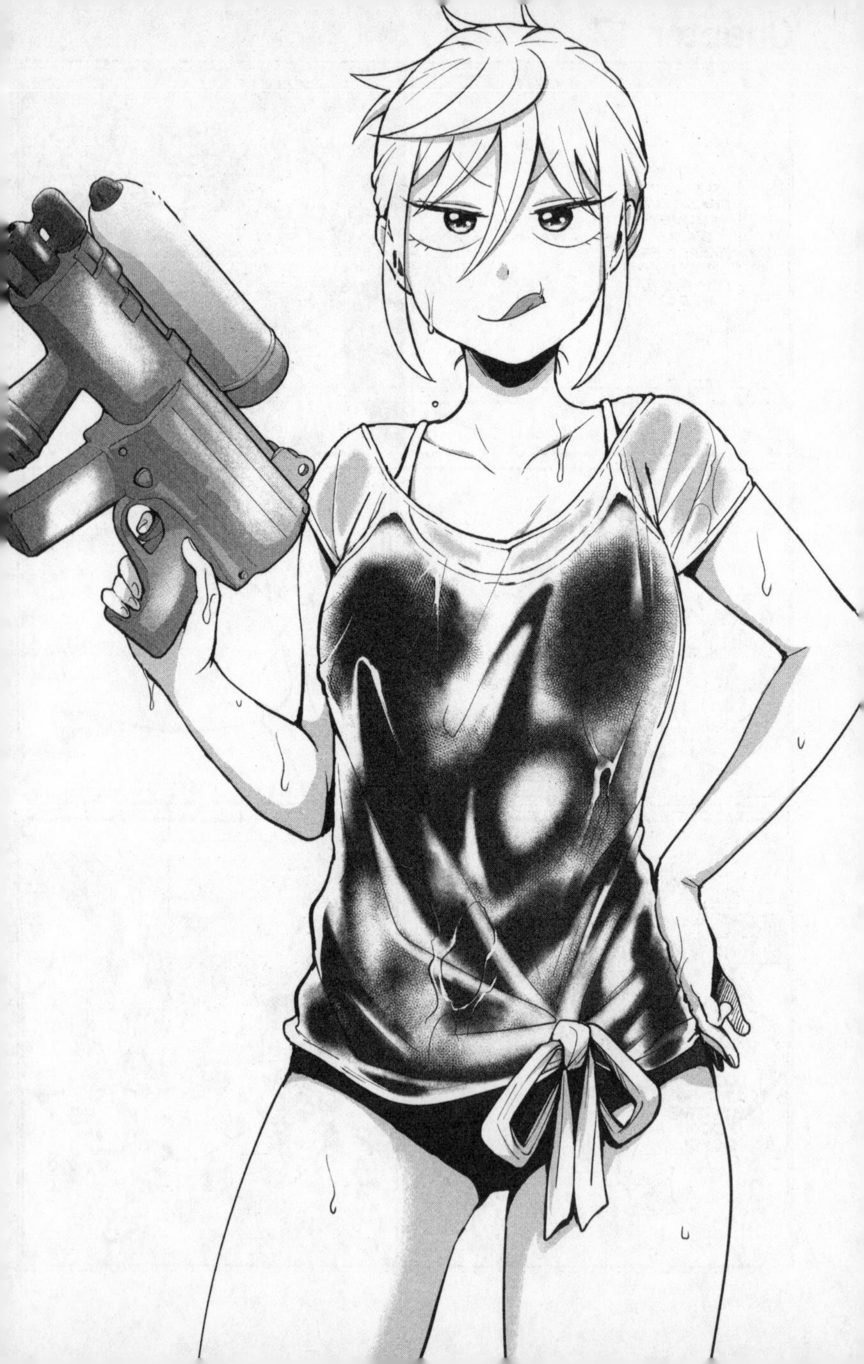

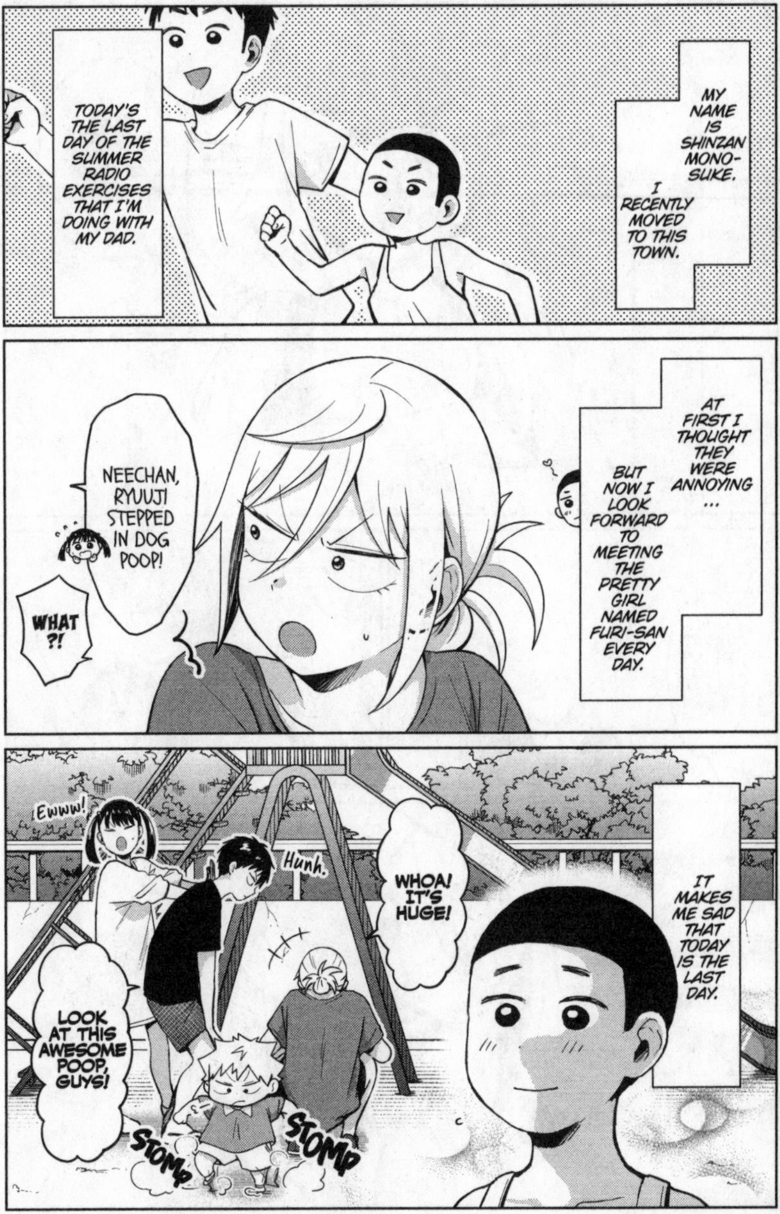
MY NAME IS SHINZAN MONO-SUKE.
I RECENTLY MOVED TO THIS TOWN.
TODAY'S THE LAST DAY OF THE SUMMER RADIO EXERCISES THAT I'M DOING WITH MY DAD.
AT FIRST I THOUGHT THEY WERE ANNOYING ...
BUT NOW I LOOK FORWARD TO MEETING THE PRETTY GIRL NAMED FURI-SAN EVERY DAY.
NEECHAN, RYUUJI STEPPED IN DOG POOP!
WHAT ?!
IT MAKES ME SAD THAT TODAY IS THE LAST DAY.
WHOA! IT'S HUGE!
Hunh.
Ewww!
LOOK AT THIS AWESOME POOP, GUYS!
STOMP
STOMP

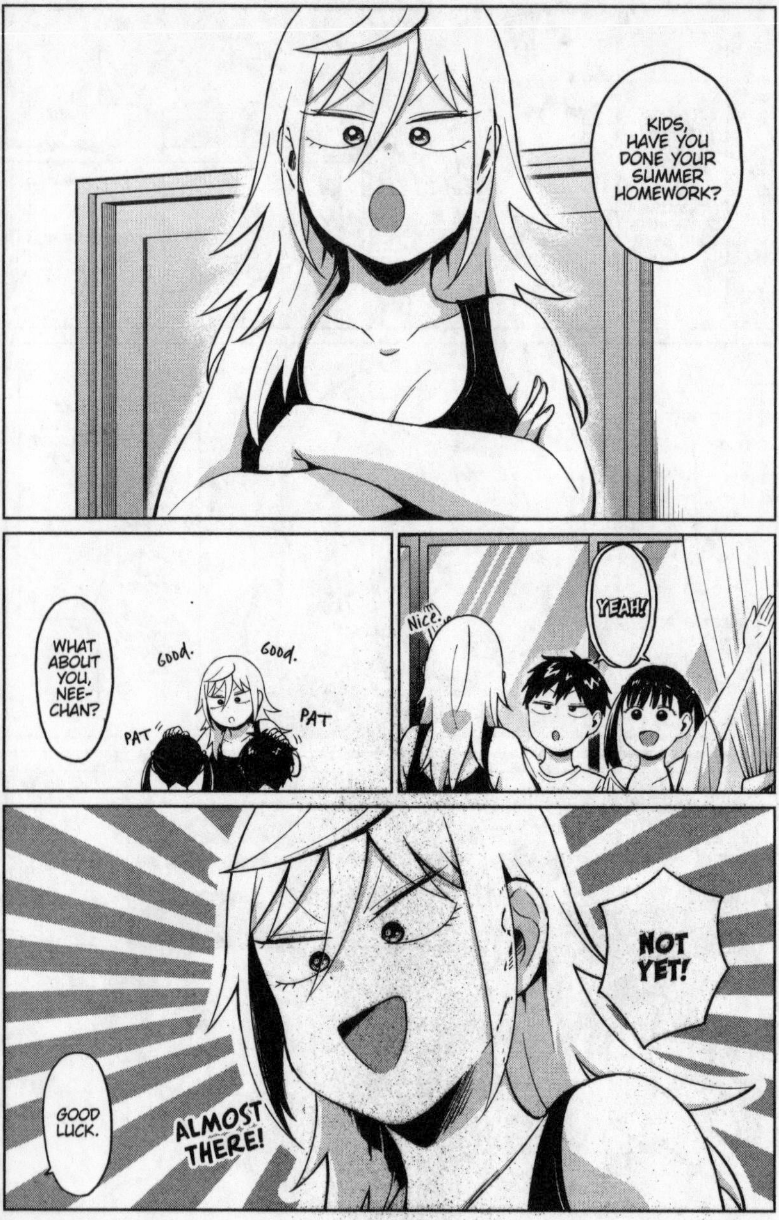
KIDS, HAVE YOU DONE YOUR SUMMER HOMEWORK?
YEAH!
Nice.
Good.
Good.
PAT
PAT
WHAT ABOUT YOU, NEE-CHAN?
NOT YET!
ALMOST THERE!
GOOD LUCK.

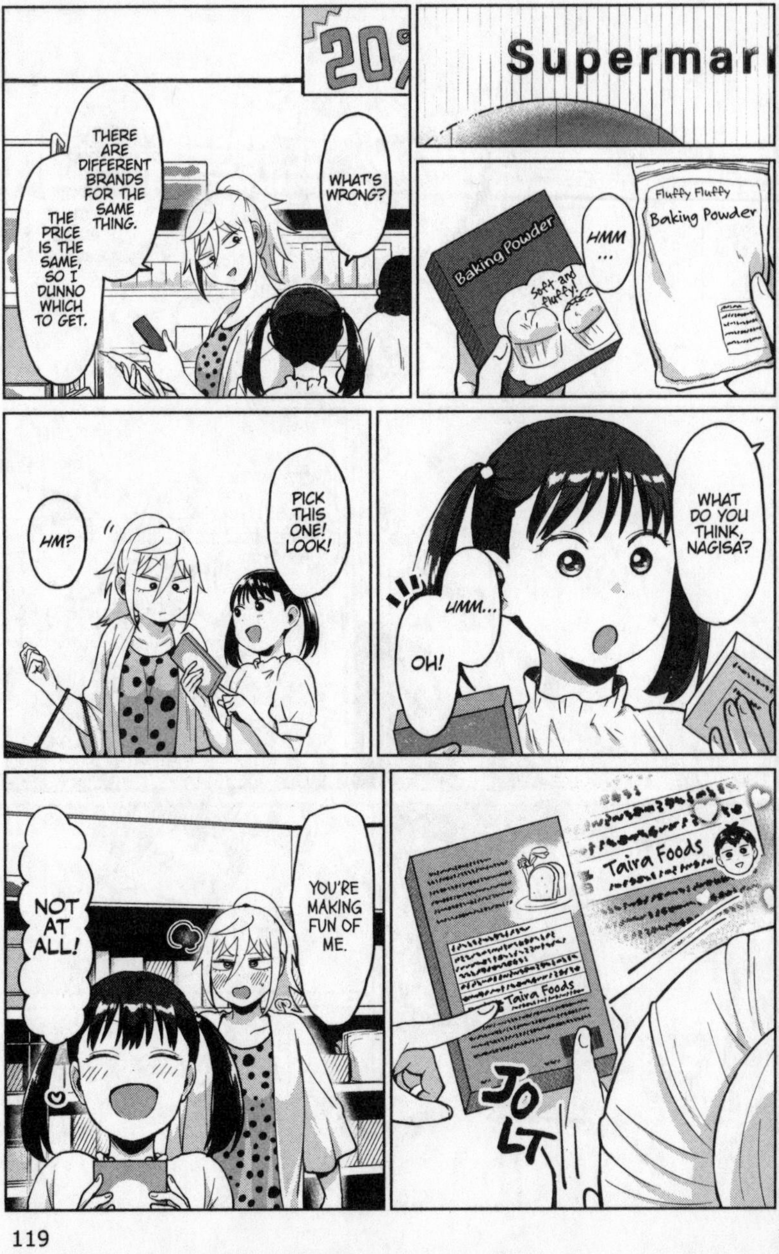
Supermar
HMM...
Fluffy Fluffy Baking Powder
Baking Powder
Soft and fluffy!
20
WHAT'S WRONG?
THERE ARE DIFFERENT BRANDS FOR THE SAME THING.
THE PRICE IS THE SAME, SO I DUNNO WHICH TO GET.
WHAT DO YOU THINK, NAGISA?
UMM...
OH!
PICK THIS ONE! LOOK!
HM?
Taira Foods
Taira Foods
JOLT
YOU'RE MAKING FUN OF ME.
NOT AT ALL!

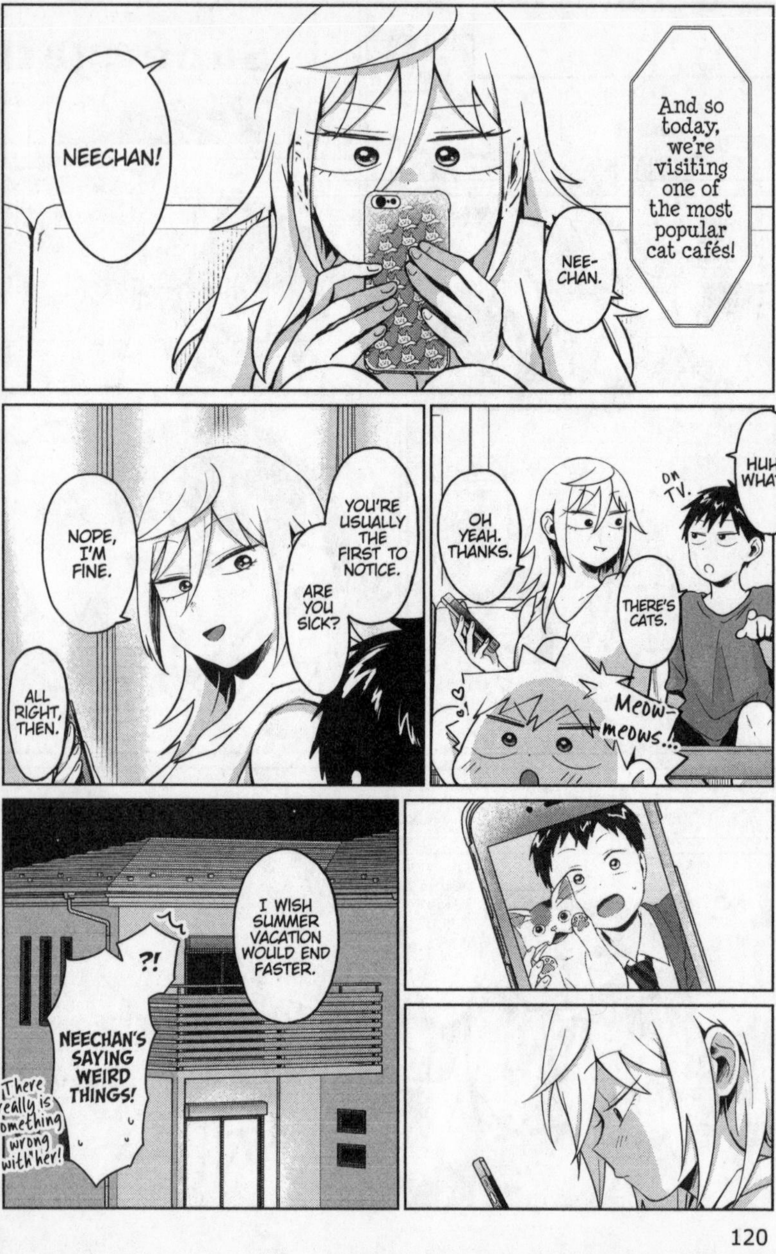
And so today, we're visiting one of the most popular cat cafés!
NEE-CHAN.
NEECHAN!
HUH? WHAT?
ON TV.
THERE'S CATS.
OH YEAH. THANKS.
Meow-meows...!
YOU'RE USUALLY THE FIRST TO NOTICE.
ARE YOU SICK?
NOPE, I'M FINE.
ALL RIGHT, THEN.
I WISH SUMMER VACATION WOULD END FASTER.
?!
NEECHAN'S SAYING WEIRD THINGS!
There really is something wrong with her!

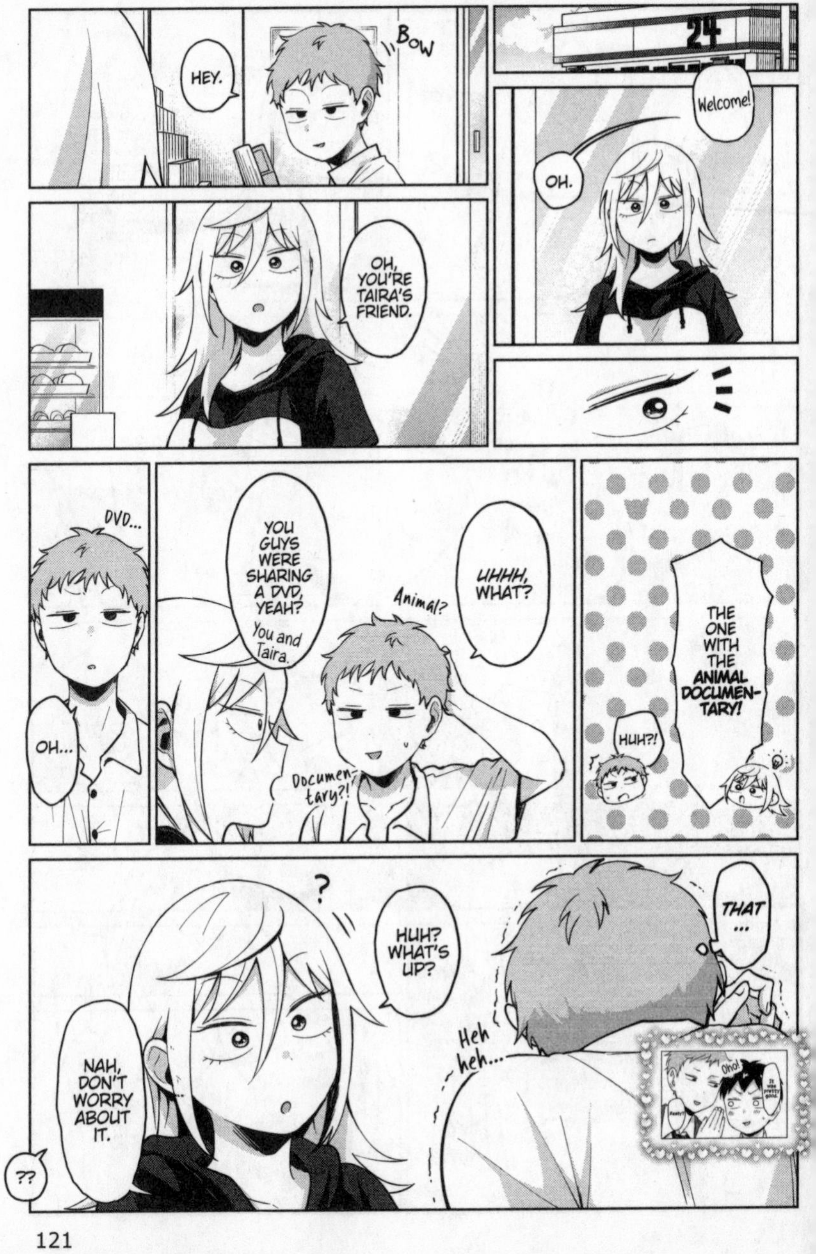
24
Welcome!
OH.
HEY.
BOW
OH, YOU'RE TAIRA'S FRIEND.
THE ONE WITH THE ANIMAL DOCUMENTARY!
HUH?!
UHHH, WHAT?
Animal?
YOU GUYS WERE SHARING A DVD, YEAH?
You and Taira.
Documentary?!
DVD...
OH...
THAT...
Heh heh...
HUH? WHAT'S UP?
?
NAH, DON'T WORRY ABOUT IT.
??

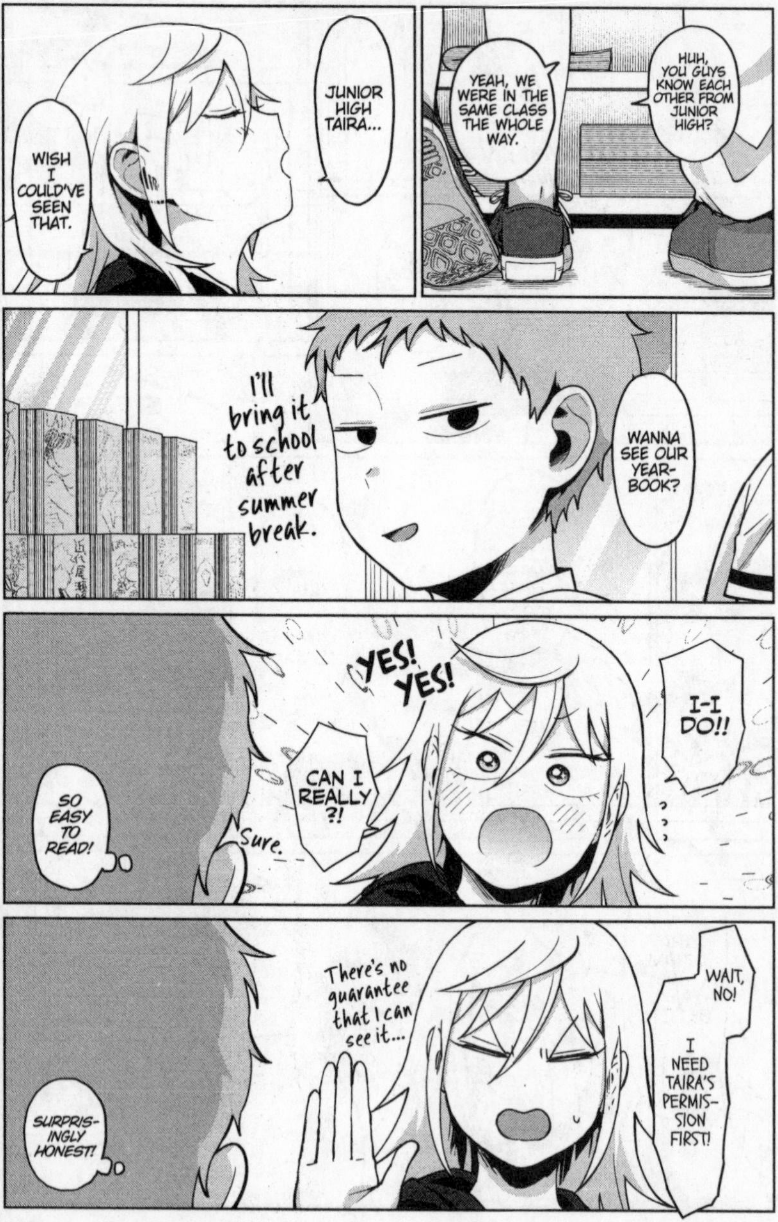
HUH, YOU GUYS KNOW EACH OTHER FROM JUNIOR HIGH?
YEAH, WE WERE IN THE SAME CLASS THE WHOLE WAY.
JUNIOR HIGH TAIRA...
WISH I COULD'VE SEEN THAT.
WANNA SEE OUR YEAR-BOOK?
I'll bring it to school after summer break.
I-I DO!!
YES! YES!
CAN I REALLY ?!
Sure.
SO EASY TO READ!
WAIT, NO!
I NEED TAIRA'S PERMIS-SION FIRST!
There's no guarantee that I can see it...
SURPRIS-INGLY HONEST!

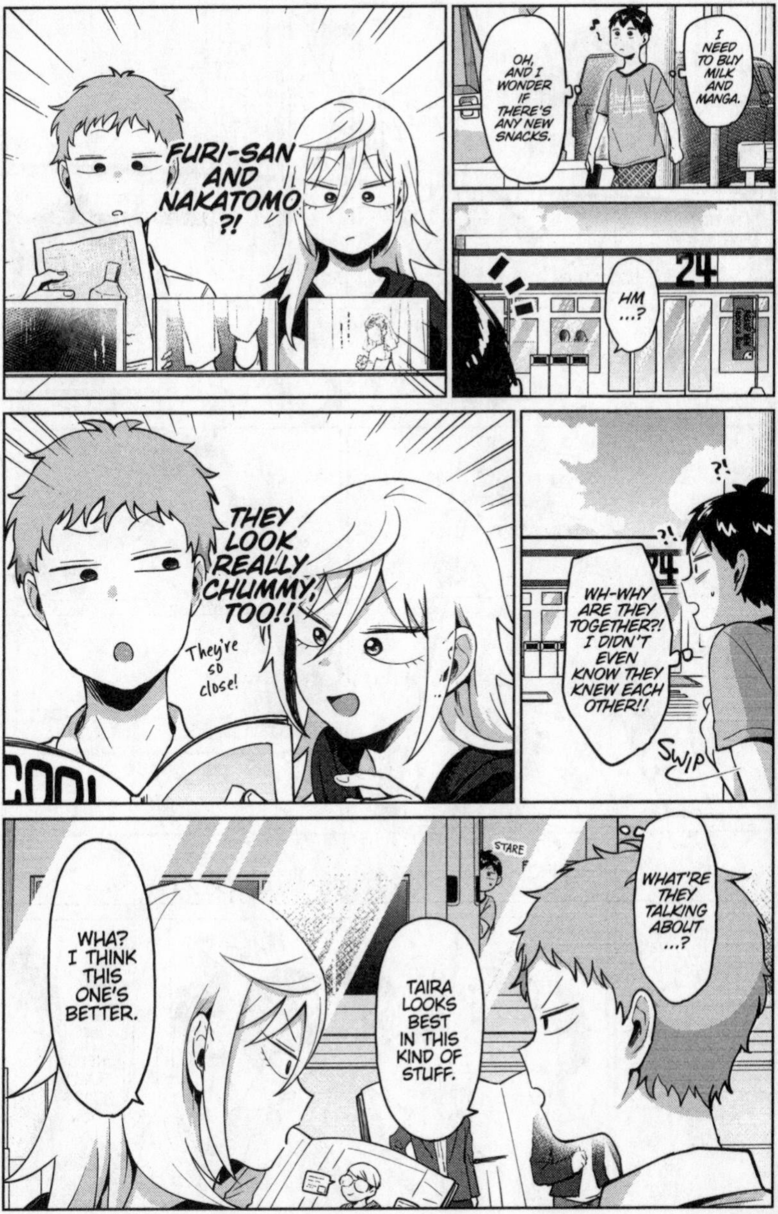
I NEED TO BUY MILK AND MANGA.
OH, AND I WONDER IF THERE'S ANY NEW SNACKS.
HM ...?
24
FURI-SAN AND NAKATOMO ?!
?!
?!
WH-WHY ARE THEY TOGETHER?! I DIDN'T EVEN KNOW THEY KNEW EACH OTHER!!
SWIP
THEY LOOK REALLY CHUMMY, TOO!!
They're so close!
WHAT'RE THEY TALKING ABOUT ...?
STARE
TAIRA LOOKS BEST IN THIS KIND OF STUFF.
WHA? I THINK THIS ONE'S BETTER.

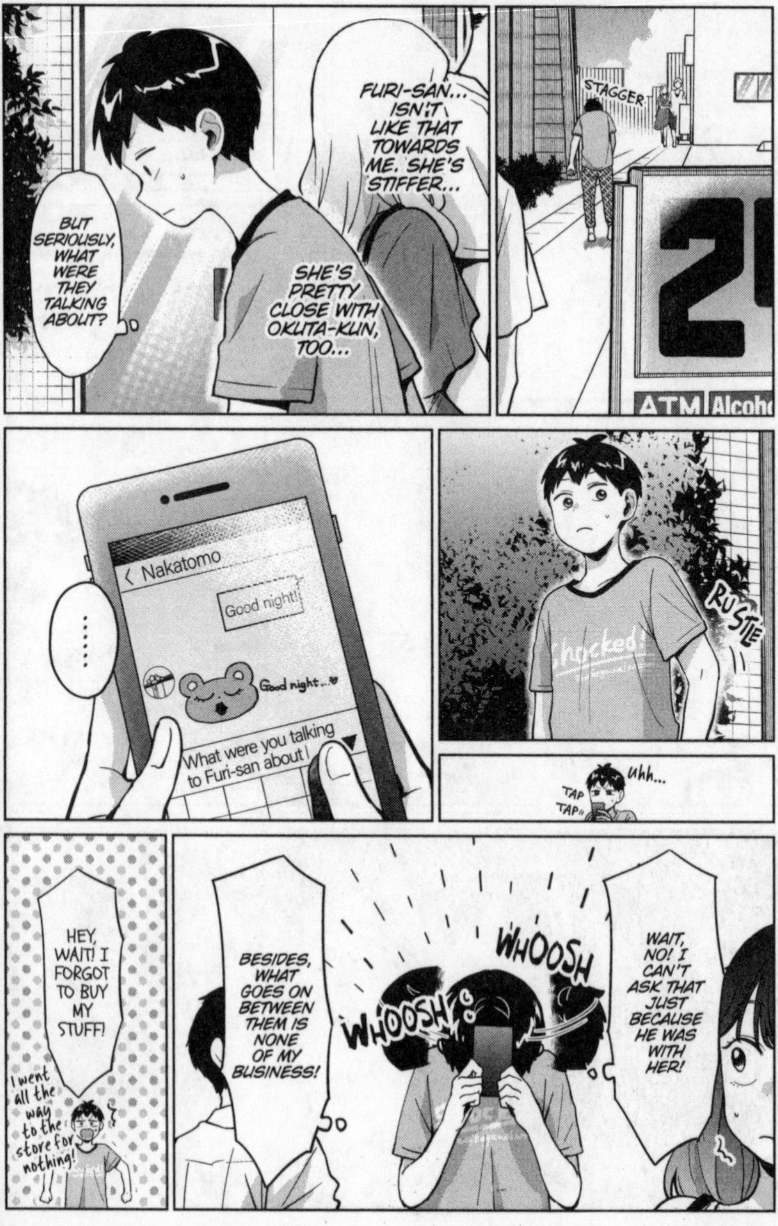
STAGGER
ATM Alcoho
FURI-SAN... ISN'T LIKE THAT TOWARDS ME. SHE'S STIFFER...
SHE'S PRETTY CLOSE WITH OKUTA-KUN, TOO...
BUT SERIOUSLY, WHAT WERE THEY TALKING ABOUT?
Shocked!
RUSTLE
Uhh...
TAP TAP
......
Nakatomo
Good night!
Good night...♥
What were you talking to Furi-san about
WAIT, NO! I CAN'T ASK THAT JUST BECAUSE HE WAS WITH HER!
WHOOSH
WHOOSH
BESIDES, WHAT GOES ON BETWEEN THEM IS NONE OF MY BUSINESS!
HEY, WAIT! I FORGOT TO BUY MY STUFF!
I went all the way to the store for nothing!

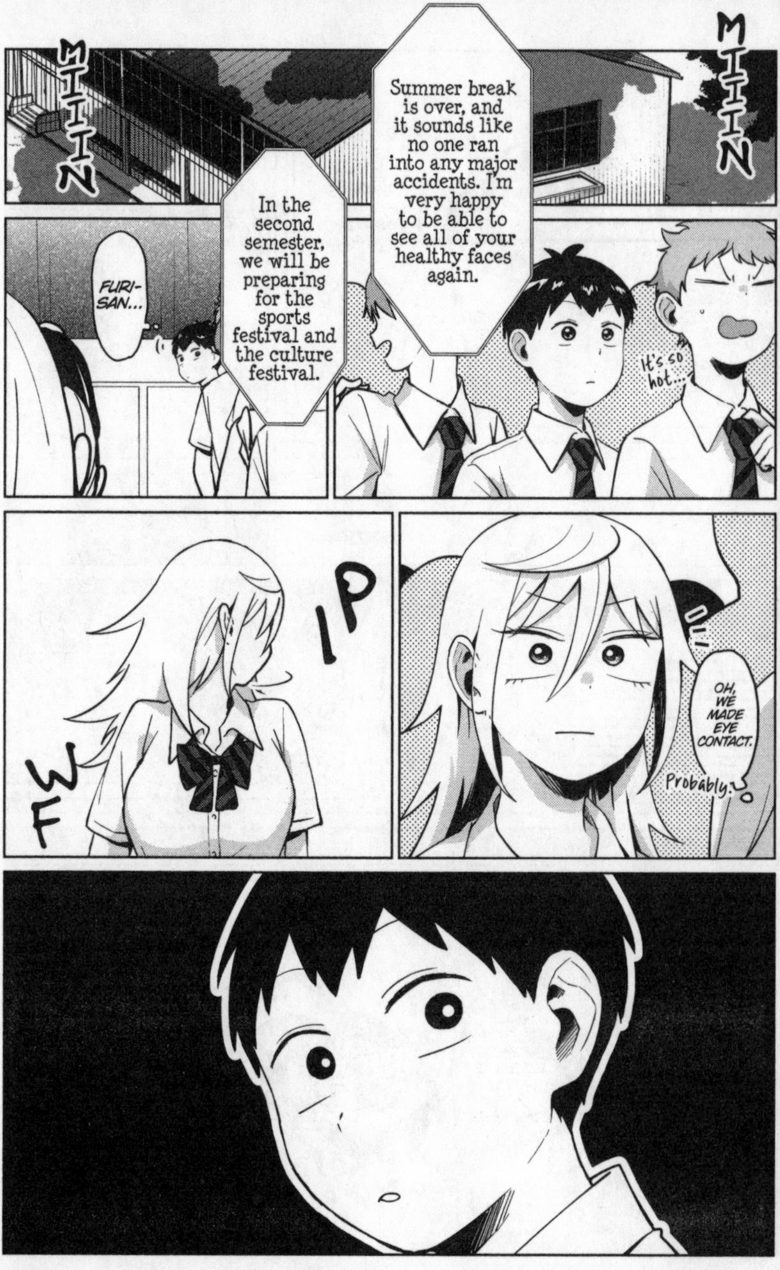
MIIIN
MIIIN
Summer break is over, and it sounds like no one ran into any major accidents. I'm very happy to be able to see all of your healthy faces again.
In the second semester, we will be preparing for the sports festival and the culture festival.
It's so hot...
FURI-SAN...
OH, WE MADE EYE CONTACT.
Probably.
FWIP

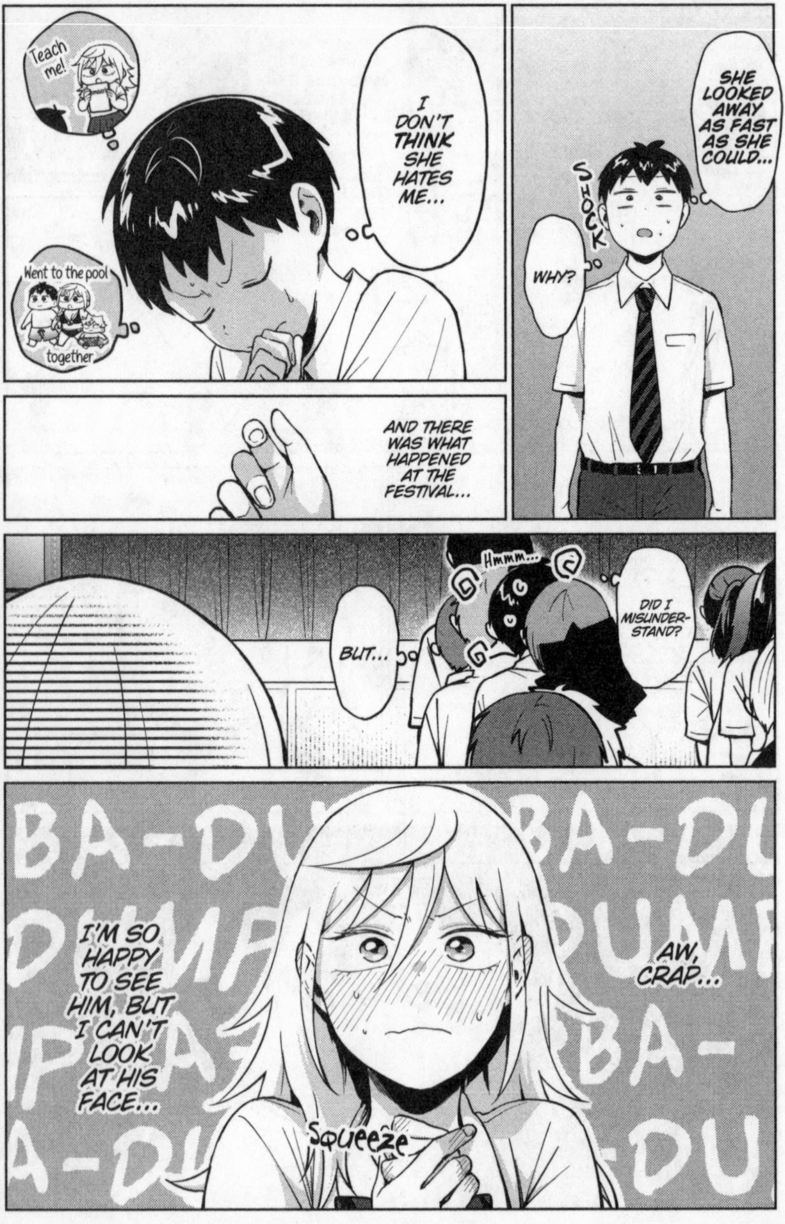
SHE LOOKED AWAY AS FAST AS SHE COULD...
SHOCK
WHY?
I DON'T THINK SHE HATES ME...
Teach me!
Went to the pool together
AND THERE WAS WHAT HAPPENED AT THE FESTIVAL...
DID I MISUNDER-STAND?
Hmmm...
BUT...
AW, CRAP...
I'M SO HAPPY TO SEE HIM, BUT I CAN'T LOOK AT HIS FACE...
Squeeze
BA-DUMP BA-DUMP BA-DUMP BA-DUMP

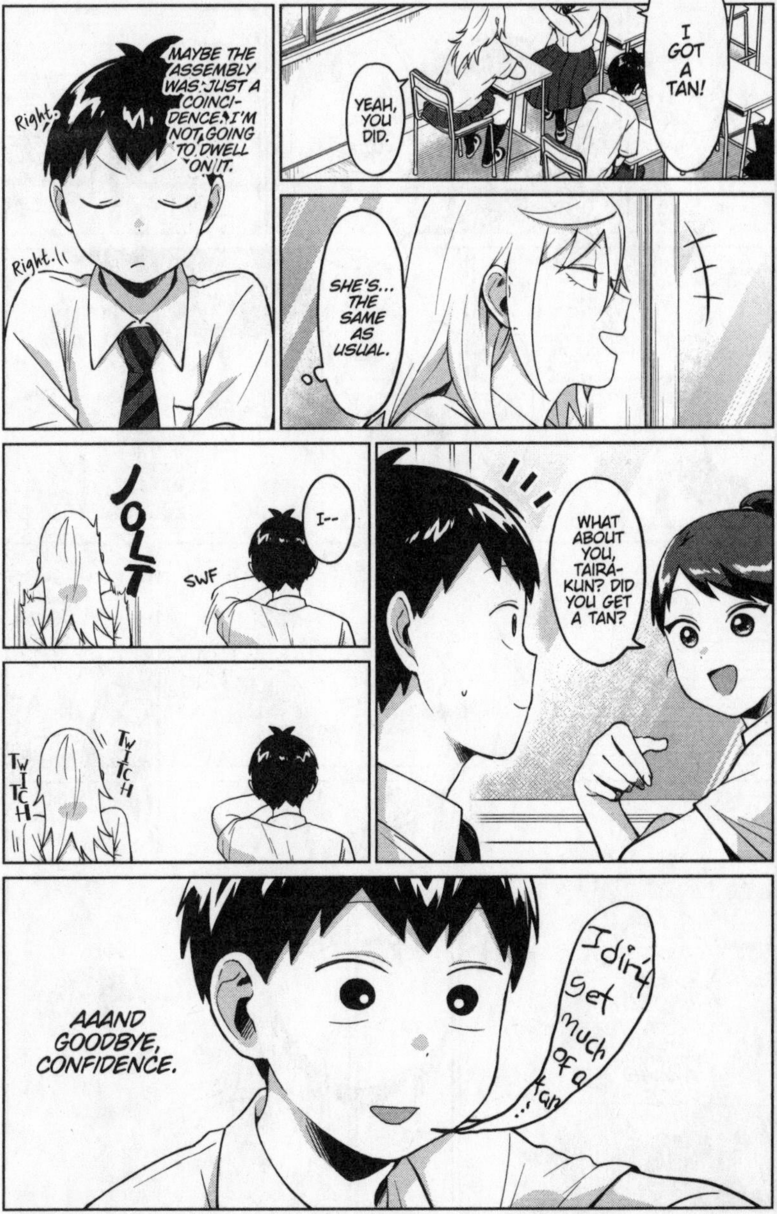
I GOT A TAN!
YEAH, YOU DID.
SHE'S... THE SAME AS USUAL.
MAYBE THE ASSEMBLY WAS JUST A COINCIDENCE. I'M NOT GOING TO DWELL ON IT.
Right.
Right.
WHAT ABOUT YOU, TAIRA-KUN? DID YOU GET A TAN?
JOLT
I--
SWF
TWITCH
TWITCH
I didn't get much of a tan...
AAAND GOODBYE, CONFIDENCE.

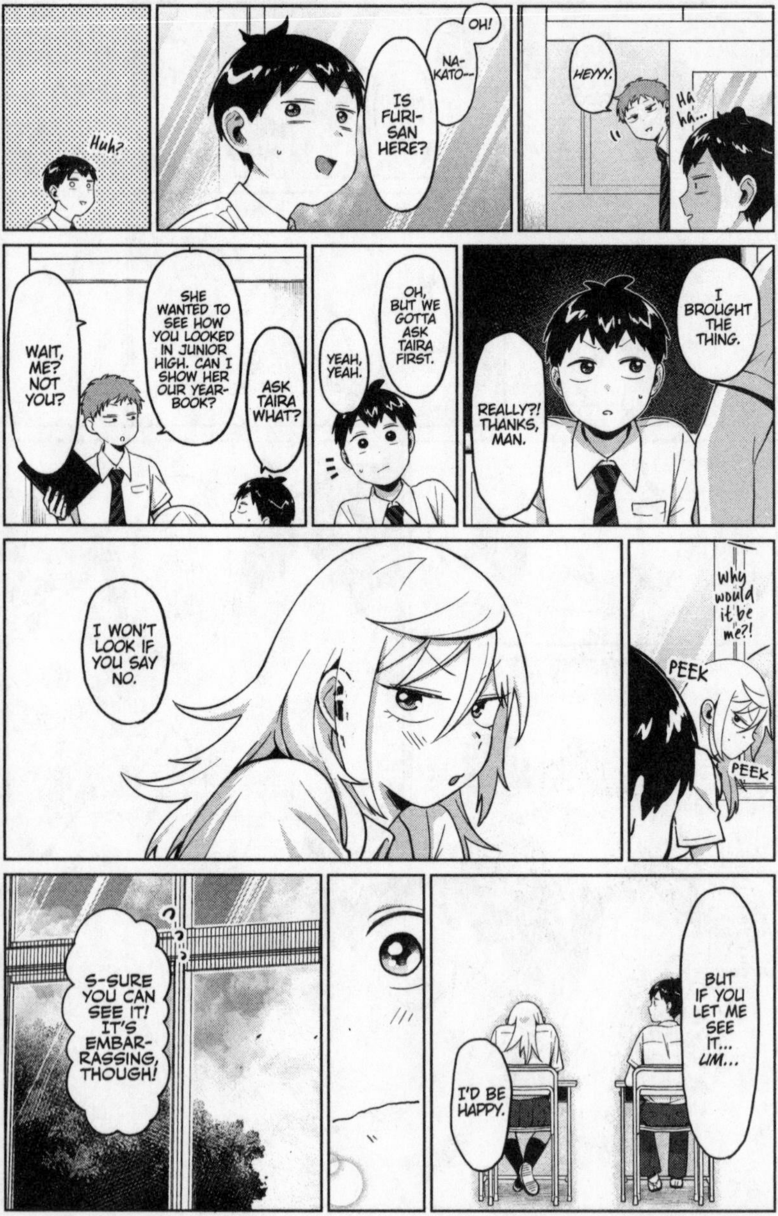
HEYYY.
Ha ha...
OH!
NA-KATO--
IS FURI-SAN HERE?
Huh?
I BROUGHT THE THING.
REALLY?! THANKS, MAN.
OH, BUT WE GOTTA ASK TAIRA FIRST.
YEAH, YEAH.
ASK TAIRA WHAT?
SHE WANTED TO SEE HOW YOU LOOKED IN JUNIOR HIGH. CAN I SHOW HER OUR YEAR-BOOK?
WAIT, ME? NOT YOU?
why would it be me?!
PEEK
PEEK
I WON'T LOOK IF YOU SAY NO.
BUT IF YOU LET ME SEE IT... UM...
I'D BE HAPPY.
S-SURE YOU CAN SEE IT! IT'S EMBAR-RASSING, THOUGH!

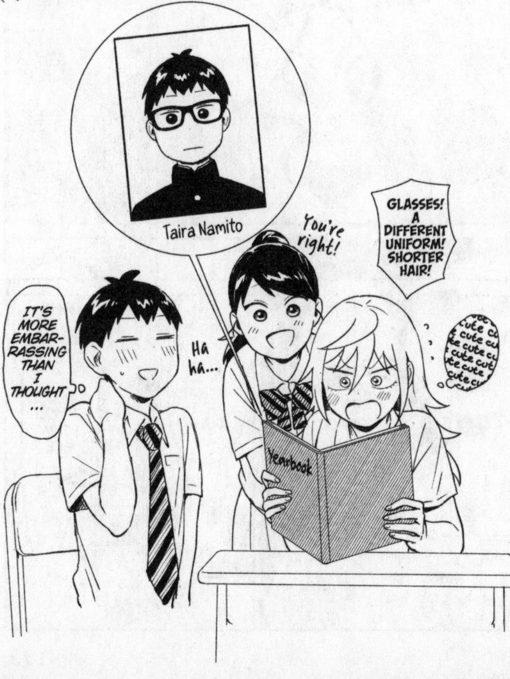
GLASSES! A DIFFERENT UNIFORM! SHORTER HAIR!
You're right!
Taira Namito
cute cute cute cute
Ha ha...
IT'S MORE EMBARRASSING THAN I THOUGHT...
Yearbook

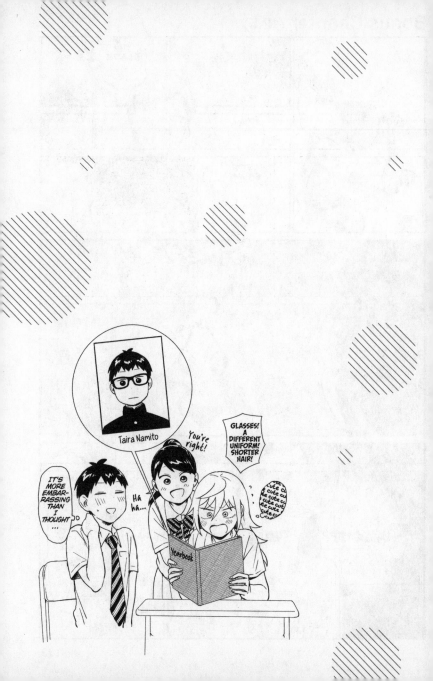

Bonus Chapter (12.5)

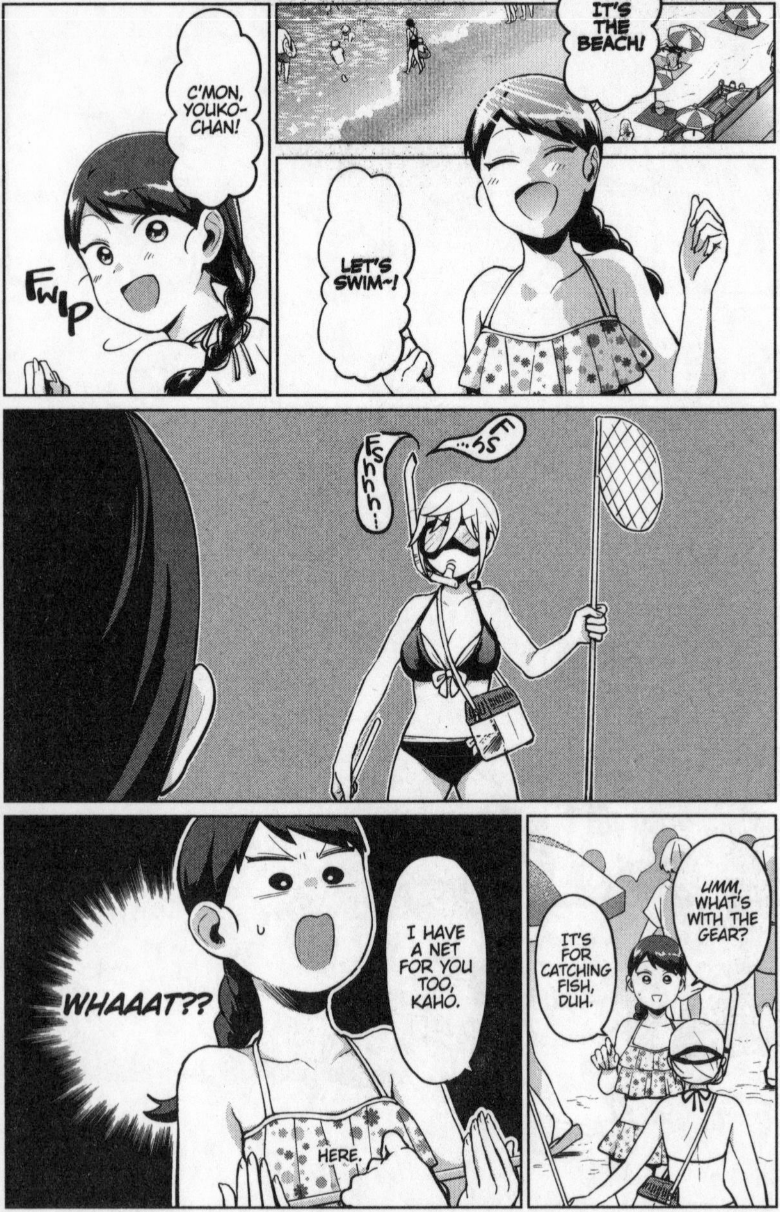
IT'S THE BEACH!
LET'S SWIM~!
C'MON, YOUKO-CHAN!
FWIP
Fshhh...
Fs...hs
UMM, WHAT'S WITH THE GEAR?
IT'S FOR CATCHING FISH, DUH.
I HAVE A NET FOR YOU TOO, KAHO.
WHAAAT??
HERE.

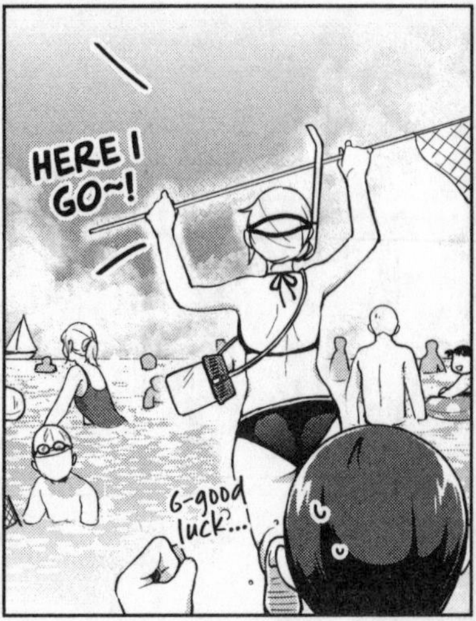
HERE I GO~!
G-good luck...!
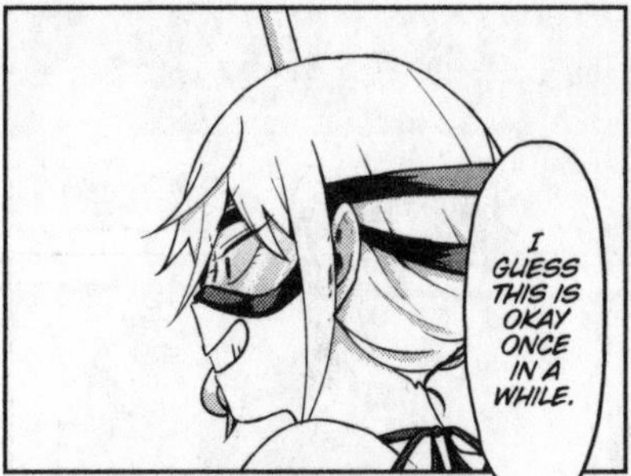
I GUESS THIS IS OKAY ONCE IN A WHILE.
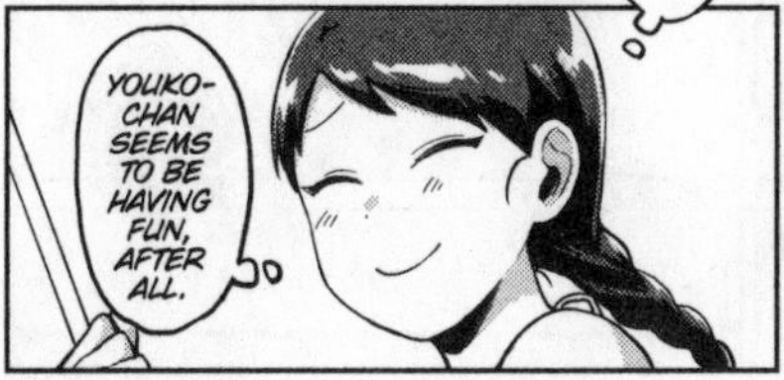
YOUKO-CHAN SEEMS TO BE HAVING FUN, AFTER ALL.
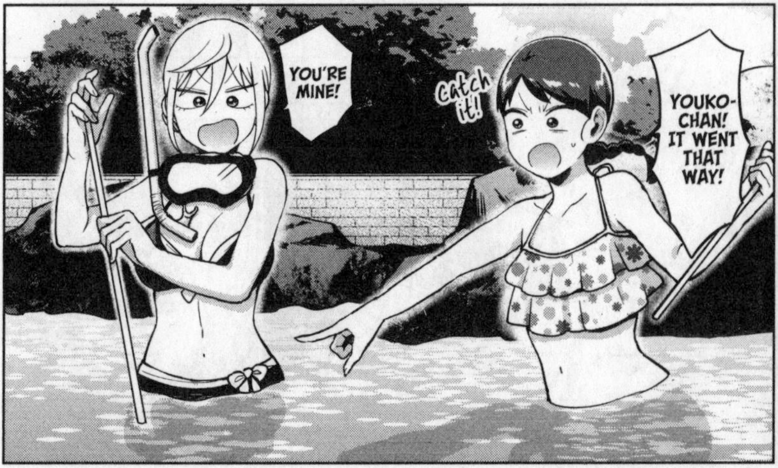
YOUKO-CHAN! IT WENT THAT WAY!
Catch it!
YOU'RE MINE!

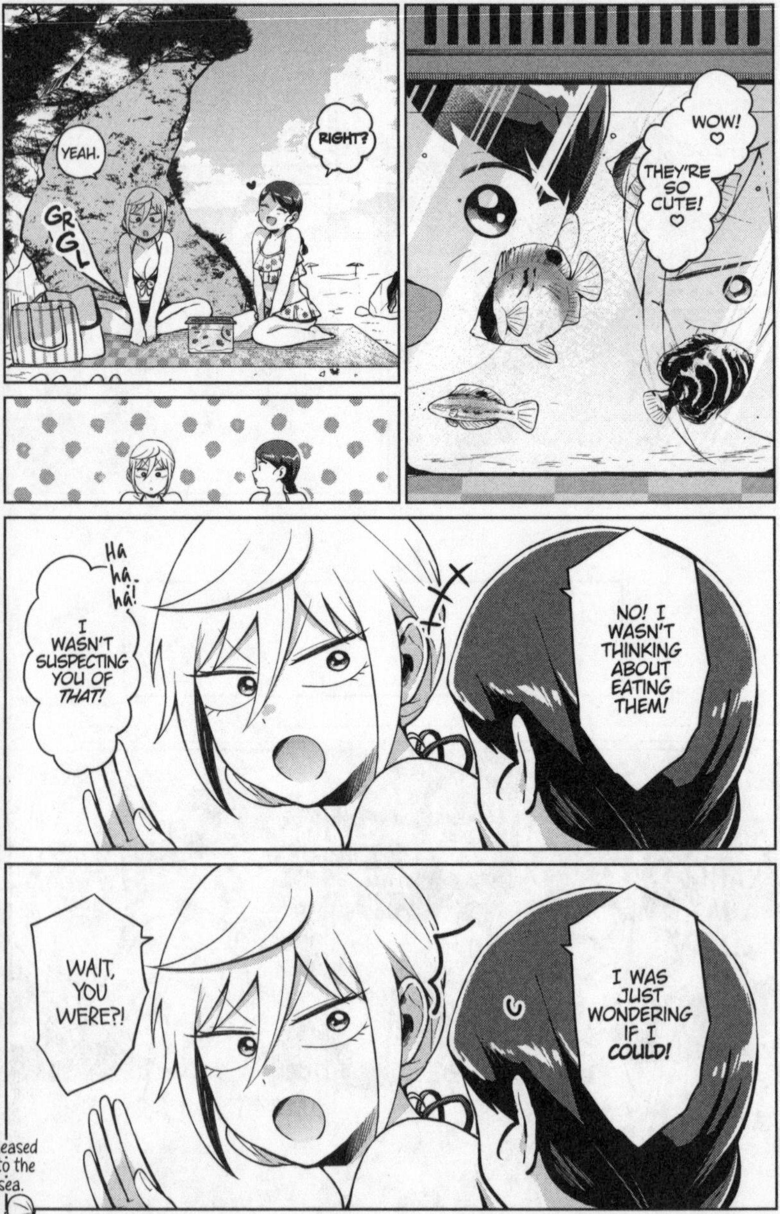
WOW! ♡
THEY'RE SO CUTE! ♡
RIGHT?
YEAH.
GRGL
NO! I WASN'T THINKING ABOUT EATING THEM!
Ha ha ha! I WASN'T SUSPECTING YOU OF *THAT!*
I WAS JUST WONDERING IF I COULD!
WAIT, YOU WERE?!

leased to the sea.

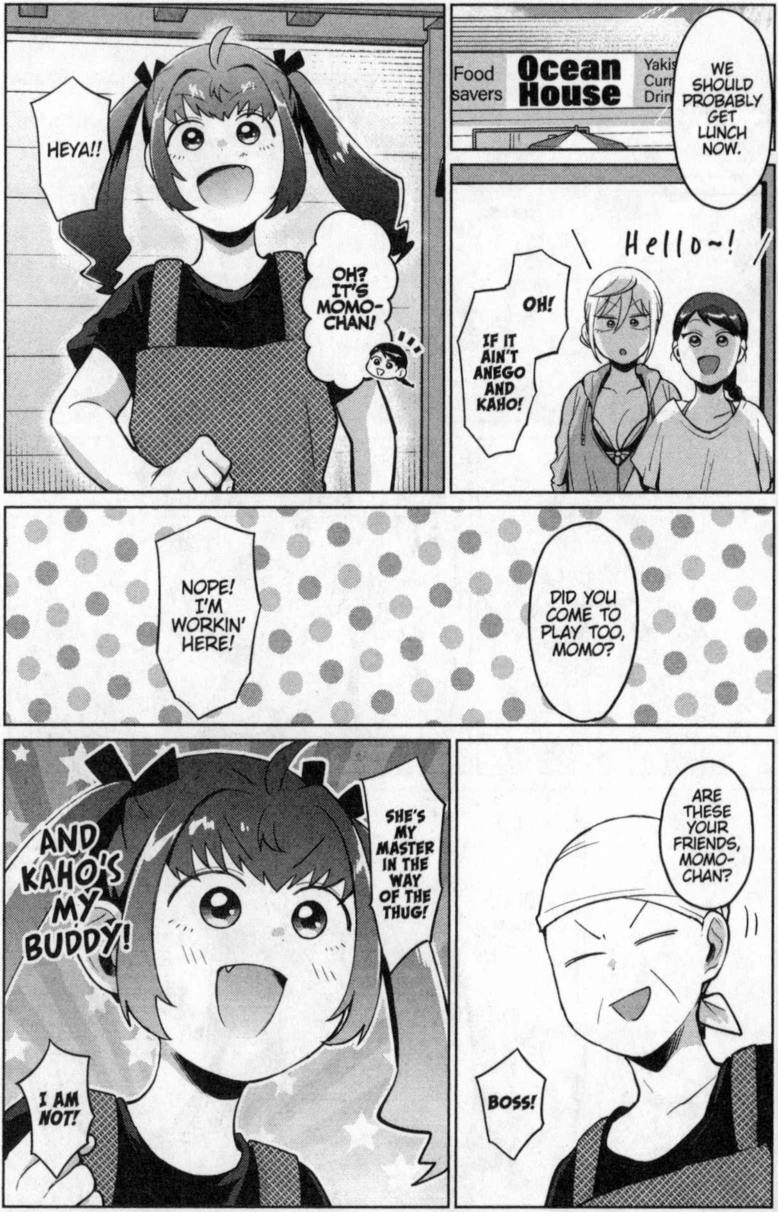
Food
savers
Ocean House
Yakis
Curr
Drin
WE SHOULD PROBABLY GET LUNCH NOW.
Hello~!
OH!
IF IT AIN'T ANEGO AND KAHO!
HEYA!!
OH? IT'S MOMO-CHAN!
DID YOU COME TO PLAY TOO, MOMO?
NOPE! I'M WORKIN' HERE!
ARE THESE YOUR FRIENDS, MOMO-CHAN?
BOSS!
SHE'S MY MASTER IN THE WAY OF THE THUG!
AND KAHO'S MY BUDDY!
I AM NOT!

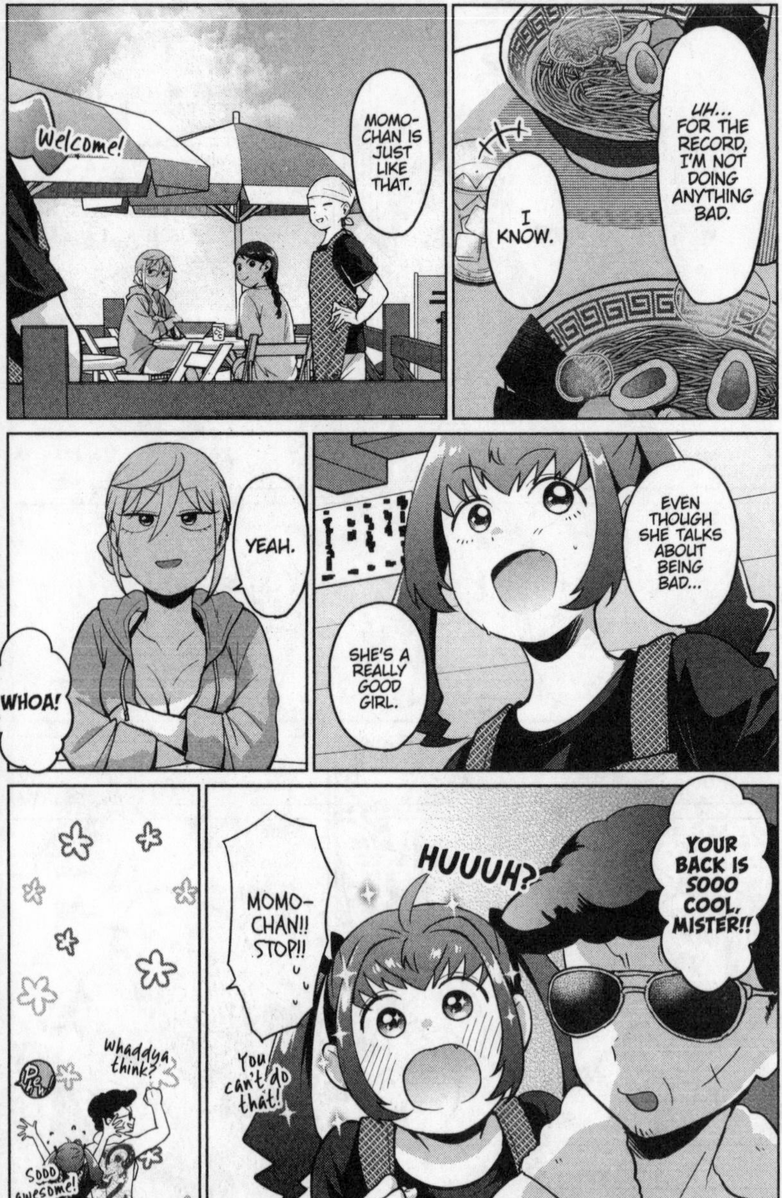
UH... FOR THE RECORD, I'M NOT DOING ANYTHING BAD.
I KNOW.
MOMO-CHAN IS JUST LIKE THAT.
Welcome!
EVEN THOUGH SHE TALKS ABOUT BEING BAD...
SHE'S A REALLY GOOD GIRL.
YEAH.
WHOA!
YOUR BACK IS SOOO COOL, MISTER!!
HUUUH?
MOMO-CHAN!! STOP!!
You can't do that!
Whaddya think?
Sooo awesome!

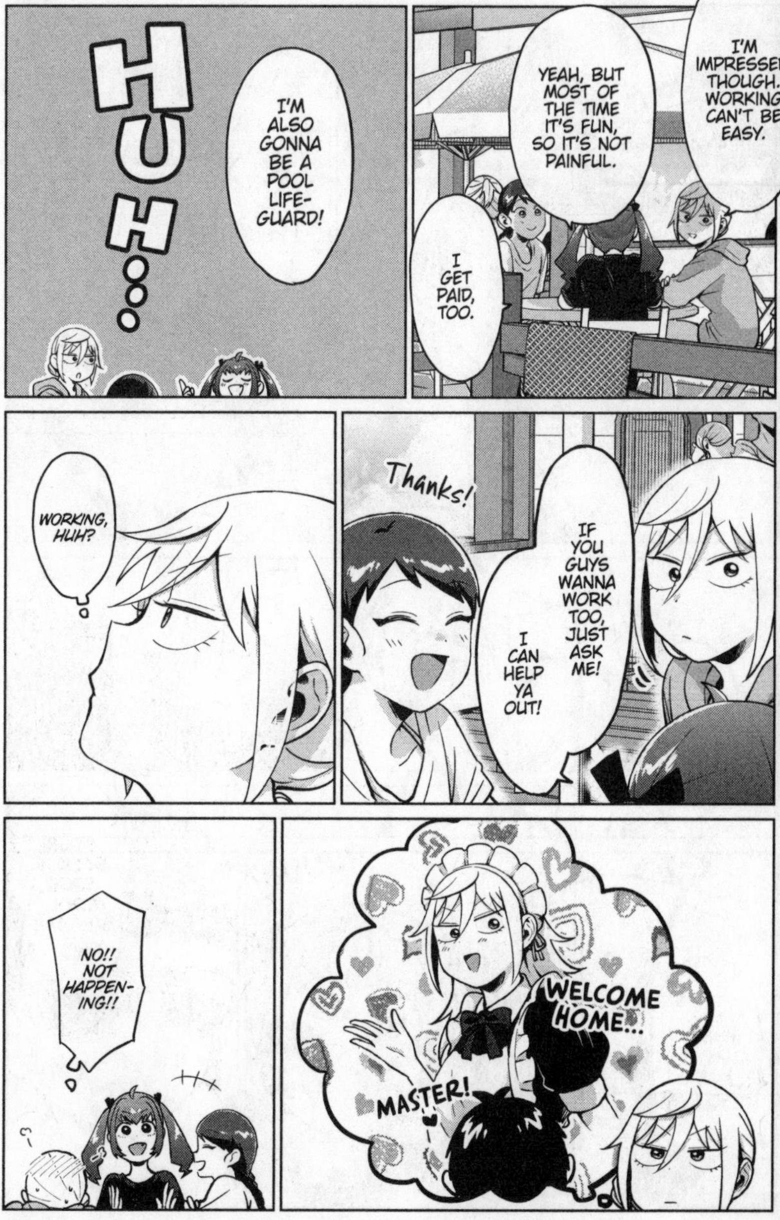
I'M IMPRESSED THOUGH. WORKING CAN'T BE EASY.
YEAH, BUT MOST OF THE TIME IT'S FUN, SO IT'S NOT PAINFUL.
I GET PAID, TOO.
I'M ALSO GONNA BE A POOL LIFE-GUARD!
HUH...
IF YOU GUYS WANNA WORK TOO, JUST ASK ME! I CAN HELP YA OUT!
Thanks!
WORKING, HUH?
WELCOME HOME...
MASTER!
NO!! NOT HAPPEN-ING!!

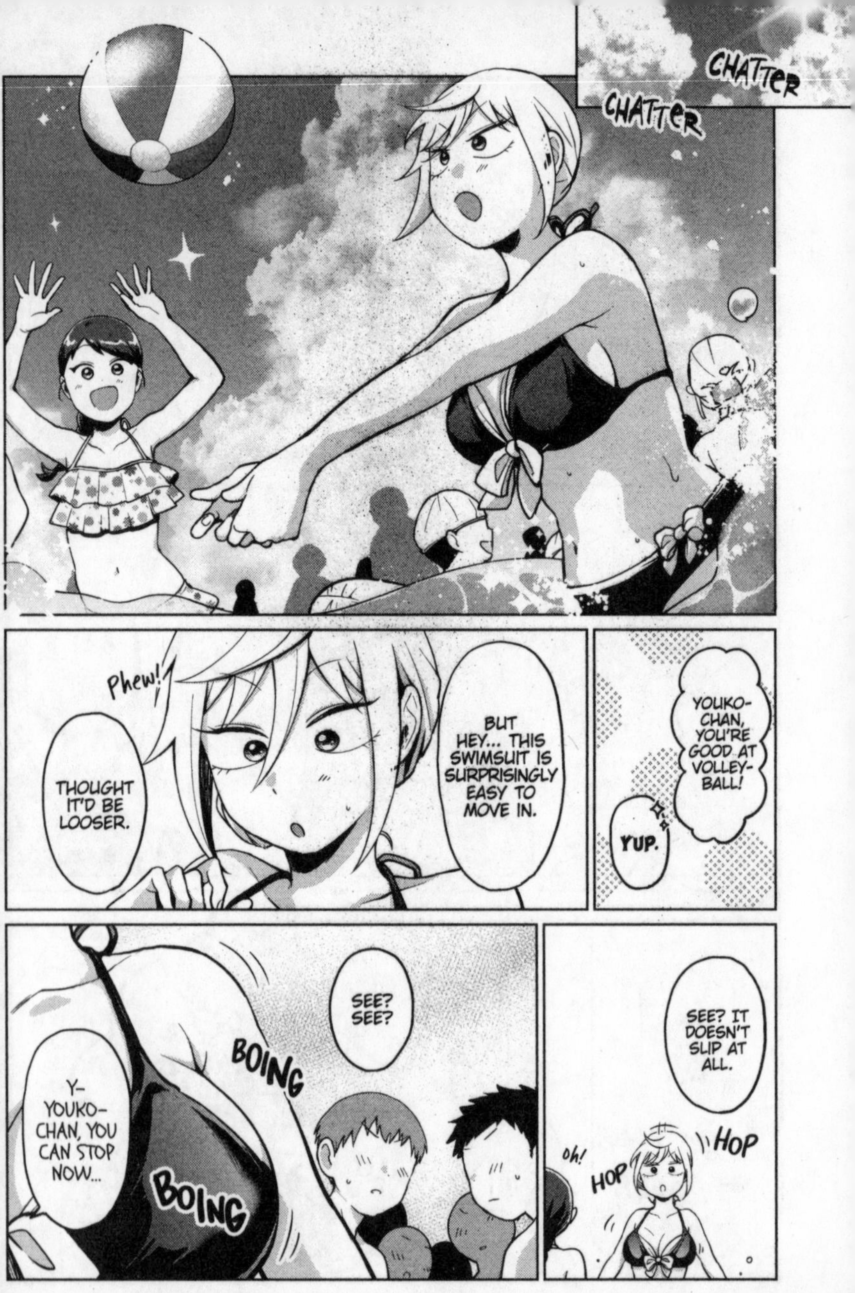

CHATTER
CHATTER
YOUKO-CHAN, YOU'RE GOOD AT VOLLEY-BALL!
YUP.
BUT HEY... THIS SWIMSUIT IS SURPRISINGLY EASY TO MOVE IN.
Phew!
THOUGHT IT'D BE LOOSER.
SEE? IT DOESN'T SLIP AT ALL.
HOP
HOP
Oh!
SEE? SEE?
BOING
Y-YOUKO-CHAN, YOU CAN STOP NOW...
BOING

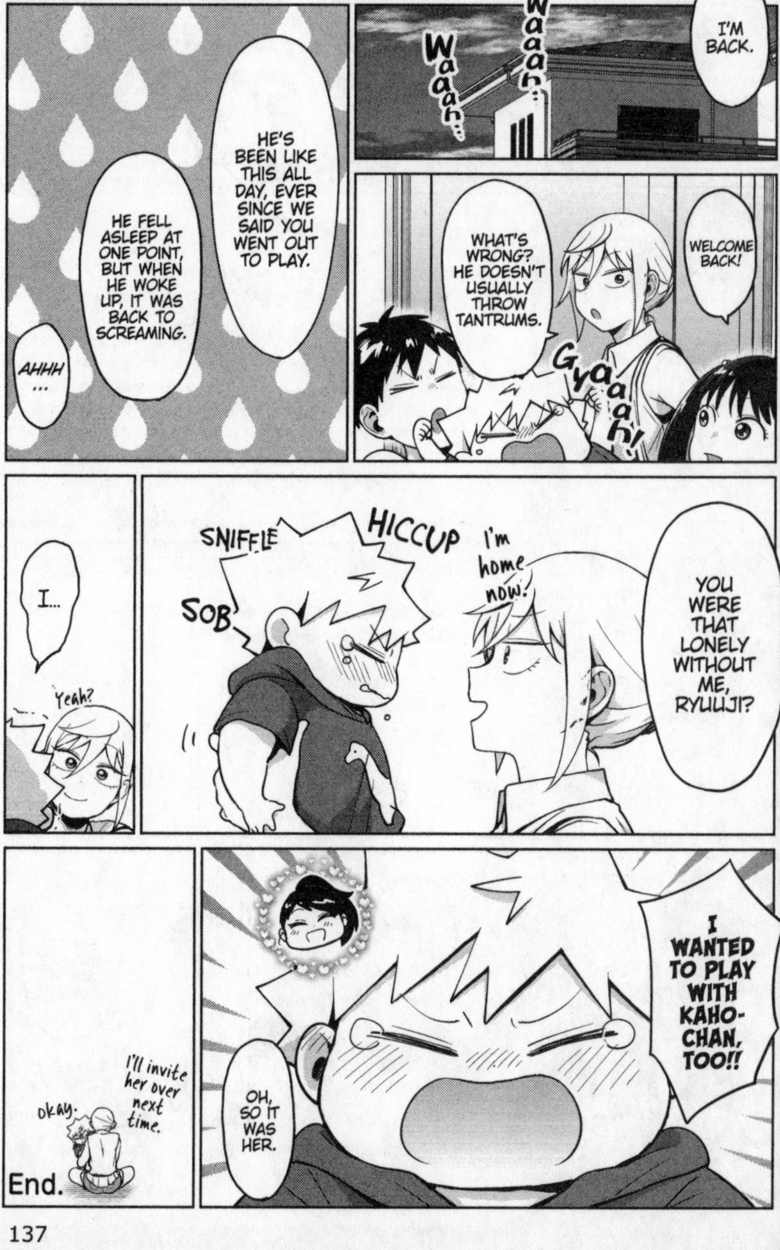
I'M BACK.
Waaah...
Waaah...
WELCOME BACK!
WHAT'S WRONG? HE DOESN'T USUALLY THROW TANTRUMS.
Gyaaah!
HE'S BEEN LIKE THIS ALL DAY, EVER SINCE WE SAID YOU WENT OUT TO PLAY.
HE FELL ASLEEP AT ONE POINT, BUT WHEN HE WOKE UP, IT WAS BACK TO SCREAMING.
AHHH...
YOU WERE THAT LONELY WITHOUT ME, RYUUJI?
I'm home now.
HICCUP
SNIFFLE
SOB
I...
Yeah?
I WANTED TO PLAY WITH KAHO-CHAN, TOO!!
OH, SO IT WAS HER.
I'll invite her over next time.
okay.
End.

SEVEN SEAS ENTERTAINMENT PRESENTS

NO MATTER WHAT YOU SAY, FURI-SAN is SCARY!

Vol. 2

story and art by SEIICHI KINOUE

TRANSLATION
Minna Lin

LETTERING
Carolina Hernández Mendoza

COVER AND LOGO DESIGN
Hanase Qi

PROOFREADER
Kurestin Armada

COPY EDITOR
Dawn Davis

EDITOR
J.P. Sullivan

PRINT MANAGER
Rhiannon Rasmussen-Silverstein

PREPRESS TECHNICIAN
Melanie Ujimori

PRODUCTION ASSOCIATE
Christa Miesner

PRODUCTION MANAGER
Lissa Pattillo

MANAGING EDITOR
Julie Davis

ASSOCIATE PUBLISHER
Adam Arnold

PUBLISHER
Jason DeAngelis

Tonari no Furi-san ga Tonikaku Kowai Vol. 2
© 2020 SEIICHI KINOUE. All rights reserved.
First published in Japan in 2020 by Ichijinsha Inc., Tokyo.
Publication rights for this English edition arranged through Kodansha Ltd., Tokyo.

Seven Seas press and purchase enquiries can be sent to Marketing Manager Lianne Sentar at press@gomanga.com. Information regarding the distribution and purchase of digital editions is available from Digital Manager CK Russell at digital@gomanga.com.

Seven Seas and the Seven Seas logo are trademarks of Seven Seas Entertainment. All rights reserved.

ISBN: 978-1-64827-669-9
Printed in Canada
First Printing: January 2022
10 9 8 7 6 5 4 3 2 1

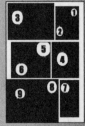

READING DIRECTIONS

This book reads from *right to left*, Japanese style. If this is your first time reading manga, you start reading from the top right panel on each page and take it from there. If you get lost, just follow the numbered diagram here. It may seem backwards at first, but you'll get the hang of it! Have fun!!

Follow us online: www.SevenSeasEntertainment.com